Reclaiming Our Lives

Reclaiming Our Lives

HOPE FOR ADULT SURVIVORS OF INCEST

Carol Poston and Karen Lison

LITTLE, BROWN AND COMPANY
BOSTON · TORONTO · LONDON

FIRST EDITION

Library of Congress Cataloging-in-Publication Data

Poston, Carol
  Reclaiming our lives.

  Bibliography: p.
  Includes index.
  1. Incest victims — United States — Psychology.
I. Lison, Karen. II. Title. III. Title: Hope for
adult survivors of incest.
HQ72.U53P68 1989   306.7'77   88-28375
ISBN 0-316-71472-0

10 9 8 7 6 5 4 3 2

Designed by Joyce C. Weston

RRD VA
Published simultaneously in Canada
by Little, Brown & Company (Canada) Limited
PRINTED IN THE UNITED STATES OF AMERICA

Contents

Acknowledgments

While the impetus and discipline to conceive and write this book were certainly ours, we scarcely could have completed a page without help from others. We want first to thank novelist and translator Lore Segal, whose frank advice, active support, and careful reading of the early text gave us courage and direction when we needed it most. An early interview with Dr. Richard Krugman at the Henry C. Kempe Center in Denver gave us valuable assistance in dealing with a complex field. We thank Jane Jordan Browne, our agent *par excellence,* who aided, advised, and stood as dragon at the door; and Jennifer Josephy, our editor at Little, Brown, who both championed our larger cause and attended to the smaller details. We also thank Barbara Roy, Carolyn Hulse, Grace White, Judith Osterman, and Linda Williams, who read individual parts and gave valuable advice on content. We are grateful to Sue Sindelar, in the Office of Academic Affairs at the University of Illinois at Chicago, who provided assistance during text production. And finally, Larry Poston served as manuscript editor, computer go-between, and cheerleader, a man for all seasons.

Karen Lison thanks her parents, Jerry and Cas Kaitis, for years of love, support, and encouragement; her husband, John, for his unfaltering confidence that she could do this and more; her sons, Christopher and Timothy, for loving their mum unconditionally;

and her friend and co-author, Carol Poston, who so eloquently put thoughts and ideas into words. Finally, Karen is grateful to all her clients — from Diana, the first pre-teen in 1966, to Marcella, the grandmother of ten in 1988 — the women who revealed their incestuous pasts and kept Karen searching for new ways to encourage their healing. Their stories planted the seed for this book.

Carol Poston thanks her therapist Patricia Dore for her gentle and intelligent care; Grace Episcopal Church in Oak Park, Ill., especially the Marriage Encounter and Lectionary groups for their nurturing of the life within; Rachel and Anne for loving their mother in all kinds of ways; friends Jeannette Crowley, Emily Kohl, Suzanne Greene, and Christopher and Elizabeth Keys for love and support; and Karen Lison, who carried out this project with insight, humor, and steadfastness. And finally, the love and support of her husband Larry have made this book — and perhaps even life itself — possible.

Most important, we thank the women who shared their life stories with us. In the interest of anonymity we do not use their actual names, but they know who they are. Their honesty, courage, and humor inspired us at every step of the way. Their lives and experiences formed the seed bed from which this book could flower.

This book is dedicated to all the women who endured incest as children, with admiration for those who survived, with sorrow for those who perished, and with encouragement for those who have yet to remember.

Reclaiming Our Lives

Introduction: How This Book Began

KAREN LISON SPEAKS:

My interest in incest began in 1966, the year after I graduated from college and began working as a probation officer at Chicago's Cook County Juvenile Court. There I was assigned a case load that averaged 35 girls between the ages of twelve and seventeen years. Many of them were on probation for running away from home, an action that only becomes a delinquent offense once a girl is already *on* probation (usually for *being* a runaway), then *violates* that probation by running away again.

Many of these girls revealed to me that they were leaving home to avoid daily sexual abuse from fathers, stepfathers, or brothers. These girls were often dubbed "promiscuous" by the states' attorneys, and it was suggested that they were accusing family members when, in fact, we all *knew* that they were "seductive nymphets trying to lure anything in pants."

The girls I worked with never received the kind of treatment they deserved. Instead, many were taken from their families and sent to the State Training School for Girls. They were *incarcerated for running away from sexual abuse.* It was a frustrating position for a probation officer in those days, especially with the scarcity of resources available.

Today we realize that these young women were being honest about what was happening, and the courts now have a variety of treatment programs designed for the incestuous family.

In 1972 I entered graduate school. Part of the requirement for graduation was to complete a supervised practicum where I was assigned a total of ten clients to follow throughout their therapy. Of the ten, seven were females and four of those had incest in their backgrounds.

After graduation I took a position at a small psychiatric hospital in a Chicago suburb. I was hired to work in the hospital's incestuous-family treatment program. Here the *entire family* was treated on an inpatient basis — an excellent but very costly alternative treatment method. The program folded, but I stayed on to work with the general psychiatric population.

As I learned more and more about the individual patients with whom I worked, and as they began revealing their histories, I again began to see stories of incest and abuse. Again I was struck by the frequency with which incest seemed to occur and the devastating effects it had on its victims.

From the hospital I moved to a social service agency to coordinate a parent-aide program designed to prevent child abuse in families judged to be at high risk. Once more, incest showed its ugly face when many of the mothers who were at risk of abusing their children began disclosing their own histories, histories laced with incest.

I couldn't get away from it. Everywhere I turned, clients discussed incestuous pasts. All of them expressed feelings of being alone and blamable for the incidents. I knew they needed a group where they could share their feelings and discover that they were not unique. They needed to see how the incest had affected their adult lives and how to put the experiences finally behind them and move on.

In June of 1982 I quit my job and threw myself into reading as much as possible about incest, attending workshops and seminars on the subject, and writing letter after letter to authors of the books I had read. I wanted to learn everything I could about incest so that I could start a group for survivors. In September of that year the first group came together in a tiny office I was subletting from an accountant friend.

One by one the women's stories unwound, each, it seemed, more devastating than the last. But at the same time, the similarities became more and more apparent. All expressed feelings of guilt, shame, low self-esteem, difficulties with sexuality and intimacy, and fears of trusting. As the women's shame lessened, their self-esteem grew. Their fear of exposure dwindled as they slowly shared their fears and vulnerabilities. I, too, although not a survivor of incest, knew that I had found my place. It was a clear realization that for the first time I was able to have an impact on the lives of these women. For the first time I was spearheading something that was working for survivors, and the women were healing. The name of our group? SIGH, an acronym for Survivors of Incest Gaining Health.

CAROL POSTON SPEAKS:

In the Gospel of Mark, Jesus asks, "Is a lamp brought in to be put under a bushel, or under a bed, and not on a stand? For there is nothing hid except to be made manifest; nor is anything secret except to come to light."

Bringing to light the dark secret of incest in my life has been difficult. The light came gradually, as the flame of a kerosene lantern, gradually fed more fuel, finally glows and irradiates even the corner of a room. It took years for me even to bring the lantern into the room of my secret. It took several hard years in therapy to uncover my eyes and look at the room that the lantern lit. Finally I was able to look under the beds and behind the furniture, even where the light did not reach.

Because I am a student of literature and a writer, I saw this story of self-discovery as a powerful narrative. I had reached my forties, and I knew that the story needed to be told, because I knew I was far from alone. So when I finally saw that room in my life standing clear in the light, I chose the further task of telling others what it looked like. People who have not experienced childhood sexual abuse have trouble imagining it.

I set out to interview people who knew about the subject of incest. The journalistic approach of interviewing experts was natural to me, and it was the only way to get good information, since there is not a massive quantity of literature on the adult survivor of incest. Much of what has been written are painful and discouraging accounts of abuse without sufficient attention to the healing process. The experience of recovery as I had lived it had not been discouraging so much as it had been one of growing and changing. I knew I was not alone. So I decided to talk with other people — both professionals and the real experts, women who had journeyed through the dark tunnel of the experience to find light at the end.

As I researched the subject and located experts, I learned about the work of Karen Lison and called her for information. She confessed to me that she had wanted to write a book as well, since she had amassed so much information and since, to her dismay, so much of the literature did not reflect the truth as she saw it being lived out.

We met for tea. We interviewed each other cautiously. We decided that our philosophies were alike. We are careful women, so we drew up a legal contract. After nearly four years of close work and discussion and disagreement, we are not only still speaking to each other, we are fast friends. Karen calls it chance; I call it grace.

HOW WE PUT THIS BOOK TOGETHER:

We found the material to date on the subject of adult survivors of incest to be of two kinds: anguished first-person accounts, often anonymous, which, while they help a survivor realize she is not alone, also can often be discouraging, depressing, and quite without hope. Other books were written by, and often for, professionals. We wanted a book written by women, for women — *all* women — a book that moved, informed, and gave hope.

Carol decided to write the headnote section of each chapter out of her own life experience. The main body of the chapters comes from information we obtained from in-depth interviews, conducted jointly, of nearly fifty survivors. Many of these women have at one time been Karen Lison's clients, but others came to us because they had heard of the project, and several therapists in the area called to talk.

Our own dialogue as authors created the text. Carol talked of her personal feelings and experiences, and Karen interpreted. Karen talked of her extensive experience with more than 200 clients over the years. Carol wrote and listened and recorded what she heard. These interviews took place weekly over a period of two and one-half years and were supplemented by some long weekends spent in a cabin in Michigan, away from the authors' respective families and households. The collaboration has been close, the study intense.

Still, differences of opinion exist between us, and we confess that the tension sometimes can be felt in the text. Where we have been at distinct odds about an issue, each pauses in the text to speak in her own voice. The role of the incest survivor's mother is a case in point. As a survivor of incest, Carol Poston has had a long struggle with her own mother, and she believes that any mother can, if she chooses, see her daughter's pain and discover the incest. She believes, in short, that all mothers share some degree of the parental responsibility. As a therapist with years of experience treating survivors of incest, Karen Lison firmly believes that there are mothers who do not have a clue about what is occurring and that these mothers in no way deserve any blame. The blame for the incest needs to be put solely where it belongs: on the perpetrator. Both of us believe that, at least in the absence of additional research, these two firmly held opinions reflect facets of a rather complex truth more adequately than either opinion held by itself.

The tension at other points is perhaps more subtle, particularly when the authors, though they diverge in some points of interpretation, do not find that their differences justify the use of alternative voices. If a reader perceives that behind a single voice lurks some authorial disagreement, the reader is probably right.

This book is, like all good stories, truth telling. There may be women who did not experience what we did, and to that we can only say that we wrote and told what we know.

CHAPTER

I

Beginnings

ONCE *upon a time I was a little girl. My nickname was "Punky" because as a child I was as chubby as a pumpkin. My brother called me "Sis" or "Sissy." None of my family ever called me by my real name or even by a nickname close to it.*

We lived in a house in the woods, and there was a creek nearby, a beautiful creek that had a steep path down to its rocky bank, and the only thing that kept me from slipping and breaking my head on the way down were tree roots that stood out of the dirt and were toeholds for a small foot.

In the summer the creek was tranquil and in its deep pool, clear and framed by granite boulders, trout swam. In spring the creek was a torrent, flooding the banks, uprooting trees, and running muddy and brown and high in its banks.

The house at the top of the hill from the creek was a two-room frame house with plank floors, a settler house with no conveniences. Drinking water came from the creek below, carried by my father, a heavy steel pail in each hand once a day, in the morning. There was a dipper, white enamel with a red ring, that lay by one of the buckets, from which I came to gulp a drink often during the day — a brief refresher from running and play around the choke-cherry bushes and jack pines.

This was the country, the mountains, beautiful in a not very populous part of the country, and the family was intact though poor. This story might have been the same had the setting been an urban highrise or a flat in a factory town or a split level on the plains of suburbia. The family might have been white or black or a reconstituted one with stepfather or even not a nuclear family at all.

As a little girl I thought that what started all the trouble was that my mother had to go to work. In my early years we had lived on a big farm, and my mother did the work of a farm wife, and she had stayed at home.

But my father had a bad temper and had gotten angry at his employers. He needed elbow room, he said, so he took his family and moved up the mountain to make a living on his own. He never had a boss again.

He did odd jobs, piecework, nothing steady, some of it grueling and hard. He came in dirty, tired, and angry. It was a frugal living they had, with few conveniences, little money, primitive living conditions.

At first this way of life didn't take away from my pleasure in play — days of tree climbing in summer and sledding in winter with my brother. But then the fights began. Even though my father was decent and respectable, he didn't make enough money. And my mother wanted things for herself and her children. She wanted to get the bills paid and someday she hoped to stop paying rent so we could have a place of our own. She was tired of the two-room shack with the outdoor privy and the walk down the hill to the creek for water even for washing — six buckets of water it took just to fill the washing machine, to say nothing of the rinse water, which, even filled high in the galvanized steel blue tub, would still look sudsy and gray-blue. I stomped barefoot in the puddle the soapy water made when my mother drained it by hose into the grass-shy yard.

My mother had tried decent and respectable work like selling Fashion Frocks door to door, and I remember with such pleasure seeing my mother dressed in one of the starched frocks she was trying to sell others, her dark hair glistening and a glimmer of coquettishness in her eye. The trouble was that the women who had the money to buy such things were not going to invite this woman into their living rooms with the carpet and matching drapes to sit on the nice sofa. When she got invited in, it was by the people who had time for a cup of coffee and a little gossip and no money for such frills as silk stockings and Fashion Frocks.

My mother was ambitious. From an immigrant family with eight children, she had her first job when she was thirteen — earlier if you counted the quarters she got for bringing in the neighbor's cows at milking time, the quarter that bought her own mother a bucket of lard or a bit of thread for darning.

Nor was she afraid of hard work. There was a good job for the asking at the dance hall pavilion, for this was a resort town. Small in population throughout the year, it swelled in summer with tourists, and the pavilion vibrated with the sounds of big bands and couples who came from afar to sway and swill under the cool summer sighing of the tall pine trees.

The job was waitressing, and there was not just salary but tips, good tips for efficient, hard-working people like my mother who still carried a twinkle in her eye. I woke up mornings with my brother and stacked the coins on the dresser in high piles and giggled, because we knew that there would be ice-cream cones or candy that day and a six-pack of beer for the folks.

So, even though her husband was furious at her, my mother continued to work long nights, which didn't end until the last customer had left the pavilion and there had been, perhaps, a drink and a bite to eat after that. All those long nights she left behind a frustrated and angry man — for his pride was damaged by a wife who had to work — at home with his small children.

So he turned to —

And he turned his fury on —

His victims, his targets, and thus began the nasty little secret. I first remember his giving me the nightly bath when I was perhaps five years old, his putting warm water from the tea kettle into the white enamel washing bowl with the red ring around the edge, and washing my little body tenderly as a mother would.

Perhaps not intending —

Perhaps very well intending —

And how did it feel to be me?

At first I didn't understand what was going on. When he bathed me, I stood one foot in the white enamel bowl while he washed the dust off my ankles from a day of play. I felt him tremble as he lifted a soaped washcloth to my crotch and saw the color of his face change and heard his voice tremble as he said how pretty I was. I felt ashamed of myself for being so pretty.

Not long after came bedtime visits. After the lights were out and my mother long gone earning money at the pavilion, I lay in terror, for he had taken to tiptoeing quietly to where I slept across the room from my parents' double bed. My bed was in fact the sofa — I never had a bed of my own. My parents had decreed that my brother and I were too old to sleep together any more. So my brother lay sleeping alone, in a double bed in the other room.

My father came and put his hand under the covers and did things to me. He whispered to me that it was our secret, wasn't it, and that I liked it, didn't I. He wanted, he said, to "play" with me. It didn't feel like play. It was not like jumping rocks in the creek with my brother or riding the scooter down the hill in the driveway and putting both feet up and trying to balance all the way to the end.

It hurt. His hands were big, gnarled with years of work, but also just plain big, for he was a big man. And he put fingers in and around and forced his way between my legs no matter how much I closed my eyes and held my legs together or prayed to Mary and to God and to Saint Jude, saint of the impossible, to make him go away. I clenched my teeth tightly and closed my eyes and turned my head away so he couldn't kiss me on the lips. I thought I might throw up on him, which would make him angry. I made my stomach hard so he wouldn't hurt me if he pushed or hit me.

He came across the room every night for years, and sometimes before he turned out the light he stood across the room rubbing his terrifyingly huge thing that looked red and ugly and fat.

Nightmares began.

I woke up screaming, and then he would get out of his bed and come over and "comfort" me by stroking me all over until I pretended to be asleep and snoring so that he would leave me alone and go back to bed.

I began sleepwalking because the dreams were so terrifying that my body had to run away. The awful dream — which I told my family and they laughed — was that I was standing clutching my teddy bear as a huge crane with its chain full of a pile of long fat pine logs came swinging slowly, inexorably around to where I was standing. I ran because it was sure to crush me.

One time I woke up out in the front yard, confused about where I was. More often I tried to find my way back to bed in the dark and found the chair instead and crunched and huddled myself into it until morning broke when I could see the mistake I had made.

One dream made me immobile with fear and I could not run. I was forced to walk a tiny bridge made of green grass, but on either side were chasms so deep and dark I could not see the bottom. I clutched my teddy bear and carefully put one foot in front of the next and walked straight ahead.

Teddy was my only comfort, and I liked to reward him for being so good to me. When we were in bed together teddy drank make-believe chocolate milk shakes. That's what he craved most of all. He got all the kisses and hugs and tears and squeezes I gave to no one else.

Then mother decided teddy had to be taken away. I was getting to be too big a girl to sleep with a silly furry animal, although teddy by this time had lost his fur and become almost smooth. His original pink had become shades of dirty brown. His nose was pushed flat with hugging.

And so the morning of my ninth birthday, when I folded the blankets off my sofa bed and put them in the trunk across the room where they were stored during the day, I put teddy in the bottom instead of the top. And there he stayed, across the room, so near but yet so far, for when I was frightened in the night I was not allowed to go and get my bear to hug. I was a big girl now.

So I developed new strategies. I began to menstruate at age eleven, and I discovered that he would not touch me when I was all done up in Modess and elastic belt — a modern-day chastity belt, it turned out.

I began having phenomenally long menstrual periods. I found this ruse amusing in later years, a sign of pluck and courage.

For what, after all, kept the sorrow at a manageable level? Only pluck and courage and books, long books that took me out of my own place and time, like Les Misérables. *It made my life seem O.K. by comparison.*

But my courage began to run out, because things were getting worse. I had stood years of bed sneaking at night and now I had hard work by day as well, for my mother now cleaned other people's houses, worked at night waitressing when she could, and took in laundry. After I came home from school, I was expected to start dinner and clean the house and bring in any laundry on the clothesline.

One winter night I came home from school with a mountain of homework. The house was cold; no fire had been made in the fireplace, our only source of heat except the kitchen stove. I went out into the snow to get the frozen diapers off the clothesline and bring them into the house, where I had to string them, stiff as boards at first, upon an indoor clothesline. The room was full of the dank, urine-tinged smell of baby diapers.

Cold, feeling unloved, burdened with work, and choking with tears, I decided to put a bullet through my head.

I walked to the bureau on his side of the bed where, in the bottom drawer, he always kept the loaded .38 pistol to ward off intruders — he had the reputation of protecting his family — and I held the gun's compact, cold heaviness awhile in my hands.

I decided to kill myself in his presence so that he would know why I had done it. Weeping as I went, I stumbled out to the garage where he was bent over a chain saw, trying to fix it — he also had the reputation of being able to fix things, though broken items strewn around the garage remained until after his death.

He looked up. I sobbed, "I can't take it any more!" And I can remember the eyes heavy and lined with grime like a coal miner's and the dark jowls in the face that looked up at me from where his greasy and heavy hands rested on the saw.

He leapt up and with one motion seized the gun from me with his right hand and with his left crushed me to the ground. I lay crying in the coal slack and pine needles. He stomped into the house and put the gun back into the drawer, where it lay until after his death. My mother has since removed it for fear small grand-children would find it and have an accident.

I found new ruses to stop the horror. Now he cornered me by day, since the pavilion was long closed and my mother was gone all day working at a store. He often came back home early from his odd jobs or did not go to work at all. Everyone knew he tried to support his family, although his heart condition required that he have a two-hour lunch and a small nap during the midday.

One afternoon he surprised me by coming home earlier than expected. I was waxing the kitchen floor. Recognizing the soft-in-the-jaws look and silly grin that announced a pinching and fon-dling episode, I began methodically to wax him out of the room and, of course, to wax myself into a corner. I saw that he was angry at my trick. In earlier times the sea of wax would not have rebuffed him, but there was something different now — my new baby sister sleeping in the far bedroom. He turned on his heel and went into the bedroom and got the baby out of the crib. I heard him sit down in the rocking chair in the living room and begin to rock and murmur to the baby. I did not look. I did not want to see. I turned my face to the corner and my stomach was seized in a cramp. I could no longer cry. I could not let in anything that hurt too much.

The long golden days of summer vacation were spelled into ways of maneuvering to get out of his reach. I tried putting the ironing board between us if I was ironing in the same room where he was sitting. I read and even typed outdoors under the trees rather than take a risk of getting cornered inside. I could do nothing about the way he invariably wakened me in the morning, a pinch on one or both of my developed breasts.

I got work out of the house and left as early in the morning as I could. One day we both came home for lunch, and no one else was home. I made scrambled eggs. And he got me up against the sink, rubbed and pinched me and pushed his hard and lumpy groin against me. It took years before the man I finally did love and adore was able to approach me for a kiss from the back, particularly if I were standing at the sink.

Full of revulsion and anger and tears, I said across the living room where he stood lighting a smoke, "Why can't you just be a regular father?" And then I stopped sputtering, paused, and said in a lower voice,

"You know, I could take you to court and call you — almost anything."

And he turned and said softly, "If you ever do, I'll kill you."

And I believed him.

· ✳ · ✳ ·

BUT I survived.

And so did countless other women, adult women who will continue to live in silence about the enormous crime done them as children, a crime that affects nearly every facet of their lives as adults. The statistics, revised upward nearly every month, make the chances very good that you either know one of us or are one of us. As you drive down a country road to the small-town shopping mall, every third woman you see as she is hanging out her washing or pushing her stroller or checking out your groceries may have experienced sexual abuse as a child. As you bustle down a busy street bumping elbows with Christmas shoppers, every fifth woman you touch may have had some experience of incest. The overwhelming majority of those incest cases were perpetrated by a member of her nuclear family, nearly always her father or step-father. As a child, the incest victim is far less at risk in school or on the streets than she is in her own home, surrounded by those who "love" her.

Estimates vary about how large this crowd of incest survivors is. Susan Forward and Craig Buck say ten million American women have been incest victims; Sandra Butler puts the figure as high as twenty-five million.

The numbers are staggering, however we look at them. The numbers are people, real people, who carry around with them the shameful secret that they may never reveal — even anonymously to a Gallup pollster. For the yet more alarming fact is that sex abuse is a seriously underreported crime. Both the FBI and the Justice Department estimate that only one in ten cases is reported. It would be fair to say that sex abuse is almost a commonplace: it happens so often.

And we can no longer pretend that incest, long-called by social scientists the "universal taboo," is really taboo. If one in five women has been a victim, the secret pain of incest must lie behind the eyes of a woman you know. That victim may have been you as a child.

Incest has begun to come out of the closet of late, it is true. It has been covered in the nightly news and the large newspapers, often with sympathetic and sensitive reporting. But the emphasis in the popular press has been overwhelmingly directed to the juvenile victims and to the adult perpetrators. While this new interest in the sexual abuse of children is welcome and necessary, very little has been accurately reported about the adult who survived incest as a child.

We must remember that incest was not invented in this decade. If we are now hearing more about it, we can only conclude that it happened just as often in generations past but was kept secret. It was the lifelong burden of a victim who never told anyone because she was so ashamed, abetted by a society that never asked because it chose to remain ignorant and therefore unconcerned.

When adult incest victims *are* described in the popular press, they appear to be profoundly damaged people. If we are to believe these accounts, possibly every fourth woman in the population will grow up to be an abused wife, will resort to beating or neglecting her own children, and will be unable to succeed in a career or to tie a marital or other intimate bond as firmly and healthily as could a "normal" person. More cruelly, incest victims are said to be doomed to sit behind prison bars, to crowd the bus stations as runaways, to walk the streets as prostitutes, or to populate the mental institutions.

Many of those grim reports are true, of course. A study in 1983 showed that 100 percent of women in one penitentiary were victims of sexual abuse as children. Studies show an alarmingly high correlation between sexual abuse and women who become prostitutes, as well as children who become runaways and delinquent adolescents.

But the fact remains that *most* of us are *not* behind prison bars, although we may have constructed bars within ourselves, and most of us do *not* work the streets as prostitutes, although in most cases sexual adjustment has been a hard-won victory. We do *not* run away. In the majority of cases, we do *not* beat our children or abuse them, though many health professionals believe we do.

Who are we — the adult survivors of incest?

We are not psychotics and social misfits.

We are probably more like a woman we shall call Sabrina.

She has learned that we are writing a book about survivors and has volunteered her knowledge. She comes into the office quietly, wearing a friendly smile, removes her fur hat and pea coat. She is slim with strawberry blond hair, and looks ten years younger than her forty-four years. She has been in individual and group therapy for about two years, and she has learned to talk easily about her experiences, although she admits she often finds herself fearful and not confident in situations where she must speak in front of anyone she does not know; she is shy and insecure.

When we ask about the actual incest (as we routinely do), she says, "I'll try to remember. I only remember it partially. The first time I was eleven and the first time it was not intercourse; it was touching, and my mother walked in and saw it and she walked out again. She asked my father what he was doing and he said it was none of her business and he had to explain the facts of life to me because she didn't."

The mother subsequently left alone for a trip abroad. Sabrina implored her mother to take her along. "I begged her to let me go," she reports. During the mother's absence her father had intercourse with her in the same room where her brothers were also sleeping. She thinks she must have blacked out during the actual event, since she remembers his starting but not his finishing: "That's the funny part; I remember him doing it, but I never remember the finish. But afterwards I remember his saying to me, 'You're not to tell this to anyone; otherwise I have to kill you and me.'"

More intercourse, fondling, touching, oral intercourse, and verbal abuse continued until she left the house to marry at age eighteen.

Is there anything to distinguish Sabrina from the so-called normal doctor, teacher, homemaker, librarian, or accountant you see every day? Nothing distinguishes her on the outside. Sabrina is a hairdresser who loves her job, a mother who loves her children, an attractive woman with a good marriage and a seemingly happy life.

But let us ask Sabrina.

Incest has affected Sabrina as an adult in both mental and physical ways. She has suffered physical symptoms that were hard to explain. A physician prescribed an antiseizure medication for a year thinking she was possibly epileptic because she continued to black out unpredictably and for no apparent reason. The fainting ended once she remembered that the episodes began when her brother, upon being forcibly ejected from their parents' house, came to Sabrina's door and asked to live with her and her family. She refused, because space was tight with two small children. The brother then beat her badly and threatened her by saying he would get back at her by telling "what you did with your father."

"That brought it all back," she says, and she passed out for the first time in her adult life. She now theorizes that she used to pass out during the incestuous intercourse as a child and that being reminded of it as an adult caused the same result. The blackouts were her defense against intolerable pain.

Having such severe pain as a child taught her to dissociate — to remove herself mentally from what was happening in order to avoid feelings. She admits that, as a child, the only way she could survive was to deny that she even had feelings. As an adult she still has problems with feelings: "I can't get angry enough or feel as strongly as other people," she says. She is having to work hard and with single-minded effort to assert herself and to communicate her feelings.

She has permitted herself to be victimized as an adult because she was forced to be a victim as a child — her brother's beating taught her that. Had her childhood been different, she would not have had to struggle so hard with mature self-esteem and self-respect.

The incest has had a profound impact on her relationship with her parents. Even though her mother lives in the same city, Sabrina does not see her. The mother will not admit that she could have protected her daughter better, and Sabrina is still longing for her mother to say, "I'm sorry." She knows she may wait forever.

Her father lives in another country. Sabrina has written him a letter calling him to account for what he has done, and she has gotten no answer. "I'm furious," she says, "and I'm going to write another letter about the incest and how I feel, how angry I am, and if I get no answer, I am going to let his relatives know what he did to me." She is resigned to the fact that he may never admit his crime.

What cries out from the example of Sabrina is the tremendous resilience and courage that seem to characterize incest survivors. They live with truths many "normal" people can hardly bear to hear. Therapists and researchers close to the subject sometimes marvel that people damaged so severely can survive, much less flourish. Not unlike victims of a concentration camp, their lot has been to submit to degradation, violence, and pain, and finally to try to transmute those experiences into life-giving ones, to exchange the paltry currency of an abused childhood for the relative treasure of a satisfying adulthood.

Sabrina exemplifies the incest survivor who triumphs over tawdry and painful sexual experiences with courage and will. That burden can only be lightened by the truth that finally comes to incest survivors: "You didn't deserve this and it isn't your fault. Make yourself as happy as you can be now, despite the fact that this happened to you."

It is time to put to rest some of the pernicious myths about what we are like, to start telling the truth about our lives, and to show that we are not monsters and misfits.

But it is time to talk about our pain, too, and the ways we learn to integrate that pain into our adult lives.

This book presents that talk, the accounts of incest survivors themselves, who tell what it is like to have been victimized as children, to grow up to be victimized as adults, and then, painfully and with great labor, to learn to choose not to be victims any longer.

The experiences of incest that we discuss here vary tremendously, ranging from perhaps one person's years of exposure to her father's exhibitionism resulting in no physical contact to the most brutal and violent scenes of rape and sexual perversity. Both are incest; both result in pain and damage to the survivor.

Experts and nonexperts have given widely differing opinions about what must happen before incest can be said to have occurred. We have taken as a working definition of sexual abuse the one provided by the National Committee for Prevention of Child Abuse: "Sexual abuse consists of contacts or interactions between a child and an adult when the child is being used for the sexual stimulation of that adult or of another person." Lynn Daugherty's definition in *Why Me?* expands the definition in a helpful way for survivors: "Sexual abuse takes place any time a person is tricked, trapped, forced or bribed into a sexual act."

Incest adds to these definitions one additionally devastating dimension: the offender is related to the victim. Here, again, we have drawn no fine lines. It seems clear that the absence of bloodlines in a stepfather does not measurably reduce the pain of incest: this person is no less a father to the child because he is not her genetic father. This is the kind of distinction that adults quibble over; to the child it is equally a betrayal of familial trust. So incest we have dealt with includes stepfathers as well as genetic fathers, uncles, brothers, and grandfathers.

Nor have we here tried to provide a sliding scale of seriousness of damage: there is no simple way to predict how incest will affect a person. Often what sound like "mild" offenses seem to have created havoc in a woman's life, while exceptionally severe and grotesque acts have left a reasonably intact person. Each person's history involves combinations of factors in the millions. Factors that researchers are investigating, however, include degree of violence used, age difference between perpetrator and victim, closeness of the relationship, frequency of abuse, and availability of stable role models outside the family. But these variables are hard to put into an equation that will predict adult problems. Each woman comes already equipped with her own biologically predetermined personality characteristics, so each woman reaches her own creative conclusions about the abuse, and the variations are many and the solutions admirable.

What a woman should understand is that it was not a flaw in her that caused the incest. Many grow up saying, "Why me?" "What did I do to deserve this?"

The brutal answer to these questions lies in the mind of the perpetrator and his accomplices, if he had any. We have not chosen to plumb the mind of the abuser; we have interviewed none, questioned none. Such possible closed-mindedness would be objectionable if we were researchers trying to discover why incest occurs and what its dynamics are. Our purpose here has been to hear from *the experts themselves — the women to whom it has happened* — what it is like to be adult female survivors of incest and how it is that they have coped with the pain and conquered the shame.

What do we mean by a "survivor"? Mental health workers have drawn up lists of requirements about what a real survivor should be able to do. Incest self-help groups list categories or stages of survivor growth. Manuals are written about steps to take in order to become a survivor rather than a victim.

Checklists of what a woman must do to qualify as a survivor put a heavy burden upon women who are growing and functioning as adults in this world. Most have struggled very hard to achieve any degree of "normalcy," so it is particularly thoughtless, even cruel, to say to a woman, "These are the remaining steps you must take before you have *really* survived."

We feel that any woman who is not in a cemetery is a survivor. Even the institutionalized women have, in a way, survived, because they developed a mental disorder to escape an intolerable situation — although, unfortunately, that disorder has rendered them incapable of living in the outside world. The fact that they have all chosen *life* over self-inflicted death makes them survivors.

We did not need to develop litmus tests of genuine survivorhood in order to interview and to write this book. If women were so damaged that they could not talk to us articulately about their experiences, we simply did not hear from them. Some came forward; others are surviving on a level that only they know, and far be it from us to label them arrogantly as nonsurvivors. The judgment of the human heart must be that survival of such pain is a complex matter carried on in myriad ways within the lives of millions of women, ways we can never hope to understand perfectly.

When we talked to the women who had grown to adulthood with their secret, managing their lives despite the damage it did to them, we came up with some general conclusions. And we also found a central truth: incest always results in damage of one kind or another.

Further, we found that the type of damage was reasonably predictable. There was a surprising consistency in the problems incest survivors had all struggled to overcome. Not everyone suffered the same symptoms in exactly the same way, of course. The range and diversity of experiences were wide, as was the variety of mechanisms women developed in response to them. It is around those issues that we decided to write our account: the issues women face and how they learn to survive through them, how, in short, they reclaim their lives after the crime done them in childhood.

The first issue, of course, was sheer survival of the actual incestuous incidents themselves. Every survivor remembers feeling trapped as a child, like a small animal cornered by a predator. Sexual advances from an adult constitute a power game. Not only is the adult much larger and physically more powerful; he also has emotional authority. Inevitably the child feels confused and has to look about for a means of escape. Every woman had to survive this critical situation by developing some mechanism, ranging from pretending that the event was not happening, to taking bribes, to pretending to enjoy it, to actually separating her thoughts from reality and dissociating mind from body.

Actual physical survival was the issue for women who experienced violent incest, where the fear of being murdered or beaten badly or where the wish for death by suicide all lurked in the context of the offense. We saw here a range of survival skills that developed out of *necessity* as a refuge or coping mechanism, which quite literally saved these women's lives. Some simply took bribes for the acts they performed, a fairly common tactic that permits the girl to think at the time that she has at least some control over circumstances. Some developed multiple personalities that permitted them to escape from their bodies during the episodes. Many report out-of-body experiences that allowed them, as one survivor put it, "to lie like a rag doll that I watched things happening to." Survivors need to realize that these escapes were *necessary* for survival. They had little choice, and whatever they could do for survival was acceptable.

This sense of entrapment is well explained by psychiatrist Alice Miller, who has written extensively about child abuse:

> Adults are free to hurl reproaches at God, at fate, at the authorities, or at society if they are deceived, ignored, punished unjustly, confronted with excessive demands or lied to. Children are not allowed to reproach their Gods — their parents and teachers. By no means are they allowed to express their frustrations. Instead, they must repress or deny their emotional reactions, which build up inside, until adulthood, when they are finally discharged, but not on the object that caused them. The forms this discharge may take range from persecuting their own children by the way they bring them up, to all possible degrees of emotional illness, to addiction, criminality, and even suicide.

We agree with Miller that incest does result in damage and some degree of emotional illness in adulthood. But we do not believe that being trapped in childhood means being condemned in adulthood. To escape the web of pain woven over them in childhood, women can choose as adults not to victimize themselves or others.

The first clue that women are ready to change is that the childhood survival mechanisms do not work as well any more, and in fact may actually become destructive. Cutting off feelings to avoid pain during abuse kept many a little girl alive. Cutting off feelings when she becomes an adult deadens her and keeps her from feeling alive. And so she must develop new ways to survive since the old ways are no longer effective. And she must learn to confront the adult issues that emerge as a result of child abuse.

The most important — the central — issue she faces as an adult is trust. A woman who has been coerced by a male she should have been able to rely on may have a hard time ever trusting men again.

As an adult she may actually fear and hate men or she may end up feeling dependent upon men for her sense of self. The extremes range from sexual aversion to sexual addiction. Since she fears risking her whole self, she withholds genuine love and trust.

But it may not be only men she fears to trust. Often she cannot trust women, because in the survivor's mind the mother who allowed the abuse to happen is seen as a nonprotector, so that women become suspect and untrustworthy as a result. Finding and keeping friends may be difficult, and when she has them, she may make intolerable or burdensome demands, which, when they are not met, prompt her to sigh and say, "See, I told you so. All people are alike — untrustworthy."

Women who have survived incest often cannot, finally, trust their own selves. There are always the fears that one will be rejected, used, abandoned — a rag doll left crumpled on the floor once again. A response to such fears is to keep her "real self" hidden (as witness the fact that we hear so little from survivors and so much of what is revealed is anonymously written or spoken). The woman may fear to let go or to trust her feelings. After all, in the past the child was often told exactly how to feel and was required to deny her own feelings and any demands she had for herself: "You and Daddy have this little secret, now, that we like to play and you won't tell anyone how much you like it, will you?" The survivor's own forcibly repressed feelings that have nothing to do with the father's fantasy could stay buried a lifetime.

The issue of trust is a central one for survivors, and when victory comes, it is hard won. Women who have survived have nearly always had this particular struggle. They first learn to trust themselves, to admit finally that they have feelings. These may be "bad" or uncomfortable feelings that they wish were not there, but accepting themselves means accepting those feelings. Trust of others and finally of men can be a long time coming, but it nearly always has to do with realizing that the offender was but one male (or at most a few) and that he was sick or perverted. Other people may or may not be sick or perverted, but at least every other person is not that same man who perpetrated those crimes and those damages upon the woman's young body and mind. Other people deserve to be judged on their own merits.

The issue of self-esteem or self-confidence is the next one that survivors face — grappling with their own value as people. From the time a woman has the awareness that what was happening to her does not happen to everyone else (and this feeling can be present at the outset of the incest if a child realizes, for example, that Daddy is acting odd or is making unusual demands), she will feel "special" or "weird." She nearly always grows up with that feeling, which makes her, as an adult, come to believe that she is not quite like other people. Because she cannot trust her own feelings, and because she is not sure how normal people act, a woman who was an incest victim as a child may become the subject of repeated victimizations in adulthood. If she begins thinking she is nothing but damaged goods, a piece of junk, she can be victimized again by the rapist and wife-beater. Some survivors let themselves be used in relationships, even prostituting themselves in repeated sexual encounters from which they get nothing. Others settle for an unsatisfactory marital relationship from which they think they deserve nothing.

Lack of self-confidence and low self-esteem can lead to unassertiveness in social situations, submissiveness in close relationships, inability to express anger and resentment in legitimate ways, and even years of utter hopelessness and despair, a feeling, as one subject put it, that "I'm flawed right to the core of my being and I'll never be well."

These women have learned all kinds of new survival techniques for their feelings of low self-esteem, most of which are useful for the rest of the population at large. Assertiveness training, careful monitoring not to let others walk all over them, learning to get out into the world and take risks — all help women to survive. One woman chuckles over a button her therapist gave her which says, in beautiful italic script, "Eat shit; get sick." It helps her to remember never again to submit supinely to people who want to weaken her and use her.

Only after a woman begins to grow in self-esteem can she start putting together a healthy sexuality for herself. Severe sexual dysfunction as a result of incest ranges from sexual addiction to complete aversion. But the incest survivor may have other less dramatic problems with sex. These may occur against the backdrop of a fairly well-adjusted sex life. Many women mention being unable to stand the smell or taste of semen; many are turned off by overtly "sexy" men; still others find certain sexual positions or "looks" or acts of lovemaking intolerable or disagreeable at best.

Recognition of the problem provides the basic groundwork for survival. The woman who finally realizes that oral sex from her father contributed to her inability to perform those acts with the person she loves may find that the memory frees her — either for all kinds of lovemaking or for the realization that certain kinds of sexual acts can never be in her lexicon of lovemaking. If she informs her lover and that person understands and acquiesces, she has survived quite capably indeed.

A largely unrecognized aspect of the survivor's sexuality is the larger issue of her attitude toward her own body. We find an array of eating disorders among incest survivors, from anorexia and bulimia to compulsive overeating, with stops at all ports in between. The extremes of obesity and anorexia are both possible outcomes for incest victims, because both can act as denials of the physical side of oneself. Some women want to make themselves unattractive either by overweight or underweight so as to repel sexual advances. In the case of obesity body weight becomes a way of shielding one's ego inside a castle of flesh. It can also reflect the desire to be physically large and powerful. One obese survivor said she wanted "to be bigger than he is so he can't push me around any more."

Closely allied with eating disorders is the physical damage that a woman may sustain and, to her peril, deny. These range from

severely damaged and scarred reproductive organs — some resulting from early intercourse are serious enough to render an adult
woman unable to have children — to venereal disease and bladder
irregularities.

A visit to a gynecologist can strike terror into the heart of a
woman abused as a youngster, not only because of the nature of
the examination but also because she does not want to have any
genital mutilation verified. The survivor has usually faced up to
this terror and is in possession of the facts about her physical
health; she might even need to accept physical deformities.

Not so easy to diagnose or treat are rampant psychosomatic
disorders: headaches, lower back problems and pain, muscle tension caused by stress and by forcing oneself to smile and look normal, and all manner of sleep disorders. Alcoholism and drug abuse
also occur frequently. Again, most survivors have faced at least
one of these symptoms, and some have learned to use them; when
these problems pop up, chances are that stress levels are on the rise
and some self-nurturing is in order.

Nurturing is, in fact, a key word to survivors, stemming nearly
always from the fact that they were never nurtured in their childhood by either father or mother, for the mother has frequently
abandoned her daughter psychologically. Having to take an adult
role at an early age may result in a range of problems, including
the phenomenon of the "little mother." Because of the mother's
psychological remoteness or actual physical abandonment, the
daughter often steps into the mother's role, taking over the child
care and housekeeping duties as well as sexual pacification of the
father. This role reversal isolates her. Not in touch with her peers,
she does not learn social skills.

In the absence of a mother, survivors are inventive about finding
substitutes, both during their childhood and after. How many
kindly next-door neighbors, loving aunts, and wonderful teachers
have rescued a young girl's life unawares? Many survivors have
sought out the mothering they needed as a young child by attach-
ing themselves to a mother figure. Others lavish that mothering

on their own children as a way of compensating. And finally, nurturing oneself by way of small physical attentions has been a useful technique for many — a walk in the woods, a bubble bath taken at leisure, a class in ceramics, all are ways of helping a woman feel good about herself. The survival techniques in this area are almost as numerous as the survivors themselves.

The lack of healthy mothering shows up as an issue in survivors' attitudes toward parenting and marriage. Many confess to avoiding or delaying marriage or having children for fear that they will fall into the same patterns of abuse — that history will repeat itself. For those who do marry, having children can be fraught with stress; since survivors did not learn effective mothering from their family mode, they often feel confused about how mothering is to be done, a confusion that can lead to too much severity or too much indulgence or simply to the feeling that they must not mess up — *ever* — an undue strain on both parent and child.

A minority of survivors we talked to actually batter their own children; for other individuals, being abused seemed to be a vaccination against doing it to their own children. The problems most women faced were what all parents face about the difficult task of childrearing. The difference for an adult survivor is that she can make it harder for herself by continually questioning what she is doing. Since she may have had a negative role model herself, she often feels at sea about what a mother should do.

Even though many survivors find it difficult, they have learned to seek out help, whether from a self-help group, a small band of fellow-survivors, or a professional. And even in the cure, there are hazards: in our interviewing we always asked the question, "How did the mental health community treat you and your history of incest?", and the answers were far from reassuring. Many therapists are simply not comfortable with the topic and cannot, therefore, deal competently with an incest survivor. Avoidance and denial appear to be widespread among mental health professionals. Many would sooner ask a client if she is hearing voices than ask her if she has sexual abuse in her background, even though figures would indicate that the chances of an abusive background far out-weigh the occurrence of hearing voices.

Male and female therapists seem to encounter different sets of problems that may render them unable to treat survivors of incest effectively. Although some therapists appear unable to treat the adult female survivor, there are also many competent and caring ones.

Finally, much therapeutic advice as well as folk wisdom and religious thinking mandates that an adult survivor needs to confront her offender. How does one go about such a confrontation? Is forgiveness ever possible? Exactly what does accepting incest as part of one's life mean?

What shines forth from these stories of struggle is the resilience, sensitivity, and courage of the women who survived. The survivor cannot ever completely put away the incest experience: being a survivor means carrying the experience in different ways all through her life. But the process of surviving and changing as a result of incest teaches a survivor her strengths, and she is freed to live a little more deeply and appreciatively when the sunshine of acceptance finally can illuminate the years of suffering and anger.

How Children Survive Incest

M Y MIND *was my escape when I was a child. I used my mind to take me away from the impossible life I was being asked to lead.*

I did this in many ways. I was, first of all, a dreamer. I consciously induced dreams or fantasies in bed at night to transport myself to another place and time. I could start them at will, like flipping the switch on a movie projector, and a travelogue film began: the scenario was always me, grown up, doing what I wanted to do, with none of my family around.

My fantasies were not glamorous by any means. They usually featured me wearing a flower-sprigged dress (understand that I was almost never permitted to wear a dress as a child), walking to my blue car in a city parking lot after my day's work as a secretary. This little cameo felt like glorious freedom to me, and I dwelt on each tiny feature of it again and again — the color and style of the dress, my coiffure, the door handles of the car, the gravel in the parking lot, my handbag, my feelings as I waved to a friend driving by on the street.

I have tried in vain to remember precisely what went through my mind while the actual physical and sexual abuse was going on, and the only answer I get from inside myself is "prayer." That stands to reason because I had an elaborate prayer life, so uncon-

ventional that it was more magic than prayer. I forced myself to go to sleep at night with my hands folded as if in prayer in case I died during the night. I made elaborate bargains with God that if He would keep my father from my bed that night, I would say not one, but three rosaries. I hoarded holy cards of martyred saints, and I doted particularly on the story of child martyr Maria Goretti who died at age fourteen trying to resist a rape. Stabbed fifteen times by the aggressor, she died forgiving him. Maria Goretti was the patron saint of children who wanted to be pure.

When my father came to my bed at night, I said my "Hail Marys" bead after bead on the rosary I held in my head not my hands. It was like a prayer mantra that rendered me oblivious to the physical world. To this day when I have dental work I automatically begin saying the rosary as the dentist drills and fills a tooth.

During the years that my mother was a waitress who worked late at night, I recall trying to get her to stay home so that I would be protected (she doesn't remember that I did). I do remember the tremendous relief I felt when I saw the car lights in the driveway signaling her return; I could at last go to sleep. I had been feigning sleep, eyes closed, consciously snoring softly, and now I could really drop off.

Daytime abuse was trickier. I couldn't close my eyes and pretend sleep or go into a dream trance, and prayers didn't work as well with my eyes open. What I did instead was to build an emotional wall around myself, and I lived inside that little castle. I studied deeply, losing track of time and not heeding the conversation around me. I read voraciously to keep myself securely in the world of the book rather than the place where I was, a place of violence and insults and degradation.

I am proud of these abilities, and I realize as an adult that there is nothing far-fetched about them at all: people kept hostage or imprisoned often resort to similar tactics, losing themselves in study or maintaining a rigorous reading program to keep themselves sane.

The problem was that I carried these survival skills into adulthood. The emotional snow fort I had built around myself did not melt, and the numbing dreams and prayer mantras became a way to escape the present, even when my adult life showed itself to be safe and good.

Some of the childhood skills developed into infirmities and illnesses in my adult life. I was a student well into that life, and I suffered for years from what I called "test syndrome": I clenched my jaw tightly, ground my teeth together, and furrowed my brow to get through it — and the situations were not limited to tests. Each day, no matter how sunny and joyous, seemed a trial; I had to grit my teeth and forge ahead.

Finally, racked with face, head, and jaw pain, I went to a doctor. I discovered that I was suffering from TMJ, or temporo-mandibular-joint disease, a painful inflammation of the jaw joint on one or both sides of the mouth that makes, let us say, eating an apple or chomping into a hotdog physically impossible. I lived on yogurt, soft scrambled eggs, and aspirin until my jaw improved. But it was never really cured, because TMJ disease is caused by grinding and clenching the teeth, both during sleep and unconsciously during the day. What was happening was that in trying to keep out pain, I was causing myself pain.

Over the years there were migraines, spastic colons, lower back pains, appendicitis alarms, and chronic bronchitis. But despite my illnesses, I seemed unable to feel any real pain, and that was the most terrifying symptom of all. I was always in control. I was the one to keep a cool head in emergencies; I had the unlined face and efficient manner of a paramedic, or at least that was what I thought until I noticed that ambulance and fire personnel in press photographs of emergencies often look stricken even as they are doing their job. It is not normal for a person to be unaffected all the time by any strong emotion. I began over the years to realize that I was protecting myself from pain by a nearly total want of feeling — anger, sorrow, unhappiness on the one side, and laughter, peacefulness, or bliss on the other.

These were the unhappy legacies of skills learned in childhood when they comprised the only protection I had. As a child, I had learned to shut out emotion; why should I feel it as an adult? As a child, I made myself numb by repeating my prayer mantra over and over; as an adult, I was often numb to the world around me. As a child I had spent countless nights pretending to be asleep when I was not. It was a lie, a ruse — and also the only thing my child mind could think of to do to protect myself from molestation. When I became an adult I had a lot of practice denying. It was not terribly hard, therefore, to pretend that what I was experiencing was something other than what it really was: if I felt angry or fearful or sad, it was really something else, and if I ignored those unwanted and unhappy feelings long enough, they would finally go away, as my father always got up and disappeared back into the night.

I was an emotional stoic, never letting myself go either to suffer pain or to experience joy. That was no way to live.

· ✳ · ✳ ·

THIS is a grim chapter, and necessarily so, because in it we must detail actual case histories of childhood incest. We do not do so to be voyeuristic or sexually titillating, nor do we like to paint men as nothing but wicked perpetrators. We do it by way of explanation. People who prefer not to read accounts of hurt and abuse may even want to skip this chapter. Particularly if you were abused, this chapter may prove painful, so you may want to delay reading it until you feel safe enough to do so.

It is necessary for us to go into this kind of detail in order to look at what happened to survivors as children so that we can understand them as adults. We need to discover the genesis of these survival tactics. What does a child do to try to escape the pain and shame of incest? How do those techniques persist into adulthood? We will divide the kinds of responses into the psychological, the physical, and the manipulative, while recognizing that most children use all three of these methods at one time or another and that it is sometimes difficult to distinguish among them. Child victims grow up and carry into adulthood a complex of survival skills, some of which are useful. Others need to be slightly transformed to make for real courage and strength. Yet others must be discarded in favor of new and more effective ways of dealing with life.

Before we begin, we must try to cast our memories back, to drop our sophisticated adult ways of responding to the world, and to visualize how it feels to be a child being abused. *Not an adult* being abused, because adults have more power and a larger range of choices than children have. *Remember: a child being abused.*

To begin the picture, how old is the child in question? Doctors Ruth and Henry Kempe, who were pioneers in the field of child abuse, estimated a decade ago that "the median age for incestuous behavior in recent years has been between nine and ten years of age." That is an old number in this rapidly changing field, but professionals still do not widely dispute it. If anything, they lower the age somewhat. Child abuse expert David Finkelhor states that abuse peaks for girls between ages eight and twelve and that "children under the age of five have a fairly serious risk of victimization, yet the public is not aware of it."

Remember that "median" means that half of the cases are below that age and that half are above it, so that the Kempes' figure of nine or ten would mean that half the abuse occurs before that age. Our studies include people who have some memory of abuse that happened before language developed, perhaps at age three or four or even earlier. We also saw cases of physical sexual assault beginning at the onset of puberty, although in many of the later-developing cases there had been present for some time the subtle communication by the adult that the child was sexually desirable, whether in body language, such as gestures and looks, or in speech.

Even if sexual abuse occurs during the teen years, it probably began much earlier. It is estimated that on the average, incestuous episodes usually last three and one-half years, so that when the adolescent is being abused, the likelihood is great that incest began in her prepubescent years. The implications of these figures need to sink in before we can ever hope to understand adult incest survivors. We must try to see through the eyes of a child as we attempt to visualize what effects forced adult sex has on her. We are not talking about adolescents, for the most part, since most incest begins to occur before the time when the majority of us remember the stirrings of what was to become adult sexuality.

Adult sex practiced upon young children confuses them, makes them feel trapped and powerless; and, like hunted animals, they escape by whatever means they can.

Let us try now to see the world through the eyes of a child, an exercise far more difficult than at first it might seem. For example, parents and teachers take it to be charming inventiveness when a child draws a picture of a bus or a car with wheels nearly as tall as the vehicle itself. These pictures, however, are probably an accurate representation of a child's world. From the perspective of someone, say, thirty-six inches tall, real bus wheels are, in fact, taller than one's head and loom as much more important than the windshield or steering wheel, which might be the most important parts of a car or bus to an adult.

In sexual assault, the child has a visual perspective that is different from that of the adult as well. A man looking down at his own genitals sees a sight quite different from what a small child does who looks up at them or has them thrust into her face or mouth. She may see the penis as something scary or wiggly that comes at her across the room, and she may not connect it with her father or with any pain. One survivor thought her father kept in his pocket a small creature or animal that got bigger when he stroked it. She was completely mystified as to what it was, but she remembers the humiliation she felt when he came into her room at night and put the creature into her mouth "and it peed inside my mouth," she remembers. Children know about "peeing"; they do not necessarily know about ejaculation. And they certainly know the humiliation of being "peed *on*."

One incest survivor has an artistic capacity to recapture this child's view of life. Barbara has multiple personalities, one of whom likes best to communicate as an artist and mutely draws pictures that show the fearful figure in her childhood. It is a stick figure with three noticeable features — a pair of glasses, some hair standing straight up on end, and a long, fat triangle at the bottom of the picture, nearly as large as all the rest put together. Sometimes the figure is clad or adorned in some way, but when the personality (whom Barbara calls "Babs") is angry about what happened to her as a child, the drawn figure is reduced to the three basic elements — glasses, hair, and penis. "Babs's" starkly reductive pictures suggest the enormous terror a full-grown person can evoke in the child.

Let us look at Barbara's case history more carefully to see both the childhood experience and the adult survival techniques that emerged. Barbara's case was the most physically severe we heard about and it seemed the most shocking to us partly because her father is a minister.

Barbara's father was brutal and sadistic and liked to inflict pain. Because she was so young, there was no place to escape, and she became a puppet under his complete control, kept at the mercy of his painful and cruelly perverted behavior:

When I was a small child he would come in and play with me as if I was a doll, and he would stick his middle finger into my rectum and his index finger into my vagina and hold me up over his head as if I were a puppet or a doll or something. I can't put things in sequence, but times after that . . . I have the memory of his changing my diapers, fondling my clitoris and sticking his finger into my vagina and it hurt.

My father varied, you see, which makes it difficult to summarize. He would be this demanding sexually active pervert and then he would come back and he was a prude, he shifted 180 degrees. [After the diaper-changing incident] he came back and it had hurt so I had placed my hand down there to comfort myself and he said that I was a filthy slut and God would punish me for touching myself down there. So he positioned a fan next to my crib and he tied my arm near the elbow on the bar of the crib and my index finger to the edge of the fan and turned the fan on and said God would make sure the rest of my hand would fall into the fan. He didn't even need to be there. God was going to do this.

Barbara managed to keep her hand from falling into the blades of the old-fashioned electric fan. But at other times she found herself helplessly brutalized. He tied her with his belt to a shower rod when she was four or five and raped her anally; he put her head and face under her tall four-poster bed, covered them with a pillow, then raped her.

He also made otherwise "safe" or unlikely situations hellish. She remembers him masturbating on her as she lay on the desk in his church study. When he was finished, he cleaned the semen off her with his pocket knife, telling her she was a "filthy slut" and that she must have been "rotten to the core inside because of this filthy stuff [coming out of her]." He did everything in his power to say that *she,* not *he,* was intrinsically evil, vile, and to blame.

The message got through: Barbara began to think that she was so filthy inside that she could never get clean. She had watched her father use the knife to get the semen off her, and even to remove it from under his fingernails. In her childish desperation she began to think that the only way to get clean was to cut herself open and scrape her insides out. "I learned about this in therapy, later," says Barbara, "when I kept saying 'Cut along the dotted line,' a line I felt from my forehead straight down the front of me. I had gotten the phrase from my father when he was teaching us to carve turkey and he would always say, 'There's a dotted line along the inside that you cut along.' I kept feeling that, and it was hard not to destroy myself; I felt like a garbage dump inside."

Not only knives but other objects became tools of torment to her. On one occasion her father suspended her from the staircase upside down over the landing and beat her with a wire catbrush, then raped her. "He was extraordinarily inventive and imaginative," she says with a grimace.

Barbara's whole childhood had become a living hell, for if she was not actually being abused, she was wondering when it would happen next. Her father's sadistic episodes recurred every few months. They were not a daily occurrence, so she faced each day with trepidation, wondering what might be in store for her. Managing the fear about when the abuse was going to occur became almost as important as managing the pain during the abuse.

She came up with a solution that worked: she divided up the pain among several personalities, so that no one would have to suffer the contradictions she saw in her father's behavior. "The sides of my father were so widely divergent that I had no way to pull them together as a child. I could not look at him and say that he was both my wonderful and kind father and the sadist who tormented me," she says.

Each of the personalities had a piece of her difficult life and dealt only in that context. A first personality, "Barb," was the girl who functioned in the workaday world of school and church; she was the model "good girl" who made honor roll grades and happily received the praise and encouragement her father gave her. This is the personality that permitted her to function until she entered into therapy at age thirty-one; it was the one who used her intellect to obtain a Ph.D. A second personality (whom she calls "Barbie") chose to live in a closet much of the time because it was safe and warm; this personality collected stones and shells and was inventive and quiet in her play. "In therapy this is the little one who trusted the therapist enough to ask help to keep alive 'Barb,' the adult who had fallen apart," says Barbara. The third personality was "Babs," the artist who liked to communicate through pictures and who drew the stick figures in therapy years later. The fourth personality, Barbara, was the one created in therapy to function and to mother the original personalities while they faced the past. "'Barb' had been the previous functioner, but was at one point in therapy in too much pain to function, so Barbara was created," she explains now.

"There was," says Barbara, "no intercommunication between

the personalities, no agreement. When 'Barb' couldn't tolerate things, she 'went away.' This was not planned. She just willed herself on the ceiling and there she could watch 'Babs' or 'Barbie' and feel guilty." Barbara describes this technique as a kind of self-hypnosis; each personality had to deal with the contradiction of father and tormentor. "Barbie" suffered the pain alone, shutting down as much as possible, by shallow breathing and no movement whatsoever. The "Babs" personality, the artist, did have fear, for she saw and drew pictures of two different men: her daddy, whom she loved, and the mean rapist or, as "Babs" describes him, "the man with the sticky uppy hair." The child "Babs" had to have a nice daddy, and she insisted that the abuse was caused by a stranger. The "Barbie" personality, the high-achieving student, saw only the supportive and estimable minister/father. "Barb" had no emotions.

As a child, Barbara "left herself" in order to survive, parceling herself up into different people to handle the trying segments of her life. As an adult, however, when she tried to function in this disjointed and unintegrated way, she was miserable. "Each personality had a piece of me and I couldn't put them together," she says now, a touch ruefully.

Barbara is now in her midthirties. Although she is a multiple personality, there is nothing frightening about her; her face is gentle, her hand and body movements slow and deliberate, and she fixes the listener with soft brown eyes as she talks about her experiences.

She will receive a Ph.D. in Germanic languages soon. She is at work on her dissertation. She holds a good job as a book editor, and she lives alone now. The extreme abuse to the contrary, she has decided that she does indeed like men, but she hastens to add, "I haven't exactly begun to date any yet." She has been in therapy for five years.

Despite her academic achievement, Barbara felt doomed as an adult. She got through her dreadful childhood, but she very nearly did not survive her adult life. She had completely lost the ability to feel, a fact of which she became aware only later in her life.

Now she has discovered the reason. "If my father thought he was causing me pain," she says, "he would redouble his efforts." Since showing any response caused more pain, Barbara learned to batten down her responses most effectively. And learning to deal with emotion as an adult has been unbelievably difficult. "I will be talking to my therapist, and she will say 'You look angry,' and I have to sort of go inside myself and feel where my muscles are and then I say, kind of surprised, 'Oh, so *that's* anger.'"

After she had attempted suicide as an adult three times and had been physically assaulted once by another man, she decided to seek help. Had she not had that strength and courage, Barbara might well not have survived to her thirtieth birthday. "I went into therapy to find out what the problem was that made me 'go away' the way I did, and there I learned, in a safe place and with a friend." Barbara had no recollection of the incest until she entered therapy.

Her comment about how she decided to go into therapy belies the struggle that preceded the step into professional help, and it understates the courage it took to face herself and her problems as an adult. Only with the greatest effort has Barbara been able to begin the struggle to overcome the horror, shame, and fear of her childhood, and to see herself as worthwhile and the world as a good and hope-inspiring place to live.

Barbara became able to perceive that *survival techniques learned in childhood can become disabilities in adulthood.* "I was the victim of the abuse well into adulthood not because of my father but because I wasn't treasuring myself," she says. She had been using the same techniques of escape even though she had no similar need to escape in her adult life.

It appears that tremendously severe physical and sexual abuse calls for the most radical protection a child can muster, and developing multiple personalities is certainly an extreme response. But there is a whole continuum of both abuse and response from which the adult survivor can learn. It is ironic that the most helpful and beneficial way an incest survivor can improve her life often comes from acknowledging unpleasant, unattractive, or even disabling parts of her personality. She might not like to see herself as a cold, unfeeling person, or as a highly manipulative and controlling wife and mother, or as someone who seems totally unable to keep women friends. But confronting those disabilities or difficulties seems to be the first step toward understanding how the patterns may have developed in childhood. It is crucial to realize that when these tactics were called up and implemented in childhood, they were necessary and useful. In most cases they spelt survival and sanity for a child being used, hurt, and deprived, physically and emotionally as well as sexually.

The inquiry is painful. Maybe we do not like how we see ourselves today; we may be locked into patterns that we keep repeating even though they hurt us. This difficulty is the survivor's key to understanding. She will begin to see how the abuse she suffered as a child led her to view herself and her world in a distorted fashion, when the distortion was necessary. Living through her childhood was like looking into the wavy circus mirrors that flatten and fatten, elongate and compress one's reflection, though the reflection shows a recognizable person still. As the adult survivor discards the circus mirror for the real one, she comes to see how warped and out of shape her previous world had been.

Psychiatrist Natalie Shainess speaks about such child and adult reactions in her book *Sweet Suffering:* "What was an appropriate response for a child vis-à-vis a threatening parent is inappropriate when it occurs, for instance, between employee and boss, doctor and patient, husband and wife. What may have been necessary, and useful, adaptive behavior for a child can become a terrible liability when it continues into the adult."

The child survives abuse and neglect with a whole range of responses: truly, we have to be amazed at the remarkable courage, pluck, and imagination children show in such attempts. Children exposed to such a severe trauma as incest were not meant to survive. They manage to do so *only* by means of extremely creative behaviors — their functional adaptations to an unlivable environment. To survive, such children had to be resourceful and find a new dodge when the old one did not work well any longer. An abusive adult is merciless; he has everything on his side: power, authority, physical strength, even credibility (for who believes a child?). Like an agile Oliver Twist outwitting Fagin or young David facing down the giant Goliath — or even a rabbit being hunted down by a mountain lion — the child has to have the wit and courage to invent ways to survive against tremendous odds.

Remember how Huck Finn casually tells why he decides to run away from home? Though we readers rarely view it that way, Mark Twain's young hero is *escaping abuse,* however humorously the author puts the words into his character's mouth:

> It was kind of lazy and jolly, laying off comfortable all day, smoking and fishing, and no books nor study. Two months or more run along, and my clothes got to be all rags and dirt, and I didn't see how I'd ever got to like it so well at the widow's, where you had to wash, and eat on a plate, and comb up, and go to bed and get up regular, and be forever bothering over a book, and have old Miss Watson pecking at you all the time. I didn't want to go back no more. I had stopped cussing, because the widow didn't like it; but now I took to it again because pap hadn't no objections. It was pretty good times up in the woods there, take it all around.
>
> But by and by pap got too handy with his hick'ry, and I couldn't stand it. I was all over welts. He got to going away so much, too, and locking me in. Once he locked me in and was gone three days. It was dreadful lonesome. I judged he had got drownded, and I wasn't ever going to get out any more. I was scared. I made up my mind I would fix up some way to leave there.

Huck Finn escapes physically by running away from home and floating down the Mississippi River into the arms of adventure, in one of the greatest stories in American literature. But real-life children escape too, and from abuse perhaps worse than Huck's. And many never leave home to do it. In fact, physical escape is usually out of the question, because they are so young and dependent that there is nothing to do but stay put and tough it out.

Psychological Escapes

One form of running away without leaving home is that which we saw in the case of Barbara, who developed new personalities to run to. Related to this phenomenon is another attempt to abandon one's body during the pain and humiliation, to dissociate from — and leave — the hurt and shame.

This type of experience is a common survival tactic and is well described by Patsy, whose early abuse began with bathtub "games" inflicted by her father, an officer in the military. It escalated to very severe and perverted behavior at age ten when her uncle (her father's brother) joined in the abuse:

We [Patsy's father and herself] always had oral sex; from the beginning I can remember that. When my uncle joined it changed quite rapidly, because my uncle was more sadistic I guess you'd call it. My father kind of went along with him, I don't know how to explain. My father was starting to get mean and cranky about it, you know, rough with me — like before he would tell me what we were going to do. Then he wouldn't tell me, just throw me down and do stuff and force me to do stuff. Before it was more gamelike. With my uncle it was like do this, do that, and they talked *about* me not at me, I mean like, "What are we gonna do?" and "Are we gonna do this?" I mean that kind of thing, as if I wasn't there.

But by then I started this new game I played where I would turn off my senses completely. I remember I'd go, "Okay, I can't hear them and I can't see them, and I can't smell them." I would just turn everything off and just lay there. Completely dead. And I remember laying there and not feeling any pain or anything just going to sleep practically, you know, like you're in a little coma for awhile. I felt like I wasn't there. I put myself, like a self-defense mechanism, like I remember one time thinking, "I'm over there in the corner of the room and I can hear them grunting and groaning and carrying on over here," and it was kind of weird really that I could totally dissociate myself from the whole thing, you know. When I talked to [my therapist] about it, I thought I had become schizophrenic to a certain degree by splitting off. I remember leaving one part of me behind [and] going on as a different person.

Patsy's behavior is not schizophrenic nor does she have multiple personalities. Professionals call Patsy's experience "dissociation." According to the most recent *Diagnostic and Statistical Manual (DSM-III)*, the manual used to diagnose psychological disorders, the essential feature of dissociation "is a sudden, temporary alteration in the normally integrative functions of consciousness, identity, or motor behavior."

Frequently survivors experience various forms of amnesia. In "*localized* amnesia, there is failure to recall all events occurring during a circumscribed period of time, usually the first few hours following a profoundly disturbing event." For example, some survivors cannot recall happenings from the time of the sexual assault until hours or days later.

More common in the women we interviewed was "*selective* amnesia, a failure to recall some, but not all, of the events occurring during a circumscribed period of time." For example, Sabrina is capable of recalling the events *leading up to* the sexual assault, Cheryl recalls the details of cartoons playing *during* the assault, and Ruth remembers seeing the blood on the bedsheet *afterwards*. None of these women recalls the actual occurrence of the trauma each time it happened to her. Their amnesia is "selective."

Many women relate that they protected themselves as children by mentally moving outside their bodies, floating onto the ceiling or into a corner where, occasionally, they could watch themselves being abused. "When it was happening, I felt my head going outside the window," is the sensation described by Roberta, a thirty-two-year-old emergency-room social worker. Her father was having intercourse with her from as early as she can remember, and it ended only when she left home to go to college.

"Floating away" persisted in Roberta's case well after the abuse ended. And the technique she learned as a child has, as in the case of Barbara, made life difficult as an adult. Roberta has to work very hard to respond to people and situations personally. When she is under extreme stress, she often finds herself staring into space, still "going out the window," and shutting out her listener as a way of battening down her own emotional responses.

This "floating away" happens most frequently when Roberta feels her anger getting out of control. Rather than expressing her anger, she dissociates. Not long ago she took her car in to be repaired, only to have it break down on the expressway on her way to work a few days after it had been "fixed." Furious, she called a tow truck, but when she got back to the service station and was facing the repairman, she found herself unable to show anger, upset, or even mild concern. Her whole self left her, and she stood shy and wordless, even though she had been seething inside only an hour before.

Such conditions come close to what is described by professionals as post-traumatic stress disorder. Again according to the *DSM-III*, "Characteristic symptoms involve re-experiencing the traumatic event; numbing of responses to, or reduced involvement with, the external world." Symptoms of this disorder include the painful nightmares and flashbacks many survivors experience, diminished responsiveness to the external world, or "psychic numbing," and the frequent "feeling of being detached or estranged from other people." Survivors report the loss of any ability to feel emotion, especially in an intimate or sexual context.

All survival skills are efforts on the child's part to protect herself, but in an attempt to escape, some children end up destroying, or nearly destroying, themselves. Children sometimes use tactics that could only be called "last-ditch attempts": it is the rare incest victim who did not try, threaten, or fantasize suicide when she was a child. And suicide is one way to respond to a really horrible situation. The child does not see any option except to try to end it all. She is totally dependent on her parents for her life; she does not have the option of saying, "I don't like the way things are going here, and I want better treatment." She cannot take her credit cards, hop into the car, and move to the local motel until things get better.

Although many a child trying suicide is doing so to stop the intolerable pain, another may be saying, in essence, "Pay attention to me; I'm hurting." Or maybe she is thinking, "Wait till I'm gone; *then* they're going to miss me. Just let them wait and see." The child is trying to say that she knows she has been mistreated, that she deserves better, that she would like to punish her tormentors.

This sense of injustice that the abused child feels comes through loud and clear in the fairly common desire for martyrdom that we saw in women who were abused. Even if they thought about suicide, what they really wanted was to die, but not to be responsible for their own deaths. In that way they would get the attention and sympathy, but they themselves would be innocent. Patsy, whose case we discussed earlier, remembers jumping into the deep end of a swimming pool before she knew how to swim and sinking to the bottom. "There I was on the bottom," she says, "and I thought to myself, 'How nice to die.'" She was disappointed that her father rescued her.

It is certainly the case that many children want simply to die, and it is sadly also the case that a good number succeed one way or another in doing just that. We cannot know their stories. Of the women who survived to adulthood and thought about or tried suicide as children, the motive seems to have been to want to escape misery and pain and to call people's attention to the fact that they were suffering. That is surely an understandable response. When they become adults and the abuse is no longer occurring, it is not as understandable, because usually adults recognize the existence of more options for themselves.

A related and likewise destructive survival tactic is self-mutilation. Although it occurs in children, it is likely to appear in its more destructive form in the adult survivor. Health professionals are seeing increasing numbers of women who cut, burn, or slash various parts of their bodies in response to their emotional turmoil. In the women we interviewed the relationship between self-mutilation and incest appeared frequently.

Self-mutilation can be an attempt to feel better inside. Women who mutilate report that seeing the blood flow is reassuring to them, because they then know that they are alive; they are so numb and unresponsive emotionally that otherwise they are not certain that they *are* alive. They also say that burning or cutting themselves hurts far less than their emotional anguish inside, and it forces them to concentrate on the physical rather than the emotional pain.

Cheryl is an example of a woman who is using adult survival tactics that put her at risk, even though they were effective in childhood. Cheryl is a nineteen-year-old middle-class woman whose parents worked, her father as a trainman and her mother as a teacher. Her uncle babysat her during the day, and began raping her from about age five onward. Cheryl survived by inducing a catatonic state watching the television set that was always on as her uncle abused her. Even now, she remembers the cartoons better than she does the pain or details of the abuse, physical abuse so severe that gynecologists who have treated her doubt that she can ever have children, so traumatized were her reproductive organs.

As an adult Cheryl still numbs herself to any feelings, just as she did when she watched cartoons as a child. She does not join her emotions to what is happening to her body, so she can quite calmly cut herself with razors; she carries numerous scars along her inside lower arms where she has slashed herself with a series of shallow cuts. None has been life-threatening — yet. She reports that she felt relief at seeing blood and having the physical pain to concentrate on as distraction from her real agony inside. Her self-mutilation is not an effective "survival skill," since it could result in physical damage, even death, but it is a way to attempt to avoid feelings, just as dissociation is.

For the adult, as well as for the child, the ultimate mutilation is suicide, and Cheryl thinks about that too. She often closes her eyes for short periods of time while she is driving, just as she closed her eyes to her uncle as a child. She flirts with potentially dangerous situations such as walking down dark inner-city alleys at night. She has gotten into deep water in the swimming pool even though she is afraid of it and does not know how to swim well. As a child she wished just to vanish, and thoughts of death are still with her constantly: she fantasizes about life after death, wondering if she might be more at peace in another world.

Self-mutilation and suicide attempts are extreme and dangerous ways for the adult survivor to deny her feelings. Another psychological escape that is less dangerous is the practice of going completely unconscious during abuse — fainting or blacking out. Sabrina (whose case was described in Chapter I) now believes that while her father was forcing penetration on her as a child, she must have completely lost consciousness, because despite her best efforts she can remember her father's beginning but never finishing. It is highly unlikely that the father was practicing *coitus interruptus*.

Sabrina was able to discover her childhood defenses when she became an adult and began to black out suddenly and with no explanation. With careful work in therapy she began to put together her mental state at the time of the unconscious episodes and saw that they had to do with the abuse. Having worked back to her childhood abuse from the adult symptoms, she was able finally to begin the process that would help her change her adult behavior. "Swooning" or "fainting" might have been all very well for heroines of Victorian fiction, but they are not very effective ways of dealing with pain in our modern twentieth-century world. So Sabrina learned new ways.

Some women we spoke to were able to numb, or shut down, parts of their bodies during the abuse. Pam is a good example. Rather than mentally dissociate or black out, she had physically denied that part of her body to which the abuse was being directed. "I made myself numb from the waist down," she says.

Pam discovered this survival tactic from numerous psychosomatic illnesses she suffered as an adult, after marriage, particularly from being occasionally stricken with paralysis from the waist down. She was in the care of physicians who were mystified by the phenomenon: one could only guess that a particular type of cheese may have contained a bacillus that reacted with an antibiotic medicine she was taking at the time.

The best clue finally came from looking at her childhood. During therapy she discovered the link. At the time Pam was experiencing paralysis, she and her husband were trying very hard to start a family and were having frequent sexual intercourse. With the help of her therapist (and the patience and gentleness of her husband), she connected the paralysis with intercourse and then worked backward to the truth of the incest she had experienced as a child.

Physical Escapes

We need to remember that not all escape attempts are psychological. Children physically escape as soon as the opportunity presents itself. It might be getting pregnant in order to marry and leave home or it might mean studying hard to get a scholarship to a college far away. Increasingly, it means running away or hitching a ride to the nearest large city, where these young people inevitably run into the arms of even bigger trouble as teenage runaways — for drug addiction, prostitution, and violence await the unfortunate children who think that running away might solve the problems they are having at home. It seems obvious, but it usually remains unstated, that runaways are *running away*, presumably *from* something, not *to* something.

Running completely away is usually out of the question. Even so, many children find ways to run, physically, by staying out of the abuser's path and getting out of the house, if they can, when they sense danger. The psychological escapes we have just discussed are the survival tactics of the physically trapped and cornered child: "psychological escape" is what women did as child victims when there was no place else to run.

Most ran when they could. And when some survivors are able finally to make a physical escape, they keep running and never look back, even though confronting and dealing with incest might make for a more pleasant and adjusted mature life. Nan was sexually victimized for years by her widowed father. "There was nothing he didn't do," she said bitterly, her lips set firm and her eyes welling with tears; "he used me however he wanted." She escaped the small midwestern farm town by getting such good grades that she won a full scholarship to college. She never went home for vacations, either staying on at the deserted campus or going home with friends.

When she graduated *summa cum laude,* she did not even stay in America to pursue a career. She had casually met a foreign man on a Greyhound bus trip between her junior and senior years. Even though their friendship was brief and superficial, he wrote to her devotedly and finally suggested that she come abroad and marry him. Such a long-distance proposal was risky at best, but she wanted to put as many miles as possible between her father and herself. So upon graduation, despite the fact that they were worried for her safety, her friends bought her a trousseau and sent her off alone to another country, where she in fact married her beau, had several children, and taught in the schools there. She never returned to America and she never communicated with her father again. Her survival meant getting away from home as soon as possible and then, as an adult, never dealing with her childhood.

Kathleen Marie chose a time-honored escape method: she tried to enter the convent. Her mother died when she was twelve, leaving her with her stepfather and half-brother. The night of the funeral her stepfather came in as she was crying in her room and, at first pretending to comfort her, he ended up forcing sex upon her. Afterward, she told her story to her cousin Bette, a girl about her own age. Bette sounded shocked and implored Kathleen Marie to come live with her and her family (Kathleen Marie's aunt, uncle, and cousin).

Once in her new home, Kathleen Marie began to experience abuse again, this time from the "savior" uncle, who was also a policeman and a respected member of the small community. He demanded that she perform sexual acts in exchange for the most ordinary services, such as a ride home from band practice. Since she had already confessed to Bette about her stepfather's abuse, she was too ashamed to confide again in her cousin — and this time she would have to identify Bette's own father as the abuser. Kathleen Marie was certain that Bette would see *her* as the guilty culprit: since the abuse kept happening, she felt that she herself must be guilty. Years later, as an adult, she found out that Bette too was being abused by this same man, her own father.

Twice betrayed by family and motherless, Kathleen Marie decided to enter the convent so that she would never again have to deal with men. Her family priest refused, however, to give the recommendation required. There was, he thought, a spiritual dimension lacking: Kathleen Marie seemed to him to desire the religious life to escape something rather than to embrace a vocation.

Except for the insight of the priest, Kathleen Marie would have forced herself into a lifestyle that she might have come to regret. As it was, she found a man she wished to marry. As an adult she had no memory of the abuse until flashbacks began to occur. She then found herself uncomfortable with intimate sexuality, and her husband urged her into therapy, where she was able finally to recall the damage done her as a child by abuse from two trusted men. Her terror of being abused again impaired her functioning as an adult. When she discovered the source of the damage, her therapist supported her in writing angry, vituperative letters to her stepfather and uncle that put the blame exactly where it belonged — on the perpetrators. Much of her guilt was alleviated through the course of her letter writing.

Physical Escapes: Plotting and Planning

Even though physical escape from the household is usually out of the question for younger children, most incest survivors report trying — and sometimes succeeding in — manipulating the threatening environment in an attempt to make it more safe. Nearly all young children want to believe that mother will protect them, and they experiment with ways to get her to stay at home or to make her play a more protective role. Later the abused child may give up on the mother as a source of protection, but in the early years she nearly always gives it a try.

Patsy, who, as we saw earlier, learned to dissociate in order to cope with the abuse she was receiving from her father and her uncle, longed for and tried to get the protection of her mother, but she realizes now that her mother was unavailable. Because the father was an alcoholic and was frequently home on "sick leave," Patsy's mother often held two jobs, one as a night nurse. In addition, her mother had eight miscarriages and bore four babies, so much of the time she was pregnant, hospitalized, immobilized with a new baby, or recovering from a miscarriage. Still, as an adult Patsy is upset that her mother was not there when she needed her: "I have asked her about it; I've said, 'Mom, where were you?' And she says, 'If I had any idea I was leaving home to go to work with such things going on, I would never have done it, but of course he's your father and I never thought he would ever do anything to hurt you kids. I mean I knew he wasn't a good father; I knew he drank too much, but he never gave me any indication that he [would do what he did].'"

For one reason or another, the mother fails to protect her daughter, although the daughter may have tried to get her to intervene — and many women stay angry all the way into adulthood about the fact that mom was not there when she needed her. But what happens when there is no mother? When the mother is gone for reasons of divorce or is dead?

Gerri's mother had died when she was three years old, and she was raised by an aunt and uncle because her father said he was unable to care for his children alone. Not being able to live in her own home, she was dependent on the good graces of her uncle and aunt for the roof over her head. She was terrified of her uncle and had sustained many beatings from him and witnessed his countless acts of brutality against other family members. The aunt had children of her own and worked outside the home to support them all, so she was none too inclined to aid Gerri in any way; the young girl knew better than to look her way for protection.

She felt even more trapped when the sexual abuse from her uncle began. One time when she was about fourteen and they were riding in the car, her uncle stopped for a drink. "When he got back in the car he started to touch me everywhere. I didn't know what was happening so I just sort of sat there. Then he said, 'Why don't you come to my bed tonight?' I didn't see how I could refuse." Soon the abuse became an established pattern and there was no place to run and no one to turn to. She had to submit. "I recall in the evenings the kids would be outside and he would want to have sex, and I remember him going on top of me in a chair we used to have, a red one, and I would ask him not to, but he would, he would do whatever he wanted to do."

Gerri cast about for protection, even trying to get it from the cousins, younger than she, with whom she had been raised. "My feelings at first in the car [had been] panicky — like, 'What is this?' and 'Why is he doing this?' Then it changed to scared. You want to be away from the person and you hope that the kids won't go to the show that afternoon and you're hoping your aunt stays home or comes home sooner or you're hoping you can do something away from the house so you don't have to be near that person."

Managing to have people stay home to protect one, hoping for the miracle of a mother's early return home from night work, even taking a younger child to bed for protection all demand a great deal of the child incest victim: she is always in the position of trying to organize or arrange events to protect herself by whatever means she can. And this continual tension is made worse because, inevitably, she fails much of the time. Grown-up schedules mandate that the child is often left unprotected as a matter of course just in the place where she needs the most protection: in her own home. And she is left, as Patsy and Gerri were, with a person who ought to be expected to take care of her, not abuse her. Even if he is an alcoholic, as Patsy's father was, mothers frequently assume that he will do at least a minimally acceptable job of caring for his children.

It should come as no surprise that problems with power, control, and manipulation are major issues to most survivors of incest. So pervasive and difficult are these issues that we have devoted a whole chapter to their discussion (Chapter 5). But once again, survivors need to remember the *source* of these tactics: in their poignant bid for power and attention, these powerless children manipulated the physical environment however they could in an attempt to make it safe and to survive. It was all they knew how to do.

Mind Games

We have seen how children use psychological escapes, such as dissociation, to escape their childhood pain during abuse, and we have glanced at some of the adult issues that are a possible outcome of those techniques. And we have looked at a few ways of physical escape, including actually leaving home, but also ways of maneuvering to get out of the way of the abuser.

A final category of escape combines the two: these are actual physical situations that have behind them a mental dimension, a peculiar kind of childhood reasoning. Some children strike deals, accept bribes, or otherwise fix things to give themselves the illusion that they are not completely powerless. They seem to find some solace in this illusion of power that helps them survive until adulthood, at which time they frequently come to regret their actions, because it appears that they have been party to the abuse by complying with a deal that they themselves helped to make.

An example might help. Marianna, frustrated in all her attempts at self-protection, finally put into place an elaborate system of sacrifice that probably would not occur to an adult. By striking a deal with her father, she thought she was protecting her mother and sisters, and that made her feel better.

Marianna does not remember when the incest began, but she guesses that it was about the time she was in second grade. Marianna's mother was of little help, because the father actually left the bed where she was sleeping to go upstairs to molest Marianna. Cornered, Marianna moved into the bed with her sister, which she thought might thwart her father's plans, but he came at night to molest her anyway. "He would come upstairs after he and my mother were in bed. [There he would be] in my room and I often wondered why [my sister] didn't know he was there. And I found out recently that my sister *did* know he was there, and she always wondered as a child why he didn't come and visit her too."

Even though Marianna's mother was at home and her sister in the bed beside her, Marianna had no protection. So intolerable was her life at home that she remembers as her happiest times her frequent hospitalizations for kidney and bladder infections (quite possibly the result of intercourse). When she could escape to the hospital she was safely away from her father, she was able to get her mother's attention, and she could always hope to die — an instance of the martyr/suicide pattern we discussed on page 48.

When she was given a room and a bed of her own, Marianna knew that she had no chance. She obviously would have to devise other self-protective tactics:

> When I was about ten years old my grandmother decided I needed my own room, and she bought me this beautiful solid cherry bed and headboard and got me a really nice desk, I mean just a beautiful antique, and I didn't even want it, I didn't even want to go in there, because I knew it was just going to make things worse, by being easier for my father to get me in a bedroom alone, but I couldn't even explain to her, because she thought she was really doing something nice. After that happened, as I explained, it just got worse, I mean it was every night. There had been some protection with someone else in the room.

So Marianna made a deal: "We had an arrangement. I told him I would do it. I didn't want to do it, but [I would do it] if he would just leave her [my younger sister] alone."

Marianna also got the verbal assurance from her father that he would never *kill* her mother, a demonstration of the level of desperation at which the child was operating. "After awhile the secret was kept because he said if I told anybody that he would kill Mom. And me, too, but I didn't care about that. But my mom was — I mean she was just the most important thing to me in the world. And I would have done anything I needed to protect her so there was no way I was going to tell."

When Marianna was eighteen years old, she came into her parents' bedroom to find her father attempting to strangle her mother. She saw his hands around her mother's neck, and went to the phone to call police. As soon as her father saw that she was in earnest about the phone call, he fled, and that night Marianna and her sister bared their souls to each other and discovered that they both had been molested over the years. They told their stories to their distraught mother the next morning and pleaded with her to divorce their father, which she finally did two years later.

Marianna was crushed when she found out that her father had not even tried to keep his end of the bargain: "He promised me he would never hurt sis and he promised he'd never kill my mom, and I know if I hadn't walked in there then, that would have been it for her."

Marianna had entered into a deal with touching honesty, so naive that it could be held only by a child — that a man who would sexually abuse his own daughter was also capable of honor and of keeping such promises to her.

As an adult, Marianna is a rescuer and laughingly refers to her Joan of Arc complex: she wants to save everyone, including her sister. Marianna has wanted her sister to come and live with her and her husband, even though such an arrangement would put considerable strain upon her own marriage. She may be unable to

have children, but Marianna is willing, she says, to adopt a severely handicapped child, possibly one with abuse in its background.

Marianna still wants to protect people, even at her own ex-
pense. In the last year she has been working in her free time at a
crisis hotline, which, among other emergencies, deals with suicide
and incest. After one phone call from another incest survivor,
Marianna unwisely gave out her own home phone number and
continued to receive the woman's frantic calls, often at two or
three o'clock in the morning. Marianna was unable to protect
herself sufficiently to understand that she needed to preserve
her own personal life from the desperate pleas of another, albeit
another person who had suffered as much and in much the same
way as she.

Marianna is now an intelligent, spirited, attractive woman and
is becoming cognizant that she must be very careful not to cross
the line that divides sensitive caring for people from martyrdom
and self-destruction. She has to work every day to tell herself the
truth about *how she really feels.* Her abuse-laden background has
taught her quite the opposite — to misrepresent or avoid her own
feelings.

At base, it is this dishonesty, this having to misrepresent her own
feelings in order to survive, that does such lasting harm to the
adult woman. As a child she had to lie or at least disguise the truth
in order to live through the humiliating and hurtful abuse: keeping
the secret meant living a lie. The truth hurts, and as an adult she
may be unable to see what she needs or feels in any situation,
because she avoids pain.

This dishonesty or pretense that things are different from what,
in fact, they are is best exemplified by one of the most common
survival tactics used by children, that of feigning sleep. Imagine an
eight-year-old child, lying in bed at night, cognizant of every footfall, fearing the turn of the doorknob that signals the approach of
the perpetrator. What is she to do?

She pretends to be asleep. Remember that this is a child, and so we witness her touching and naive belief that a man who would commit the crime of incest could be a man unwilling to interrupt a child's sleep.

We can question how effective a technique this is, because it probably does not deter a perpetrator who wants to have his way. At best it forms a kind of state of hypervigilance in which the child is then ready to dissociate or otherwise prepare herself for the pain.

As adults, survivors of incest are plagued with sleep disorders. Being hypervigilant is a pattern that was set in place early and frequently continues into adulthood. This habitual hypervigilance before falling asleep can cause severe insomnia in the adult survivor. Seeing shadowy figures at the foot of the bed, interpreting the sounds of the house — the radiator gurgling or the floor creaking or the wind blowing against the shutters — can strike terror into her heart. Fear of night intruders is common.

Bed is not a friendly place for many an adult survivor of incest. Memories abound there. Some survivors are even unable to sleep in a bed. Cecily can fall asleep only by sitting up in an easy chair; if she wakes in the middle of the night, she retreats to the bedroom, but not before she pushes a chair in front of the door. Other women need to fall asleep watching television on the sofa — anything to avoid the darkened room. Many need night lights or a light on down the hall to make certain that no one is creeping in.

Survivors often feel physical touching or indications that the abuser is still present and in bed with them. Roberta cannot sleep on her back because she feels a heaviness on her chest as if a body were on top of her, and she feels shooting pains in her vaginal area. In group therapy Joan reported with much embarrassment that she felt breath on her cheeks at night, but she lay frozen in her bed, terrified to get up and turn on the light for fear of finding that someone had crept into her room unknown to her. She was surprised and relieved that others in the group reported experiencing the same phenomenon.

Living with Hope

So much for the grim stories. We have tried to show a whole range of abusive situations as well as a whole range of responses children use to conquer their terror. There are surely other responses, other ways women invent to survive the hurt, pain, and shame. And there are thousands more stories of abuse just as humiliating and hurtful as the ones we have told here.

We need to remember, through this sorrowful recitation, that these are stories of triumph, courage, and the will to survive. As children, these women invented a refuge right in the midst of their purgatory — or even hell — and learned to hold on to life even as they were being told that they had no value and that life was not worth it. A therapist who has worked with incest survivors, including those in the prison population, said to a conference audience recently, "After a uniformly horrifying early life, these women developed layer after layer of coping strategies. Only the most powerful instinct to survive can explain them."

The sobering issue for adult survivors is that they have often learned their lesson so well that they continue to embrace all the old ways that used to keep them alive. Women who have survived incest cannot erase the frustrations and pain of their childhood experience — that is part of them. But they may feel a need to deal with the dysfunction in adulthood. As the survivor battles, she needs to cherish herself by understanding that what happened to her as a child conditioned her to do what she did; she had no other choices.

We do not believe that the story must end in illness and horror. Many thousands of women have found the freedom to cast off childhood shackles and to survive as newly regenerated adults. Hope and optimism are the best companions on this new journey.

3

The Lost Childhood

I WAS *fourteen years old at the time. It was about ten in the morning when my father came ashen-faced from the hospital to my grandmother's house, where I had been taken two days before.*

My mother had come "to town" from the remote rural area where we lived and had just given birth to a stillborn child. There were serious medical complications, which I did not understand. I knew only that I had been on my knees for what seemed hours the night before imploring God — who dwelt for me at that time in the sky with the crisply shining winter stars — please not to let my mother die. I told Him I would exchange anything, absolutely anything, for my mother's life.

That morning my father came in and asked to see me alone at the kitchen table. He looked haggard and shaken with his all-night watch. Sitting on the edge of the wooden kitchen chair he said, "What are we going to do? They want us to name it before we can bury it."

I comprehended little of the statement then. Now I think the legal requirement that dead infants must be named before burial is grisly. What my fourteen-year-old brain did take in at the time was that the we in "What shall we do?" meant my father and me. I was being consulted as an adult. I can remember even now the shock with which I took in the knowledge. I could comprehend only that my mother had nearly died or was near death. And yet I was being asked to respond in a grown-up way to a very mature, complex, painful dilemma.

As an adult I have been through the death of one of my children and in sympathy I say that I know something of my father's grief at that time. What still astonishes me, however, is the thought that a child — for a young person of fourteen is still a child — could be asked to cope with the naming and burial of a stillborn baby sister.

But in other ways I am not astonished. For years before and years after that, I listened and tried to understand all the financial worries my mother confided to me. She could never talk to my father about them, she said, because "he would just fly off the handle." I always knew how "deep in the hole" our family was and witnessed with great sympathy her slaving, pinching, saving attempts to chase away the wolf that crouched at the door.

Besides, my father probably considered me an adult, as I think my mother did, for I had long been doing adult work right beside her. After a grueling day's labor cleaning other people's houses, she brought home ironing to make a little extra money. I remember baskets loaded with twenty or thirty shirts, a good number, since she was paid by the piece. When I became a master launderer as a teenager, I helped her iron shirts (I had done the family ironing as early as I could hold an iron and do a handkerchief). This was in the days before wash-and-wear fabrics and steam irons. It was also the Era of Heavy Starch; I can still recall the Argo smell that steamed up from the damp, just unrolled shirt before I touched the hot iron to it. There were to be no creases or scorched places: neither my mother nor her employers would stand for it. It required concentration and skill, and it was hard on the feet and shoulders after about an hour. I still feel a little queasy when I walk into my local cleaners and smell the just ironed fragrance that emanates from the back of the plant.

The fact was that I had long been helping my mother out because she had so much to do; she was overworked, underpaid, and the main support of the family. I hoped to lighten her load, never really asking as I went how heavy my own load was or whether it was fair and just for a child to be doing so much. I was never paid for my work that I recall, nor do I remember being thanked especially for it. Only my grandmother smiled at me warmly and said in her broken English, "What a gut *girl!" when I did dishes for her or swept the floor.*

I had become a "little mother." I had been quite capably discharging duties of cleaning and cooking in my family for years. I was making gravy — considered to be the most difficult culinary feat in my family — by the time I was nine. I swept and tidied up the house by the same age, shooing my troublesome brother out of the way and kicking the dog outside first, since they would destroy my efforts as soon as possible.

The only things I did not do around the house were those things that required careful teaching and patience. My mother was a seamstress, but she never taught me to sew — and I still have not learned. I never learned needlework or knitting or gardening or how to make a cake. All the truly pleasant and creative household activities got delayed until I was an adult and had opportunities to pursue them.

The work that was a grind, I got to do. There was little time for fun, and in any case I thought I was forbidden it. My father did not allow me to date or drive, and no friends came to the house to play or listen to music as they do with my children now. My children have friends and we live in a neighborhood. I was stuck way out in the country and isolated socially as well.

I have a lingering sadness about the fact that I never had a carefree childhood or a reckless adolescence, because I can never have those years back and I can never have what everyone should have — a time to be a kid, to be cared for and loved and not to be responsible for everything in the family.

I am also bitter at the theft of my childhood. It is not fair that I not only got to be responsible for adult work but was also hit with adult sex in all its complexity before I had a chance to understand sex naturally and with time, as a child should before she grows into a young woman.

And I am angry, not just at the load I was asked to carry, but at the fact that no one ever told me thank you for carrying it. On the contrary, I was despised and insulted for doing what I did. I weep angry tears for that little girl, trying to cook and clean and understand what she was supposed to do, even as her father was yelling at her, "Who do you think you are? You think you know everything, I suppose, but you don't know nothing."

The truth — and I knew it even then — was that I knew far too much. I have missed forever the time in my life when I might have been excused for not knowing everything.

· ✳ · ✳ ·

THERE is a certain amount of sentimentality in the notion of "the innocent, carefree days of childhood." An adult, laden with care and responsibility in a complicated world of work, may stop to look back fondly to childhood when someone else was in charge and play seemed the order of the day. Then the adult leans back, breathes slowly, and reminisces, "Ah, those were the days."

Psychiatrists like Bruno Bettelheim tell us what may be closer to the truth: the golden age of childhood is not all that it is made out to be. It is peopled with monsters and wordless fears. Why else do the great stories continue to affect us as adults? If "Rumpelstilt-skin" or "The Juniper Tree" were mindless and innocent, they would not have endured. The Steven Spielberg fantasies that have enthralled our generation of children use their mortal struggles between good and evil to cast their spell on the parents as well. The best children's stories of all time are not morally uncomplicated. They speak about what people — both child and adult — experience in an evil or unfair world. So the literature even tells us that being a child is never easy, causing some adults to retort to incest survivors, "Well, so you were an incest victim and missed out on your childhood. But my childhood wasn't all peaches and cream either, and I'm not bellyaching about it and calling it a lost childhood. That's just the way being a kid is."

There is an element of truth in this reaction. In our culture few childhoods are without trouble and travail of some sort.

But the lost childhood of the incest survivor is different.

Here is a story not only of what she has lost or, more accurately, what has been taken away from her. It is also the story of what has been thrust upon her instead of childhood. Childhood is a time to learn to trust the world and the people in it; she can trust no one. Childhood is the time to learn the most crucial message for self-esteem, that she is a valuable person who is permitted to make mistakes and still be loved; the time for free growth and experimentation has been completely written out of her young life. Childhood is a time for play and carefree hours with friends. She has grown up isolated from normal kid stuff and is given a heavy load of adult responsibility to boot.

What has happened instead of childhood? We will put the issue briefly, then come back to elaborate in more detail: The combination of an abandoning mother (or the child's interpretation that her mother is abandoning her) and an abusing father, who is forcing her into adult sex, make the young victim an adult before her time. She is given the responsibility for the sexual and emotional pacification of her father. In addition, she frequently takes on the household routine that in these often traditional families would be the mother's. She does housework and child care, sometimes mothering her own mother by listening to her problems, accepting her responsibilities, soothing her feelings, or even defending her against the man who is her own abuser.

On top of this she has the job of keeping the secret; even though she is the victim of the crime, the burden of keeping this crime a secret falls chiefly on her. A terrible contradiction is operating: she is being hurt, but if she tells anyone she is threatened with people finding out how "bad" she is. The biggest sin becomes telling anyone outside the family what is really happening; the biggest virtue is keeping alive the lie that everything is fine and in order. She is the keeper of that lie.

Several effects can ensue. The victim is frequently isolated as a child because her duties keep her busy, and in any case the pain she has to conceal makes her less than playful and carefree. She learns to take adult responsibility as a child and, in adulthood, often continues to take more than her share of responsibility or, in reaction, refuses any. As an adult she often feels shaky in making decisions because everything seemed to depend upon her at a time when she, as a child, could not handle complex adult decisions.

Let us separate this tangled web of roles to examine the individual filaments, the reasons why the adult survivor of incest often feels that she had no childhood.

The Adult Sexual Role

Of paramount importance is the fact that she was forced into the adult role sexually. One only need read a list of titles of child pornography to realize that the adult male seducer of children fantasizes about a child who really is an adult in desires and capacities for sexual enjoyment: "Torrid Tots," "Horny Imps," "Lollypops" suggest a male imputing his adult desire to the child object. His abusive behavior becomes on some level justified if he can persuade himself that the child wants or needs sex; the child is then co-offender. Many women heard their fathers assign them this role when they said, "You want this just as much as I do," or "Now doesn't this feel good?" or "We need to get you ready for your husband."

Not only has the child been handed the role of co-conspirator; the offender also gives her certain adult characteristics. Humbert Humbert, the hero of Vladimir Nabokov's classic novel *Lolita,* describes the young girls who are the objects of his sexual desires: "Now I wish to introduce the following idea. Between the age limits of nine and fourteen there occur maidens who, to certain bewitched travelers, twice or many times older than they, reveal their true nature which is not human, but nymphic (that is, demoniac); and these chosen creatures I propose to designate as 'nymphets.'" To Humbert they are "nymphets"; other people accuse young girls of being "seductive" or of "sexual acting-out." Yet these are in fact children wanting to be loved, touched, hugged, or thought attractive. And even if such behavior looks to an adult to be sexually "seductive," it is the adult *interpreting* the behavior as sexual in his own terms. He does not have the right to exploit her even if she seems to him to have "asked for it."

Similarly, in the not-so-distant past rapists in our culture attempted to excuse their actions because the victim was dressed seductively or in some other way "asked for it." Both the courts and society at large today rightly reject such attempts to condone criminal behavior. Rapists are responsible for committing the crime even if they in some way *perceived* the victim as cooperating. How much less culpable, then, is the child victim: in the cases we have been discussing, incest still remains a crime against a minor, even if the perpetrator insists that she is a "nymphet" who is asking for it. But the child victims obtain even less protection because the cases so rarely come to trial. The child probably tells no one about the abuse. The abuser is left free to put his guilt on her, making her out to be an adult requesting sex.

The perpetrator can tell the child that she is asking for the sex and is thus a co-conspirator. She often grows up to adulthood thinking that what he has said is in fact the case, despite the fact that she is being told who she is by a man uncertain of his own masculinity. His fantasies forbid her the legitimate chance to experience the world for herself and to find out what sexuality is and what it requires. She is hit with a complete adult agenda when she is only a child.

Emotional and Sexual Pacification

But it is not just the sexual agenda that is at issue here. The child may be bidden at first by the mother, but perhaps later by the whole family, to keep the father *emotionally* pacified as well. She knows that if she does not placate the father in the way she knows best, all hell will break loose and the whole family will be down on her. And at the same time that she is "Daddy's girl," she may be reviled and resented by others in the family, who, while they expect her to take care of the father, also resent the special attention she gets.

Kim is a woman of thirty-nine, wife of a dentist and mother of four children. She is a physician's assistant and a student of interior design, a field in which she hopes to make a new career soon. She is a leader in school and community activities, and her healthy aspect seems to belie the extreme damage done to her for years by an incestuous father and brutalizing family. Incest began when she was seven and ended the night before she was married, when her father made what he considered his last rightful sexual claim on her. While still in high school she bore her father's child and put the baby up for adoption. Her mother and father let it be known to their friends that she was a "tramp" and that they had no idea whose child it was.

Kim tells what it was like to be the sexual and emotional pacifier of her father: "It was always up to my sister and me to calm my dad down when he came home angry. My mother would be in the kitchen cooking, and she would say, 'Go cuddle with Daddy' to us and we would. Those evenings she would have to go shopping, he would sexually play with me. I kept looking out and listening for my mother to come home." As she was growing up, Kim obeyed her mother and soon accepted it as her responsibility to take care of her father during her mother's absences and whenever else she was commanded. This behavior was approved and reinforced by her father, who made it clear to Kim that she was doing the right thing. "In the early part this was love," she says, "the feeling that this was a 'special thing.' It showed his love for me and I accepted that." As a young child she felt glad she could make Daddy happy and keep the family working smoothly.

By the time she was in high school, Kim realized that something was wrong and that what her father was doing was far from the norm. As a young child she had been quiet, shy, and withdrawn. Because she had no friends, she had not had an opportunity to compare notes with children from other families and see how unusual her own was. So it took until high school for her to see that the behavior she had taken to be love was not precisely that. "I remember then trying to tell him, 'No, this is wrong.' Then he hit me and raped me. After that, it was submit or be beaten."

Kim was under her father's sexual thrall as certainly as if she had been a slave in a harem: she was economically and emotionally dependent on this family. She knew how to "calm" her father down, and the rest of the family came to expect her to do it.

Her mother helped the situation along, not only by requiring Kim to pacify the father but by emphasizing the "fact" to her daughter that she was forever dependent on the family. Even after high school graduation Kim continued to live on at home because her mother wanted her to, and she was accustomed to pleasing mother at all costs. Her self-worth seemed to depend upon it.

"I tried to leave home when I was twenty," Kim recalls, and she had arranged to rent a room. The rental agent called her home with a message, and Kim's mother intercepted the call, learning her daughter's plans. She told the real estate agent that Kim would not be taking the room, then confronted her daughter, saying, in Kim's words, "that I was too young and could not support myself and besides that she needed me there to take care of *him*."

Fathers involved in incest are often socially isolated themselves; they typically do not have a large network of friends and colleagues to call upon in times of stress. They are characterized by professionals as dependent, immature, and insecure. Thus if stress occurs without the mother around, they often turn to the daughter, simply because they have no one else. We do not mean here to blame the abusive behavior of some incestuous fathers on the mother's absence, only to explain the circumstances under which much abuse takes place.

Roberta remembers being placed in the uncomfortable position of being her father's confidante as well as his sexual solace. Her mother had gone to care for her own dying sister; Roberta begged her not to go, fearful of the incestuous assaults that would occur in her absence, although she could not tell her mother the real reason. While gone, Roberta's mother suffered a heart attack, and Roberta and her father went to join her. Roberta remembers that her father, during the trip in the car, told her intimately many of his emotional upsets, including how afraid he was that his wife was going to die — ignoring his *daughter's* fears that *her mother* might be dying.

The "Little Mother" Syndrome

Often the child is also being asked by her mother to be an adult at the same time that she is sexually active with the father. A mother can participate in depriving her daughter of childhood. If she turns over the sexual and emotional pacification of the father to the daughter, a mother may encourage the child to give the father sensual or sexual attention a loving wife ordinarily gives to her husband. Perhaps it is the daughter who discovers what gives the man pleasure — combing his hair lovingly, sitting on his lap, or giving him backrubs. She might find that it seems to make Daddy happy if she puts her arms around him or holds his hand as they watch television.

In healthy families this can be harmless behavior. But in some incestuous families — by definition unhealthy families — the mother completely hands over adult responsibility to her daughter, and then turns her back on what happens. Several adult survivors remembered being told by their mothers to try to take care of Daddy and make him happy while Mother left on an errand or went out for the evening. Pauline had been accustomed to massaging her father's back while the mother was present. In time, the father began to request that she do it in the privacy of the parents' bedroom. Her mother did not object when the father locked the door while he and Pauline were inside the bedroom together.

Any mature woman and mother will be able to understand the kind of behavior adult survivors are complaining about here. No responsible mother permits her husband and child to retreat behind locked doors at the husband's request. Nor is it appropriate for a wife to expect her daughter to tend to her husband's sensual needs.

Survivors often feel that their mothers handed not only the sexual and emotional pacification of their fathers over to them, but a whole package of other adult responsibilities as well. Many mothers either needed to work or chose to be employed outside the home. When the daughter was left at home, she was not only at the mercy of the abusing father but also expected to be in charge of household tasks and child care that might more properly have been the responsibility of another adult, even, God help us, the father. The mother occasionally was a hypochondriac — or even genuinely ill — and abandoned the regular household duties in order to take to her bed. The daughter in this case got burdened not only with caring for an ill mother but also with the bulk of the domestic routine. Many an incest survivor we spoke to has decided never to have children of her own because the memory of enforced child care still rankles in her mind.

In today's world most women work, because they both want to and need to, and it does not look as though the future will change this much. Today's adult incest survivors are part of that labor pool, and the complaint they advanced about their mothers working when they were children must not be taken as a plea for all mothers to stay home and take care of their children rather than being employed outside the home. Rather, what we hear women saying is that their mothers left them without taking sufficient care that they had proper supervision. Additionally, the mothers expected the child to do adult labor, often without being told exactly what to do, nearly always without remuneration or even a thank-you.

We are not talking here about children being expected to keep their rooms clean and to do dishes; those are, of course, reasonable expectations in healthy families, and few survivors would have complained about having to do that kind of work. What the mother did in most of these cases was what professionals in the field of child abuse refer to as "role reversal." The nonprotecting, abandoning mother gives over household responsibilities to the child such as housework, care of other siblings, and even the emotional mothering of her own self.

Let us look at the case of Sabrina, first discussed in Chapter I. Sabrina was first raped by her father during her mother's absence on a trip abroad, then on nearly any occasion when her mother was out shopping or doing errands. At the same time that Sabrina was being sexually victimized, her father was battering his wife. When he came home late from drinking bouts, he often beat her after he had forced her to get up and prepare him some food at whatever unreasonable hour he returned.

Sabrina's mother treated her daughter as a friend during this period, confiding in her about the father's excesses. And while she was young, Sabrina listened sympathetically as her mother complained about the long list of problems with this man; Sabrina felt sorrow and compassion for her mother at the time. Later, as an adult Sabrina wondered why she had sympathized more with her mother's plight than with her own abuse — after all, the mother had a choice to leave whereas Sabrina, as a child, was doomed to stay. The mother did, in fact, abandon Sabrina to go to Europe, leaving her at home at the mercy of her father's sexual abuse. Many women felt as Sabrina did. When they were young and themselves victims, they sympathized more with their mothers than with themselves and their own plight. They come to see in adulthood that they were being victimized by the father and used by the mother, and they feel angry on both counts.

When they examine the situation, however, survivors usually see that there were reasons they themselves overlooked when they were very young. It was necessary, for the victim's survival, to bond with the mother, even to reverse roles to become the mother's mother.

Children cannot completely go it on their own at an early age. Totally dependent on their parents, they must find devotion, caring, communication, wherever they can. The emotional give-and-take of listening to a mother's problems and sympathizing about her bastard of a husband is preferable to no family contact at all.

Her mother is perhaps even an ally. The two females may unite against the abusing male in spirit, if not in total confidence, since the daughter usually has not been able to communicate the incest to her mother — or the mother has not heard the communication if the child tried. She probably still looks up to her mother because the latter is an adult, and adults have power and worth that children do not have. It might be easier to sympathize with how unfairly her mother is being treated, because adults count for something. The child may not see that she herself is of much value at all.

The time comes when it may occur to the victim that she too is being abused, but the sense of self that would tell her she is of value and need not tolerate such hurt is not sufficiently developed. Her self-esteem is so hidden under her layers of coping mechanisms that she does not take steps to end the abuse, even if she could. In the meantime, her mother may become an ally.

Part of being an ally is helping out; you help carry the burden of a friend, and you lighten the load as much as you can if you are both being hurt by the same victimizer. Because an abusing father is often self-centered, he may make tyrannical demands on the whole family that have the effect of uniting the oppressed. Sabrina's father, for example, insisted on a fastidiously clean house, but he was not willing so much as to pick up a broom or a dishcloth himself. So Sabrina stepped in to help her mother keep the house spic and span so that her father would not always be screaming at mother about it.

And so the "little mother" begins to evolve. She starts by doing small tasks to lighten the burden of someone who is being hurt as much as she is, and she probably ends up carrying half or more of the load. In time the "little mother" ends up taking care of her own mother, listening to her stories and complaints, picking up her responsibilities, even telling her mother what to do and showing off by doing things better than anyone else in the family. It is her niche, her identity, to be the one to whom everyone else looks for competence and cleverness.

It will come as no surprise that this childhood role often persists into adult super-responsibility. Sabrina was a compulsive housekeeper and took almost complete control over her children's lives, picking up after them and doing their jobs for them even when they were no longer small children. When her oldest child was a senior in high school, Sabrina was still setting her alarm clock early enough to get herself up to wake her children and make breakfast for them.

Sabrina knew that she was attacking the "little mother" issue she carried around with her as an adult when she resolutely went out to the drugstore and bought an inexpensive alarm clock for her eighteen-year-old daughter. She brought it home and told her daughter firmly, but lovingly, to begin using it.

"The Secret"

The abused child is usually sworn to secrecy by the abuser: the burden of that secret affects her life in so many ways that, in fact, we find ourselves dealing with "the secret" in every chapter of this book. "The secret" affects her childhood in a special way, however, because it keeps the little girl from being carefree and open both with her friends and with other adults.

Let us pause and think about the burden of secrets in general.

In adult life there would be no problem with gossip or scandal if it were easy to keep a secret. *A secret wants telling;* that is its power. It is hard for anyone to keep a secret.

How much harder for a child. Most of us remember being sworn to secrecy by a childhood friend; perhaps we were not to tell about whom that person really liked or disliked. And the secret usually got out, and friendships were ruptured over it. It is all part of the pain of childhood, learning that your very best friend will, in fact, "rat" on you. Few secrets are kept very well or very long.

But *"the secret,"* the deep, dark black secret of incest, is so much heavier; the penalty for telling so much more severe, the shame, blame, and guilt so acute, that it can never be told. So the little girl carries a burden with her every day, one that she is not ever able to forget or throw away. It weights her spirits down and demoralizes her.

Coupled with this heavy burden is the sense of her own fragility — how easily she could be destroyed if the secret were revealed. A high school teacher, wanting to explain to his students exactly what parental responsibility was about, took a carton of eggs, blew the insides out, and handed the fragile shells to the students, one for each young person. The student was charged with caring for the little egg for a whole week, keeping it wrapped up and protected, never leaving it alone or uncared for. If the student had to leave the egg for a time, it had to be left in the care of a responsible person. At the end of the experiment, no eggs were left whole.

The incest victim must guard the secret unceasingly and protect it as though it were a fragile egg. She may never leave it in the care of another. She is continually aware of having to tend it and take care that it not be discovered.

The super-responsibility of keeping the secret can even persist into adulthood. Some women are so overpowered by having to keep the incest secret that in adulthood they can be emotionally blackmailed. Susan was seriously dating a man, but rarely thought of him as a very good candidate for marriage. She told him about her history of incest. Later, he asked her to marry him, and she reluctantly agreed, fearful that if she did not, he would reveal her secret. Clearly theirs was a marriage built on the quicksand of fear, not the bricks of solid trust.

Laura is another case in point. Married and with two children, Laura sued for a divorce after six years on the grounds of physical abuse. Although she wanted and felt she deserved custody of the children, she gave them up because her husband threatened to reveal to the small community in which they lived her incestuous relationship with her father twenty years earlier. As much as Laura loves and wants her children, she could not fight for them. To do so would have meant that the secret would come out for everyone to see — that *she* had been a bad little girl because her father raped her.   perception of sin

Social Isolation

Carrying around the secret, being charged with sexually tending the abuser, and often bearing the additional burden of household tasks, most incest victims feel socially isolated, certainly by their teen years. "How do you do giggly girl things as a teenager," says Linda, "when you already know what it's all about?" Linda felt out of place as a thirteen-year-old at pajama parties where her friends would whisper and wonder about what "it" was like. "I already knew all the positions by experience," Linda says sadly. How do you do the natural, normal things that are the first steps in sexual discovery when you already know too much? How does a teenage girl hold hands at a movie and do innocent, age-appropriate exploring when she may be already well versed in sexual techniques, often involving activities comfortable only for the mature, sexually active woman?

So the natural development of sexual exploration is short-circuited; she is wise beyond her years. She is also robbed of the normal context for such growth. Children who grow up witnessing mutual affection between parents learn about sex easily and responsibly. The unhealthy family dynamics in an incestuous family can leave the victim isolated and self-conscious.

Ann is a good case in point. Hers was a puritanical, tyrannical father who repressed every normal joyous movement. She wasn't permitted to dance or prance to music; her father explained only by saying, "You're being too loud." Ann thinks he simply could not stand to see her having fun and being a kid.

Until age eight Ann experienced no overt incestuous behavior, although her father had been verbally abusive as long as she can remember. At this age Ann somehow had the nerve to say to herself, "I don't deserve to be treated like this." Her self-esteem still intact, she began rebelling and told her father that she didn't like being yelled at and treated as badly as she was. The father finally turned his anger toward her in a different way, saying, essentially, "You had better love me and tell me so, or I am going to make life miserable for you." She refused to comply. He wouldn't let her play outside the house after that, and at a party with relatives he forced her to sit in the corner and wouldn't allow her to join in the fun.

He was trying to break Ann's spirit and make her into the kind of puppet he needed to dominate. He succeeded one dark, dreary night when her mother went to a meeting and left saying, "You two are always at each other's throats. Make up while I'm gone." Ann's father raped her that night, and achieved the compliance that would serve him best.

All Ann's attempts to make a normal life for herself fizzled after that point. One time she asked a friend to stay the night, and when her friend came in the door, Ann's father mumbled, "As if I didn't have enough troubles." Ann's friend was surprised, but not as shocked as she became when the father said, "All right, if you're going to stay, take off your clothes right here and put on your pajamas."

Ann's friend refused. When the father, angry, continued to insist, Ann's friend asked to phone for her parents to come get her, to which the father replied, "Children are not allowed to use phones in our home."

Ann and her friend managed to sneak a phone call to the friend's rescuing family. Her friend's father learned what had happened while taking his daughter home, became irate, and went back to Ann's house to demand an explanation (which the father refused to provide by not answering the door). He then called all the parents in the neighborhood to tell them about the suspicious behavior.

As a result, Ann was ostracized, although she was completely innocent. She learned of her situation from a neighborhood play-mate who had begun playing with her, then suddenly excused her-self, saying she had to go home. When Ann asked why, her little friend said, "I can't be your friend because my mother said you're going to grow up to be a juvenile delinquent." Ann went for years without friends, while her father continued sporadically to sex-ually abuse her. In high school she was one of the first in her class to rebel by using drugs and wearing outlandish clothes. She was pregnant by her senior year.

Adult Effects of the Lost Childhood

The residue of incest always affects adult behavior, and the phe-nomenon of the lost childhood is no exception. Losing freedom and shouldering too much responsibility in childhood seems most devastating to the adult woman in her choices of marriage and parenting roles; for her as a wife and mother, incest is *always* a relevant issue.

Marriage and the decision whether or not to be a parent are surely two of life's major events. And incest survivors can be hand-icapped in a major way in making decisions in these areas. Some decide they both can and want to handle the responsibilities; oth-ers may never feel ready for marriage and family. Still others by-pass the decision altogether, which is, of course, a decision in itself.

The Fear of History's Repeating Itself

Many women choose not to marry or to have children. Often enough in our case studies we saw that an incest survivor was avoiding those life choices out of the fear that history would repeat itself, that for a terrible, deep reason not subject to rational analysis, she would become the same kind of dreadful parent or the abject and passive spouse who contributed to making her own childhood such a nightmare.

Such fears deserve respect. Learning adequate mothering skills after growing up in an unhealthy family is tremendously difficult. Those survivors who have chosen motherhood are often overwhelmed with the question "How exactly is this supposed to be done?" The question is not surprising under the circumstances, since one of the most demanding social skills — that of parenting — must be learned without practical, positive experience. Possible results include too much indulgence of one's children, or, on the other hand, too much severity, even to the extent of becoming an abusive parent herself. Being abusive may be the only way an incest victim knows how to act until she learns to break that cycle of abuse and finds new ways to deal with the unbearable stress she feels in her role.

Self-Defeating Choices

Even if the incest survivor chooses not to marry or have children, however, the responsibility-laden years of being a "little mother" take their toll in over- and under-responsibility in other areas of their life. Roberta just barely managed the responsibility of keeping her physical life together. A social worker who worked the hospital emergency room night shift from 3:00 to 11:00 P.M., she would come home, go to bed and stay there until 1:00 P.M. the next day, shower and dress, stop at a fast food restaurant, and go back to work. On weekends she sat in her nightgown watching television and eating pizza delivered to her apartment. She owned no clothing but uniforms and nightgowns; she never wore anything else. She ate no food but fast food and hospital fare, so she did not have to set up a kitchen.

Roberta feared rejection. To protect herself against being rejected, she desperately withdrew from contact with others, isolating herself. She managed a job but came as close to a break with responsibility as a career woman could have and still keep functioning in the world. She discovered a way to arrange her life so she could survive physically, but reduce the stress resulting from social interaction.

Many incest survivors decide to ignore their physical environments rather than have to take charge of cleaning, planning, organizing, cooking, or any other tasks that require them to be functioning adults. But even women who decide to marry and bear children can be avoiding choices. If they repeat the abusive pattern of their own childhood family, they are slotting an old familiar role for themselves rather than choosing a new, stronger role.

One possible decision is to "marry the abuser," a man very like the man who exacted such a toll on her life as a child. Another is to "marry a child," an emotionally immature man who wants mothering. She thus avoids the abusive, brutal, and overpowering father-figure of early years.

Gerri married the abuser. After her mother's death her father abandoned her to the care of her uncle and aunt. Gerri's uncle sexually abused her for three years. She carried a whole panoply of maladjustments into her adulthood, all of which can be traced in large part to losing both mother and father (one by death, the other by abandonment) and being sexually exploited by her uncle. "I think the biggest harm came in that I don't trust men, and I am very angry with them. I have never had a man, including my father, that I can trust. [I have not shared the incest secret with my husband] even though he at times has physically raped me, and it has only been recently, in the past year and a half, that I have realized that it has been because of my past experience [that I allowed it to happen]."

Gerri also became an abusive mother to her own children. "I

didn't know how to parent and I was an abusive parent," she reveals. "After my daughter got hurt, I was willing to take a look at what was going on." Gerri injured her child badly, and in the emergency room where the physician suspected physical abuse, she was put in touch with Parents Anonymous. Parents Anonymous is a national self-help group that operates, with volunteer help and grassroots organization, to prevent child abuse by teaching parents how to deal with stress in ways that do not harm their children.

Marrying a "child," a man who wants mothering, occurs often enough in our culture for reasons unrelated to incest, if recent popular book titles are any clue. *The Peter Pan Syndrome* chronicles the lives of men who won't grow up. The "Jewish mother" who infantilizes her son occurs with boring regularity in many novels written by American males. We spoke to many survivors who admit mothering and lavishing care upon their husbands to a degree that seems unwarranted. Why not? They had plenty of childhood training. These women take responsibility for far more than their share of household duties; shoulder nearly all the child care; work outside the home; and in addition cut their husband's hair, pick up his socks, listen to his troubles, and accept his reasons, however weak, for not treating her as a mature and equal partner.

Because they had no experience of a responsible adult male worthy of the name, many incest survivors carry a short list of their expectations of a man: "If only he isn't an alcoholic, I don't care"; "If he doesn't beat me and stay out all night carousing with other women and brings home a paycheck, I'll be doing better than my mother did"; "He's good to me and is never abusive to the kids and, yeah, sure, I'd like more attention and affection and something to do in the evenings besides watch TV, but what's a woman to do?" Comments such as these suggest women who are willing to put up with minimal decency in their own marriages. They are afraid to ask for too much out of the very real fear that they will not get it.

Childhood trained them to live with diminished expectations of men. When they lock into a relationship that gives so little satisfaction, they are carrying into adult life a childhood pattern. It is a familiar groove, and it may work for a time, but sooner or later the survivor wakes up and realizes that she deserves more than she is getting and that she is a grown person with choices, not a trapped, victimized child.

Self-defeating patterns may exist equally in the lives of survivors who do not marry. Ellen's father was in the military and was an alcoholic who molested Ellen whenever he was drinking. As a child, Ellen continued to function by telling herself, "Well, this is just what all fathers do to show their daughters they love them, so it's probably okay." She rationalized that what was happening to her was, in fact, the norm. Ellen did not want to have her vision of reality distorted by the truth. As a result she did not check her perceptions with her friends and never learned whether, in fact, that was their experience as well.

As an adult Ellen began to see some damaging life patterns that had their genesis in her childhood denial system. She still has a lot of difficulty with girlfriends, and intimacy in a friendship is hard for her. She frequently dated married men, convinced that they would throw aside their wives for her. For a period of time she dated homosexual men, convinced that she would be the one to change their sexual orientation. She was constantly duped and finally realized that she was almost consciously finding people who are not what they seem to be. What had protected her as a child — convincing herself that what she was doing was absolutely normal and right — became in adulthood an ability to distort the plainest reality.

With years of individual and group therapy, Ellen is beginning to stop and look at situations before she leaps into them. She is becoming less impulsive, making herself examine what steps she takes in a personal relationship and what they might lead to; she undertakes this examination not in a manipulative but in a constructive and thoughtful way. She is more careful about the people with whom she associates and has given up her "searching for Mr. Goodbar" approach to friendship with men.

Nurturing the Child Within

Because the lost childhood is so devastating, women who survive as adults must come to grips with that void in their lives in some way.

First of all, there is no way to recover a childhood. It is lost forever and cannot be regained. And of course, until a woman realizes that fact she is, in a sense, crippled. Some professionals believe that neurotics stay unhealthy because they possess an insatiable goal in life: there is something they missed in childhood, something they can never have, and yet they will not give up trying to get it.

So it is with the adult survivor of incest. Women who have survived must live through the terrible pain of the knowledge that they will never get back the time of innocent exploration of their own sexuality. Nor will they ever have that idyllic and carefree time we read about in children's literature or watch on the television sitcom. Television families cannot be approximated even by real-life healthy families. How much less a model should they be, then, for a woman who came from a dysfunctional, incestuous family.

The survivor gives up her childhood as lost. It isn't fair that those precious years were snatched away, but fairness played no part in the matter. Once a woman bids that part of her life goodbye, she finds new ways to recapture some of those pleasures even if she is an adult. These discoveries can be precious indeed.

Much of the unfairness is allayed when the survivor truly connects her adult self to the innocent and good child she was before she began to feel disfigured by the incest. Many survivors begin this exploration by looking at pictures of themselves as children and examining the faces, postures, and camera poses of members of the family. These pictures always tell a story, and the survivor reads that chronicle with sorrow, because she sees how helpless she was to change things in her family.

Observing other children about the age she was at the time of the incest aids other survivors. Nieces, neighborhood children, one's own children who are innocent and carefree give her a vivid lesson about who she was as a child until incest left its ugly scar. She begins to experience herself as a good person who was injured and hurt.

Stages of growth and development gather layer upon layer in the human personality. Deep within a survivor is a child who still needs to be nurtured, loved, and attended to.

Ruth wrote a letter to her child-self after she had looked at albums of pictures and wept over the tragic and unhappy person she saw there. She addressed her "child within" lovingly and promised all kinds of happy trips and child surprises. As she thought about it, Ruth realized she had never had a birthday party as a child. She organized one for herself complete with balloons, penny candy, and invitations specifying that guests "dress like little kids." Pin-the-tail-on-the-donkey, musical chairs, and other games were played. Her age? Forty-three that year.

Barbara, the multiple personality we have spoken of earlier, has one personality who stays childlike and innocent and likes toy trucks and cars. She collects toys, both antique and new, a perfectly acceptable hobby for grown men and women. When we think about it, how many parents peeping through toy store windows are looking at toys for *themselves?* Teddy bears are very popular with survivors. Nearly every survivor we spoke to has discovered some childlike capacity in herself and has developed it as partial recompense for the years of loss.

Teenage activities can be restored as well. Patsy goes to amusement parks with her boyfriend on a regular basis, and they enjoy cotton candy and scary rides with great glee. Like many incest survivors, she missed a carefree period of gradually growing sexuality in adolescence, so she loves "teen" activities, such as going to Prince movies and rock concerts.

Incest survivors cannot expect to get childhood back. It is a loss to be grieved. They can then move on to find carefree pleasures on a moment-by-moment basis. They can search deep to discover, then nurture, the child within. Survivors learn in this way to reclaim temporary moments of childhood bliss, and to enact innocent pleasures they were denied as children, thereby enriching their adult lives.

4

Learning to Trust

I AM *afraid of deep water. I can swim in and even enjoy four feet of water, but I panic when I cannot touch my feet to the bottom. I have tried to get over my fear by taking swimming lessons, where I inevitably worked my way to shallow water or clung fearfully to the side. In college a friend even gave me private lessons. She was a Water Safety Instructor and felt confident she could help me over my fear of water. Often she and I were the only people in the university's big pool as we worked to complete the weeks of individual instruction.*

Then came test time. I happily paddled through all the strokes with my teacher shouting encouragement from the side. Then I had to dive into the deep end and swim to the shallow. I went into eleven feet and finally came up gasping once, then twice. I finally saw a long white pole extended to me; I seized it and pulled myself to the edge. I have stayed away from deep water since then.

I am afraid of all kinds of ordinary things, such as merging on expressways. I am convinced every driver will surely mow me down rather than let me into the line of traffic.

Tall buildings make me giddy. Crowded elevators panic me. On mountain highways I stare into the bank rather than down the precipice. High bridges make my seat feel numb and I cannot bear to look over the side. Turbulence in airplanes (not to mention takeoff and landing) gives me sweaty palms and a catatonic gaze. I focus on the front of the cabin and try to will the plane into a steady course. I dare not contemplate the fact that there is nothing under me.

Psychiatrist M. Scott Peck says he does not think there is such a thing as an isolated phobia. My list of fears, therefore, is probably only a beginning. I have not happened on, or thought about, all the other life situations that would strike terror into my heart. The list could be endless.

For they all spring from one central conviction that endures from my childhood abuse: the world is a hostile place, and I cannot trust anything. People who were supposed to love me hurt me. Hands that came to tickle me might pinch instead. If I was pulled affectionately onto a lap, to be rocked in a rocking chair, I felt a hard lump under me, so that what looked like affection turned to something else that made me scared. Words and the realities behind them became topsy-turvy: "Play" with him was no fun. "Be a good girl and come here" meant doing something bad that made me feel dirty.

Finally, there was nothing to trust, not even my own feelings, because a big person was telling me my feelings were wrong or, worse, that they didn't matter or didn't even exist. I lived in a nightmare cottage out of "Hansel and Gretel" or "Snow White." Witches, poisoned apples, wicked stepmothers, and a mischievous dwarf might not have surprised me.

Nothing damaged me more as an adult than the destruction of trust in my childhood. I have had to work hard to build that web or net that others more fortunate than I have never had to think about.

Learning to trust people has taken years, years. And I still have to work on being open to new people and situations. My first impulse is to flee for my own protection. I have to make myself go to parties where there will be unfamiliar faces. I have to force myself to speak up in a public place. But the more I force myself to confront new people and new situations, the more I discover that the world is, if not good, at least neutral. The bogeyman is not going to get me at every turn.

But the effort is continual. So I make myself ride airplanes, and I merge with the best of them on the freeway. I let myself feel rattly as bridges rumble under me during a traffic jam and I giggle nervously with my daughter as we gather with others in the humming elevator that takes us to the top of the world's tallest building.

I try to admit my fears and even to laugh at them, though I take their source very seriously. I am skeptical of others, and I scrutinize groups for evidence that I can trust other people. I sometimes find people do not wish me well, but there are also people who are kind, do not want to take advantage of me, and can be trusted.

And just maybe someday I will be able to jump into seven feet of water and not feel my arms freeze to my sides. Then I will call the water "friend," and ask it to hold me up, and if I float, I will know that I have finally built trust.

*   *   *

Trust is also the essential component of faith.

TRUST is the cornerstone of personality development. It is, therefore, no surprise that the most significant and deep-rooted violation the incest survivor faces is the betrayal of trust in her childhood. It invades all the other areas of survival. It colors and shapes her entire approach to life.

Psychiatrist Erik Erikson in his pioneering book of more than three decades ago saw trust as pivotal in the child's development into a responsible adult:

> The firm establishment of enduring patterns for the solution of the nuclear conflict of basic trust versus basic mistrust in mere existence is the first task of the ego. . . . This forms the basis in the child for a sense of identity which will later combine a sense of being "all right," of being oneself, and of becoming what other people trust one will become.

In a more recent work Erikson holds even more firmly to the notion of basic trust:

For the first component of a healthy personality I nominate a sense of *basic trust,* which I think is an attitude toward oneself and the world derived from the experiences of the first year of life. By "trust" I mean what is commonly implied in reasonable trustfulness as far as others are concerned and a simple sense of trustworthiness as far as oneself is concerned. When I say "basic," I mean that neither this component nor any of those that follow are, either in childhood or adulthood, especially conscious.

What is this precious gift, so critical to the healthy person, that is being dispensed here? Psychiatrist M. Scott Peck calls it "the feeling of being valuable — I am a valuable person — [that is] essential to mental health and is a cornerstone of self-discipline. It is a direct product of parental love. Such a conviction must be gained in childhood; it is extremely difficult to acquire it during adulthood."

Difficult that task may be; nonetheless, the adult incest survivor must build that pivotal trust, which was destroyed during childhood. Like a bridge bombed in wartime and reconstructed piece by piece, basic trust must be built up bit by bit in adulthood. The alternative is a tremendously diminished and damaged human being.

We must begin by looking at exactly what has happened to trust in the incest victim. Here again, there is great variation from person to person and possibly no clinical way as yet of determining what kinds of acts lead to what kinds of behavior. No one is yet sure whether it is the duration of abuse — that is, a prolonged period of sexual abuse — that fractures trust, or whether the nature, environment, and circumstances of the abuse are more critical. The age of the child at the time of the abuse is likely to be an important aspect as well.

What is certain is that up to three people can be involved in this trust issue: father (usually the abuser), mother, and the abused daughter herself. The most serious damage to trust seems to occur when the entire triad of father, mother, and self breaks down.

The father's part of the trust triad is obvious. After betrayal by a trusted male during her childhood, the survivor is certain to have a hard time trusting men in her adult life. The abuser need not always be the biological father in order for the damage to occur. A whole range of acts can produce this feeling of violation in the girl child. A mother's boyfriend abuses the daughter several times when he is in the house. An uncle abuses an adopted niece; a patriarchal grandfather, much beloved by the rest of the family, takes every occasion to abuse his granddaughter in private. The reactions in adulthood to this abuse by a male who should have been trustworthy can range from ambivalence toward men to an actual turning away and the inner conviction that no man can ever be trusted.

But it is not only men who cannot be trusted. We were surprised initially at how many women have difficulty trusting other women. These survivors are functioning as adults and surviving reasonably well in the responsibility-laden world of work and family, but they have difficulty with female friendships and work relationships.

From her years of experience as a therapist, Karen Lison concludes that not all mothers knew about the incest when it was occurring and even fewer were accomplices in the physical sense of the word. But the percentage of survivors who distrust women is extremely high, and it is almost predictable that they will not get along with their mothers. Why then does an incest survivor grow up not trusting her mother and often other women as well?

Carol Poston's own experience and her discussion with other survivors, some of whose case histories are in this book, lead her to believe that a mother doing a responsible job of parenting would in fact know that her daughter was being hurt and would take steps to prevent it. Actual physical complicity in the abuse may indeed be rare, but a mother can *choose* not to know or to avoid coming to terms with ongoing abuse. This is why some survivors feel that they were abused by one caretaker with the full knowledge and permission of the other principal caretaker.

Some authorities on child sexual abuse believe that this is precisely the case: the mother *does* know. Drs. Ruth and Henry Kempe, the Denver pediatricians who pioneered work on child abuse nearly two decades ago, say "stories from mothers that 'they could not be more surprised' can generally be discounted — we have simply not seen an innocent mother in long-standing incest." The Kempes go on to say that the mother not only knows about the incest but helps it along subtly by giving opportunities — and thus permission — for it to occur. She complies with the situation, say the Kempes, because she is frantic to hold on to her husband. She sees the daughter as the one to provide the necessary bond for her own marital relationship to continue. The Kempes see most of the offenders as "socially isolated" men who often glide into the incestuous situation unawares, "given the extra push by a wife who arranges situations that allow privacy between father and daughter."

Therapists themselves, then, are divided on the issue of whether the mother knows what has been happening. Whether or not she knows is not as important as two facts: First, the daughter *thinks* the mother knows; and second, the family unit is affected in a destructive way whether or not the mother is aware of the incest.

Some professionals have drawn a "typical incest family," the paradigm of personality traits that seem likely to occur in a family where incest could flourish, with or without the mother's knowledge. Many survivors and some other professionals find this description inaccurate and misleading. The term "incest family" suggests, however faintly, that the family, not a person, perpetrated the incest. What is true about such a family, however, is that the girl suffers the incest and has to remain silent about it. It is impossible for her to be honest because the whole family may be contributing to keeping the secret.

So pervasive is the notion that incest is a family affair that Jean Renvoize entitles a recent work *Incest: A Family Pattern,* and underlines the complex of causation and effect. She cites the following as probable corollaries to incest in the family: alcohol dependency (which occurs in 32 percent of the families), the presence of a stepfather, the conjunction of a well-educated father and a poorly educated mother, a religious orientation, prudishness about sexual matters, and a long-standing generational pattern of male-female abuse. If an adult survivor feels even a shadow of guilt or suspicion that she caused the incest, it would help her to remember that once the incest has become a pattern, the family locks itself even closer to cover up the lie, and "the victim, most commonly the daughter, is made to feel the entire stability of the family depends on her silence."

Psychiatrist and sexual abuse specialist Roland C. Summit has written a superb overview of the incest victim who becomes helpless and hopeless, caught in a family and community web of denial and self-justification. In "The Child Sexual Abuse Accommodation Syndrome," Dr. Summit says that "the fact that the perpetrator is often in a trusted and apparently loving position only increases the imbalance of power and underscores the helplessness of the child." A child in the process of being betrayed is the last person capable of rescuing herself. In later years, when she is likely to feel that she did not use all the resources at her command to end the abuse, she needs to remember what a terrible burden she was carrying. Again in Dr. Summit's words:

> In the classic role reversal of child abuse, the child is given the power to destroy the family and the responsibility to keep it together. The child, not the parent, must mobilize the altruism and self-control to insure the survival of the others. The child, in short, must secretly assume many of the role-functions ordinarily assigned to the mother.
>
> There is an inevitable splitting of conventional moral values. Maintaining a lie to keep the secret is the ultimate virtue, while telling the truth would be the greatest sin. A child thus victimized will appear to accept or to seek sexual contact without complaint.

Many adult survivors believe that their complicity (if that is how they choose to view having taken part in the acts that they later see as incestuous) began with the first incestuous act. However, many therapists posit that before the actual abuse begins, a pre-incestuous set of behaviors is already in place. These may be sins of omission as well as commission. We are frequently defining what does *not* happen in this unhealthy family as much as what *does* happen.

Psychologist Karin Meiselman summarizes the behavior of the "pre-incestuous" family, where nothing seems to occur overtly, and where, in fact, some of the behavior might be acceptable in healthier families.

> Even when the mother has played no demonstrable role in setting the stage for incest, she is thought to be partially responsible for the inception and continuance of the incestuous relationship through her failure to take any action that would prevent or terminate it. In many cases, the signs of unusual paternal behavior are present long before sexual activity occurs. Obvious pre-incest paternal behavior includes an insistence on sleeping near the daughter, efforts to see her in the nude or to exhibit himself to her, and an unusual amount of physical contact with her. For example, one father in the psychotherapy sample engaged in "wrestling matches" with his fourteen-year-old daughter, causing his wife considerable consternation. In some cases, the father begins to act like an adolescent suitor in his daughter's presence; he may actually insist on holding her hand or putting his arm around her while watching television, like a young couple at the movies. (Obvious jealousy of the daughter's friends, both male and female, or an inclination to fantasize about her sexual feelings and activities are other, more subtle signs of incestuous feelings that may be exceeding the usual, well-repressed sexual possessiveness that a father may feel for his daughter.) At any rate, there are often indications that incest may occur, and a mother may react to them in numerous ways that will increase or decrease the likelihood of incest.

Linda Tschirhart Sanford thinks that the mother's *inadequacies* make the incest possible. The father can approach the daughter because the mother is not confident in her own role. The daughter then becomes the pillar that holds up the incestuous family, and is used by both father and mother:

> When the father approaches the daughter sexually, he offers her a chance to "keep the family together." He feels the mother is not meeting his needs. He does not have the confidence in himself to try to meet his own needs. So he turns to the oldest daughter. The mother, feeling overwhelmed and inadequate in meeting her husband's needs, may welcome the daughter's taking over part of her role. . . . So no adult in the family is taking responsibility for his or her own behavior. The mother looks to the daughter to fill in the gaps — to do what she can no longer do. The father looks to the daughter to make him feel important, to provide special services. The daughter accepts all this, believing she is keeping the family together.

These child abuse experts are giving us reasons why women feel as adults that their mothers betrayed them, even though most did not actively cooperate in assaulting their children. To the child needing security and trust, a mother who does not positively protect her daughter is *perceived* as being implicated in one way or another in the incest. Karen Lison has observed that survivors looking back on their childhood may see that even though they had never communicated the fact that the incest was occurring and indeed may have helped keep the secret, they often believed mother should have magically known that they were being hurt. Children often expect mothers to be able to read their minds.

All of this is by way of saying that the mother is far from irrelevant to the incest, even if she takes no part at all in the actual physical or sexual abuse. As women ourselves we do not want to fall into the old trap of saying it is all the woman's fault, that because our mothers have failed, society can lay its ills at the doorsteps of women. But the anger and upset many adult survivors of incest feel toward their mothers may be explained by the realization that the daughters consider their mothers in some way as a part of the incest triad.

The female child first learns to see the world — and her role as a woman in that world — through her mother. The complex modern relationship between mother and daughter has been ably chronicled by many authors, including Nancy Friday in *My Mother/My Self*. Those accounts do not come out of any family pathology such as incest. But we see from them that ordinary women often have tremendous difficulties with their mothers. How much greater, then, might be the conflict in the incestuous family.

In such a family, mothers frequently communicate a negative attitude about being a woman. When asked to describe their mothers, adult survivors of incest often supply the behavior or social characteristics of very troubled and depressed women. Typical comments are "She always had a messy house, because she was too tired to clean it," or "She never had any friends," or "She watched a lot of soap operas on television." Other comments show role reversal and passivity in addition to inefficient functioning: "She expected me to listen to her problems and solve them," and "She did whatever my father demanded — he dominated her," and "He abused and hit her when he was drinking." Many survivors suspect that their mothers do not like being women, because they favored the male children in the family, absorbing and reinforcing the high value modern society puts on the male. The literature teems with mothers who were themselves being abused by the same men who were victimizing the children. Perhaps it is not surprising that many incest survivors grow up with negative ideas about being a woman and feel resentful toward their mothers for being so inadequate.

It would not be fair to suggest that all mothers in the incest triad are inadequate or weak people; the subject is far more complex than that. But the *adult* survivor is frequently angry that her mother was often unable to communicate a healthy view of womanhood toward her child. Perhaps she was unable to teach her daughter how to be intimate with people, how to view her own female sexuality in a healthy way, how to value herself.

Survivors feel that want of a healthy female role model very keenly, for it perpetuates itself in the attitude the victim develops toward herself in adulthood. What makes the attitude even more difficult to change is the complicated message many mothers convey. Not only do they deny that anything was wrong in the family; they often insist that the daughter's upbringing has been perfect, a scene from "The Brady Bunch," wholesome as prime-time, scrubbed-behind-the-ears middle America. So the survivor must come to grips with two facts: first, her childhood was such that she can feel anger and resentment about it; and second, she often has to discard a myth — the pernicious nonsense that her childhood was not only good, but perfect.

The severest betrayal of trust comes from a father betraying his daughter sexually and a mother willing to distort reality. As the young woman grows up and away from this unhealthy setting, she feels unable to trust her own perceptions. This is a tremendous and crippling infirmity. Let us try to understand how it occcurs.

The primary betrayal was the father's. Even before an event the survivor can label as incestuous, his behavior might have made her uncomfortable; perhaps he just did not seem like other dads. This feeling may have caused confusion, because she was uncertain what love from him meant. For some survivors the damage is all of this uncertain, covert kind. They know something went wrong but they are not sure what.

It is hard to talk about this "pre-incestuous" behavior because it can seem just like ordinary, normal fatherly love, and one runs the risk of having people say, "For crying out loud, can't a father do *anything* affectionate with his daughter without being suspect?"

It is a matter of focus. When boundaries have been crossed, often it is not an event but a subtle matter of attitude or mood. And yet, and this must be underlined, *such behavior is incestuous* and may cause as much harm as, let us say, complete intercourse. In Jean Renvoize's words, "A child whose father does nothing more than continuously expose himself to her in a deliberately sexual manner all through her childhood may well be more damaged than an adolescent who experiences a brief period when unforced intercourse takes place between her and her father."

Examples of "pre-incestuous" behavior or covert incest include a father who spies on his daughter when she is showering or undressing. Perhaps he parades around in only his skivvies downstairs when the rest of the family is fully clothed. Or perhaps he shows unusual interest in his daughter's dates, saying things like, "Did he get into your pants?" In one case the adult survivor we spoke with had only a single overtly incestuous occasion: When she began to menstruate, her father insisted upon looking at her, spread-eagled on the bed, "to see if everything was O.K." It was profoundly damaging to the woman, who also remembers that "he looked at me on other occasions in such a way that I felt he could see through my clothes, but he never touched me."

These are situations in which the child has received the victim-message: "You exist for my pleasure at this moment." All of these actions constitute incestuous behavior, however covert.

The betrayal becomes more severe when the behavior becomes more overt. All the women interviewed said that their lives changed drastically after an overt, sexual, incestuous act occurred. However gentle the incest may have seemed to them then — or now — the point is that the act was done by a man who wielded power against a child who was not able to say "no" and could not defend herself. Her world became distorted when she was a child — and will continue to be distorted when she becomes an adult, unless she is able to recognize that *that was then* and *this is now*. In childhood her choices were limited, but there is no end to what she can choose for herself *right now*.

If the mother is strong, finds out what is happening to her daughter, and saves her from the father's exploitation, the girl may emerge less damaged. Girls reporting their abuse to mothers who subsequently take quick action do seem to have a better record of earlier recovery.

One of the survival mechanisms many women used as children

was to pretend that the mother really wanted to be supportive and strong, but she could not because she was being treated unfairly or unkindly by the father. Ordinarily this protective attitude of the child evaporates when she comes to grips with herself as an adult. She becomes aware that in fact her mother did, as an adult, have choices. The mother chose to let her daughter be placed in jeopardy, or turned away from difficult human situations so that she would not have to deal with the abuse or deprivation she suspected was taking place.

If the mother chooses to ignore the child's pleas for help, she becomes a co-conspirator. If she takes part in the physical assault, she is a perpetrator. If she denies that there is anything in the world more important than herself and confines her discussions to her own problems and the weather, the child feels her world topple. The child is doubly betrayed by father and mother. Any family sense of trust is gone, and the result is that the child will have difficulty trusting herself as an adult. If she is unable to trust her own feelings, she is unlikely to leave herself open or vulnerable for fear she will be betrayed again.

Parents who tell themselves and their child lies reinforce this inability to trust. The perpetrator may have told the child *how to feel* about the abuse. He may have said, "This is play," or "Isn't this fun?" or "Now, didn't that feel good?", using language and concepts important to a child and thereby distorting the child's reality. She is getting a double message, for the healthy child knows about fun; if a caretaker sets about, quite consciously, to substitute his adult sexual pleasure for the child's pleasure in play, she will become confused. These distortions from childhood make her insecure and untrusting as an adult. She may even lose touch with her feelings altogether because she has been instructed for so long on how she should feel.

The burden of betrayal falls on the father and mother without impunity. They have taught the child that her feelings are not only wrong; they simply do not matter. She has to deny how she really feels for the convenience of the parent's fantasy or denial — most commonly the father's sexual fantasy, accompanied by the mother's denial that anything is out of kilter in this "perfect" family. It is a living lie, however, a castle built on the sand of a father's sexual pipe dream and a mother's head-in-the-clouds view of what her family is all about.

The child might fantasize escape, the "when I grow up I am going to . . ." daydream that probably helps her survive her misery. When she does in fact grow up and move away, however, she may be ill equipped to deal with reality. She may often find herself still keeping an escape door open in every relationship.

The child has been betrayed by the closest of her early relationships. She looked for protection and for affirmation that she was valuable and lovable and got hit with an adult agenda — a sexuality for which she was not ready and the message that says what she is thinking is all wrong and what she is feeling makes no difference anyway. As an adult she may avoid closeness. She may be rejected and abandoned again. Intimacy may seem to be beyond her reach.

As a child she learned very early to hold tight to the small territory that she found safe, a territory often enough described by her arms around a teddy bear or a play area shared with a brother or sister. It will be no surprise that as an adult she is often afraid to risk certain situations, personally or professionally.

She freezes emotionally. She refuses to be vulnerable and open or to admit her fears or incapabilities. She sees the world as a hostile and threatening place, and she shrinks inside her own prescribed boundaries.

Such a world may seem safe, but it is also difficult to stay inside the suit of armor she has cast for herself. For reasons that remain as individual as the woman herself, she begins to look for new ways to solve old problems and to get past her childhood victimization. Some say that the hardest step is the first one toward a therapist's office. For others the longest breath they ever take is to say the words to tell just one other person their secret. For yet others it is looking into the bathroom mirror and seeing themselves for the first time.

The process begins. She begins to feel again. She breathes Ezekiel's prayer: "Take away my heart of stone, O Lord, and give me a heart of flesh." And she learns how to implement those three magic words that can change her life: "Take a chance."

The Case of Tracy

Despite M. Scott Peck's admonition that it is very difficult to learn basic trust and a sense of "I am valuable" in adulthood, incest survivors must do just that, and here again they are as enterprising in their methods as they were in their survival techniques as children.

We do not have an abstract concept of "the normal person." Such a notion is like survival itself; if we begin making checklists of normalcy we end up very quickly with a tight and rigid definition to which few would conform. There are many forms of survival. If a woman shows personality traits that are self-preserving, including courage to feel emotions fully and recognition of the strengths that make her valuable, she is surviving well indeed.

An excellent case in point is Tracy. She is a twenty-seven-year-old divorced woman who is now lesbian. She carries in her past one of the most complete cases of self-victimization we have seen. Raised in a severe religion that condemned smoking and drinking, she nonetheless began drinking at age eleven, the same year in which her uncle began sexually abusing her. She was a late-stage alcoholic by the age of nineteen, and she says, "I hated myself then."

A teen life filled with delinquency and vandalism ended with her being placed in a state hospital before she was twenty; she had slit her wrists. A year later migraines again led to hospitalization. The next year she not only attempted suicide several times but cut and slashed herself. At the hospital she was sexually abused by a psychiatric technician. She reported the incident, and then attempted suicide again.

By age twenty-three Tracy had begun what she now calls "manic behavior." "I was perfect. I got religion, stopped smoking, started cleaning house, stopped drinking, began jogging, became anorexic, and was working in an alcoholic rehabilitation program with kids. I was abusing laxatives and fasting. Then I became suicidal after breaking the fast." The self-mutilation and hospitalizations continued until Tracy finally found a therapist who could help.

The therapist told Tracy, essentially, that they would open up her past. "I got scared," Tracy says. "I knew I had a deep dark secret back there, but I didn't know what it was." The incest was uncovered: it included rape by a cousin at age thirteen as well as years of oral sex and genital fondling by an uncle eight years older.

"I treated a lot of symptoms," Tracy says, "but I never started getting better until I looked the incest straight in the eye." Because survivors of incest also frequently possess an array of maladaptive symptoms as adults, it would be possible to "chase symptoms" for years and never confront the emotions about the incest itself. That same denial about the emotions arising from incest which, in childhood, spelled survival, often lead to craziness as an adult. Children have few choices; adults are much freer to acknowledge the truth about themselves, and believe that change can occur.

Tracy finally looked the truth in the eye. She had not perceived any choices as a child: "I felt like I had to do it. He was bigger," she says, speaking of her uncle. As an adult, she says, "I've learned to take responsibility for my own actions . . . I can accept reality now. It's O.K. for me to have bad feelings now."

As a child she had learned to trust no one, least of all herself. "I did nothing. I learned to stop feeling. It helped at the time. But these techniques destroyed me. That's what the cutting and mutilation was all about. Now when I need something I ask for it. I'm not afraid of bad feelings. I feel it all."

She talks about the positive changes she has made: "I'm learning that I can trust other people but also that I can't change them. That's O.K. I'm also feeling better about myself because I feel I am helping others through my group for self-abusers." Tracy has become a much sought-after expert on the subject of self-mutilation. Her own experiences qualify her. She has found the courage to take both personal and professional risks.

Still, she views men with a jaundiced eye, saying, "Nothing from them comes without a cost." As a lesbian she does not feel threatened by them; she is comfortable with men in her business and social dealings. And her survival in that world is oddly more complicated because Tracy is a very attractive woman and, in her own words, "Men come on to me. But I can say 'no' to men. Some women choose to be ugly because they haven't learned to say 'no.'"

Tracy has chosen to rule men out of her sexual world; she can ill afford to rule them out of her business and professional associations, so there she deals with them as comfortably as possible. She refuses to capitulate to a dominant male notion that all attractive women are yearning for a man. Tracy refuses to make herself less attractive so that men will not notice her. She does not see her physical attractiveness and good grooming as reserved for the notice of men alone.

The Case of Barbara

Barbara has seen the same universe as Tracy and, like her, has viewed it as a hostile and dangerous place. Her decision about how to begin to trust has been quite different. The ways in which she was abused (examined more thoroughly in Chapter 2) included sadism and perverse sexual behavior. She developed multiple personalities as a way of surviving.

The incest experience left her completely unequipped for an intimate relationship with a man, because she so thoroughly internalized her father's expectations of her that she became his "son" and adopted elements of masculine behavior.

She lacked a positive and strong role model in her mother, who knew about some, if not all, of the abuse and did nothing about it. With a family of daughters, the father had hoped for a boy at Barbara's birth. Barbara complied. "I wanted nothing feminine," she says. "I tried to be as male and as adventurous as possible, and my father was delighted about that."

Her mother's powerlessness made Barbara see the female role as inferior and weak. Seeking her father's approval had a practical advantage: it was a smart survival tactic to please this powerful, controlling figure in her life.

It had not yet occurred to Barbara that she was contorting herself to please the man who had been abusing her, making herself incapable of the social graces that make dealings between male and female so much easier in our culture. She pretty much denied all sexual feeling in her single-minded pursuit of the career that her father valued so highly. "I became," she says, "a mind on wheels."

Learning to trust again means learning to heal the fractures that occurred in the relationships among father, mother, and daughter. Barbara chose to begin with her own part; she decided to learn to trust herself.

After several suicide attempts and years of despair, she made a conscious decision to be a survivor:

> I used to be a victim even after the abuse stopped because I did not treasure myself. I was a victim of rape attempts, and bosses could walk all over me. The process [of becoming a survivor] has been long. The change came as a result of starting to take care of myself. "I've been a victim long enough," I said to myself. "I'm gonna take care of myself." And now I walk differently and my eyes are more alive. It's a lot more fun this way.

After several years of therapy Barbara was able to tell her mother about the abuse, and her mother did not deny the story. Barbara felt herself getting closer as an adult to her mother, who used to appear to her as a weak, overworked housewife, a minister's spouse, who sewed, cooked, and cleaned but steadfastly refused to see what was happening to her daughter before her very eyes.

And then Barbara's mother quite suddenly died. Barbara waited at the deathbed and tended her mother with love and care, communicating by eyes and smiles rather than words, because the mother had lost her voice. Barbara felt that at the very end her mother was acknowledging the hurt that had happened to her daughter and that she was deeply sorry.

At this point Barbara finds herself attracted to men, and she would like a male/female relationship. Her biggest stumbling block is that she lacks the social skills to feel comfortable in a relationship with a man. And she is terrified of sex with a man. Nonetheless, she is hopeful and at the same time determined to rebuild her trust completely to include men. She knows she has regained her trust in herself and her own perceptions, and she thinks that at her mother's deathbed, she began to rebuild trust with women in a way she had not before. Ahead lie risk, challenge, and possibly defeat before she finds herself in that warm and loving relationship with a man.

Barbara's fear of men is real, for she was deprived of positive female role models as a child and did not learn to cultivate, as a young woman, those social skills that make a relationship with a man easier. "I can't stay at a party more than half an hour," she confesses. And she finds it hard to let herself be attractive. Over the years, she has allowed herself to gain weight, and in this she is not unusual. Behind many overweight survivors is a voice saying, "See, my weight is why people reject me." Obesity keeps them from having to think about developing intimacy or about the incest that is causing the fear of intimacy. Obesity was a wall Barbara put up around herself so that she would not have to feel the pain of really seeing herself. She is taking down that wall by losing weight, and taking a good look at herself and at what changes she needs to initiate.

The Case of Marianna

Marianna, on the other hand, is already tremendously attractive — a tall, willowy brunette with strikingly blue eyes and a lovely blush on a nearly flawless complexion. Men are a problem because they swarm about her. She has had a number of sexual encounters with men despite the years of abuse from her father, abuse which included being forced to read pornographic literature and to look at pictures to "instruct" her. "Eventually it was everything you could imagine. . . . I think one of the worst things was one which I just recently [remembered]. He used a lot of pornography. He used to order a lot of movies and books. I'd go to bed at night and there would be a 'present' waiting for me under the bed between the mattress and box springs, and he'd say, 'Now, I want you to read that.'"

As we recounted in Chapter 2, Marianna made a bargain with her father. In return for her sexual compliance, he would not hurt Marianna's mother or sister. When she was eighteen, she discovered her father trying to strangle her mother, called the police, and effectively evicted the father; her mother divorced him two years after she learned that he had been abusing both daughters. Marianna left home for business college and landed a job soon after.

But then Marianna married. Fiercely devoted to her husband and grateful that he understood and accepted the emotional damage that the years of incest created, she decided early on in her marriage not to deprive her husband of something she understood all men wanted: the belief that he was giving his wife sexual pleasure.

So she faked orgasms. She has only recently confessed to him that she has been lying. She says hopelessly, and cries as she speaks, that she will probably never enjoy sex, but that she does so much want to give her husband what he wants: "Sometimes when we're making love I just feel what's so great about it? Why does everybody make such a big deal about it? I do love him, I really do, but I just try not to think about it. I think of something else, like what I'm going to wear to work the next day or what I'm going to have for dinner tomorrow."

Marianna hears what she is saying when she talks about her fantasy during sex: she is limiting herself to a choice between the duty to please her husband in bed and the duty to be a good house-keeper the next day, all the while sacrificing any pleasure she herself might be capable of having. The choices she has set up for herself are akin to what happened to her as an incest victim. There she was torn between not wanting to be her father's sexual victim, and believing that she had to accede to her father's wishes to protect her mother and sisters. When she made the pact with her father that if she engaged in sex with him, he would not hurt her mother or abuse her sisters, she did not see that neither choice had anything to do with her own needs.

Marianna is a self-described Joan of Arc, a martyr for others, a handmaiden to duty — that same duty that was an escape route from her abuse as a child. When she was a child, it was mandatory for her to deny that she had any emotions or needs that were not being met. Duty to others spelled survival then, an escape route from feeling, and a necessity to preserve her family.

But of course she is an adult now, and more choices are open to her. And still she is frightened to admit that she might have some emotional needs that are not being met.

Why does Marianna's situation show a lack of trust? And what is she doing about gaining a sense of trust as an adult?

Enjoying the sexual act and being orgasmic require a great deal of trust. Being able to give in, relax, share, and let go are part of sexual intimacy. But to the person who is fearful of letting down the barriers enough to experience intimacy, sex is a terrifying situation.

For Marianna as a child there was no safe place, not even in the bed she shared with a sister. The only safe place was deep inside herself. The incestuous family permits few boundaries; the victim is fair game for all. The child is forced to retreat into a remote part of herself.

But letting another person come into one's personal space during intimate sex is what mature sexuality is all about. When the child's boundaries have been violated so much that she is driven to a veritable desert island of safety, the adult does not give up her one safe place with impunity.

As we seem to mention again and again, such a state of affairs leads to a tremendous distortion of reality. Marianna has a difficult time seeing herself realistically. She commonly finds herself on her desert island holding steadfastly to a tiny truth that she is valuable, and reaching out to people by saying she is willing to sacrifice herself for them.

Beautiful as she is, Marianna sometimes wonders if she is attractive — in fact, it is a preoccupation with her. When people tell her she is beautiful, she becomes embarrassed. When people tell her she is pretty enough to be a model, she pooh-poohs it. Not trusting her own perceptions, she has had pictures taken at a modeling agency to verify to herself that she exists.

She recently took a course at a local junior college in the color-coordinating techniques popularized by Carole Jackson's book *Color Me Beautiful*. She had hoped to make herself attractive. She relates:

> When I got to the class everyone there was big and ugly. Then I got embarrassed because I knew I was more attractive than they were. My instructor decided to use me as a model, which made me even more embarrassed. Everyone else was there in blue jeans and sweat shirts, and I had worn a silk blouse. I felt just awful. And I had worn high-heeled snow boots, and when the class was over I went out to the parking lot to get into the car and I slipped on the ice and hit my head and I got a big black and blue mark on my arm. I just lay there in the snow and said to myself, "I just wish someone would come here and rape me and destroy this beautiful image of me."

There are several telling things about Marianna's experience which she readily acknowledges. One is that rape, forcible sex (differing from her incest only in that the incest went on for years whereas the rape would be perhaps a single act) is something which destroys beauty. Sex, in Marianna's mind, blasts beauty and makes the fair ugly. Little wonder, of course, that she finds sex in marriage, which she recognizes as normal and desirable, to be a destructive and belittling experience. Sometimes she feels that there is something good about her, but the sexual act pulls that assurance aside and, in a deep and dark way, affirms that, yes, she is really bad!

Her lack of trust in others, particularly in men, comes from her feeling that if people, particularly men, say that she is attractive, they are only out to use her. To avoid that exploitation, Marianna tries to deny that she is attractive. In the "incest message" when she was a child, "You are beautiful" meant "I want to use you for my pleasure." Marianna still hears that double message as an adult.

Marianna is choosing to regain her trust by building it inside herself and refusing to live in a make-believe world. By telling her husband that she has been faking orgasms, she is refusing to live a lie and is allowing herself to feel, even though she does not like how she feels. Pretending is lying; until one admits the truth of a difficulty, no change is possible.

Marianna is considering a career in modeling. The photographs used to verify that she was acceptable now persuade her that she has beauty worthy of a model. She sees something valuable and is willing to use it to her advantage. At the same time she is working with the public as a medical receptionist and going to school part-time to affirm a sense of worth — to exercise both her brain and her social abilities.

Marianna is regaining a sense of trust by risking herself. Some day she hopes to trust herself enough to enjoy sexual intimacy.

The Case of Roberta

Roberta is learning a sense of trust in another way. After several discouraging encounters with a variety of therapists, she found one with whom she feels comfortable. In therapy she has chosen to try to acquire trust by arranging her life at the moment as a series of events in which she is competent and can prove her own self-worth. She hopes some day to be able to branch out and find trust in close friendships with women and intimate relationships with men. But the time, she feels, is not now.

She does not cultivate close friends. She is afraid that they might find something about her that they will want to reject. Afraid that they will not like what they see, she cannot risk rejection and limits herself to acquaintances and relationships at work and school.

She cannot trust herself with men, and her reason sounds simplistic. "I just can't make the small talk," she says, "and why should I pretend to be sociable when I'm not?" She has never had a sexual experience with anyone except her father.

Roberta's reason for not trusting men comes primarily from the years when her father wordlessly forced intercourse upon her on a regular basis. When she first sought therapy in her early twenties, she could not sleep, was depressed, and was addicted to tranquilizers. She had become fearful of sleep because of dreams of her father on top of her, suffocating her. But she frequently woke up having wet the bed or having experienced sexual arousal. She felt tremendously guilty. She is ashamed of the thought that she may have found any sexual pleasure in the past and that she continues to in her adult dreams. These are acts which, on a rational level, she finds so absolutely abhorrent that for a long time she believed she could never have intercourse with a man again.

Because she experienced sexual arousal and pleasure with her father, she has taken that guilt and transformed it into the even more damaging thought that she is not deserving of sexual pleasure, having abused the privilege in her childhood.

In retrospect she feels guilty about not stopping the abuse, which continued well into her college years, though she saw it even then as tremendously destructive. She extends her feeling of guilt back to when she was a teenager:

> I had a total of maybe three or four dates in high school, and my dad met my date in his underwear. Up until the last year I never felt comfortable being alone with a man. When I was in high school and college I had fears of being attacked. My mom had told me not to get pregnant. For several years I made no attempt to get friendly with men. When I started on a friendly basis, I would get anxiety attacks; this would happen time and time again. Now looking back I have strong feelings . . . that I should have stopped it. I feel more guilty about letting myself be sick emotionally as long as I was, even though I felt then that going along with all that was normal.

After much therapy Roberta has not yet assuaged her guilt. She can give intellectual assent to the notion that she was not at fault, that her body responded sexually although her will resisted. She knows that in reality hers was a perfectly normal reaction; if the good Lord made our eyes for seeing and our noses for smelling, surely our sexual organs were made to feel pleasure as well as produce children. And she knows as well that a child is not to be held to account for sheer physical responses over which she has no control. That innocence is surely compounded when sexual attentions have been forced upon her.

Roberta knows all that in principle. But abstract knowledge is a far cry from genuine feeling. And at the moment she feels guilt, however irrational it may seem.

Allied to that guilt is anger, rage that the abuse happened. She takes that anger out on men now that she is an adult. She asserts that she could never have sex with a man and will never trust a man again.

Nor does she trust women. Her mother lives nearly two thousand miles from her, and Roberta finds that an appropriate distance, metaphorically akin to the emotional distance she has felt from her mother all her life. She blames her mother not only for allowing the abuse to happen but for communicating a view of downtrodden womanhood that never allowed her to develop any self-respect: "Even if my mother didn't know what was going on physically, she contributed to a lot of the feelings, all kinds of negative things about being female. She even came screeching out of the delivery room with my sister that she wanted a boy because she didn't like the girls she had then."

As a child Roberta spent a lot of time literally in her closet, reading and daydreaming. As an adult she did much the same thing. Roberta was a social worker in a hospital emergency room, and after duty she did little but sleep. As we have mentioned earlier, she had cushioned herself from choices by owning only uniforms and nightgowns and by eating only fast food and hospital cafeteria fare. "I can remember going to bed at 1:00 A.M. and staying in bed until 1:00 the next day in time for 3:30 work." She became a prisoner of her own bedroom, where she retreated under stress.

Roberta is still a social worker, but she wants no more of the caring professions; she has decided to go into computer technology. She is taking a full course load in addition to her regular job, and she is making nearly straight A's, which makes her feel wonderful.

Now if she feels nervous or under stress, she walks around the block. "I have some friends at school now," she says, "and they're worth getting out of bed for. And I'm enjoying classes and college work."

It is possible that Roberta will never choose to live in an intimate relationship, male or female. She is devastated by the memory of her parents' relationship with each other and cannot imagine repeating it: "I looked at my mom and dad and how they lived. I didn't want to live like that. But they were like most people in my community. There was no choice; only one thing could a woman do — marry and have kids."

At the moment Roberta is choosing to trust herself, to gain self-respect through academic accomplishment and demanding career choices. She is beginning to feel comfortable in a once hostile-feeling world.

The Case of Beth

Problems with self-trust do not have to come out of the father-mother-daughter triad. Beth's situation shows this fact dramatically.

Beth comes from a large and close Greek family, which often shared living space. When she was growing up, Beth lived in an urban flat, and her grandfather lived on the same street, where he had a carpentry shop in the basement of his home.

Beth's parents were warm and loving to each other and to her. When Beth's friends came over, they often said what nice parents she had.

Beth's grandfather was much beloved by the whole family. During the large family gatherings so characteristic of her heritage, everyone made a fuss over grandfather. He was so funny and cheerful and affectionate. But during the week when the family was not gathered and Beth was playing around the house, her grandfather often beckoned her from the doorway of his shop. It was time to come and do his bidding.

The fondling and touching episodes that so embarrassed her began when she was a toddler, and stopped when she was about twelve. But by then she had to live with the consequences of the family secret. Over the years she had watched the family's reactions to her grandfather. They thought he was wonderful. Therefore, in her young mind she decided *she* must have been bad to make him treat her so badly.

When they moved from the grandfather's neighborhood, Beth began to fall apart. Her grades fell. She cried all the time, and she kept her sorrows inside herself even more tightly for fear "all the truth would come rushing out and people would be mad at grandpa and me." Her mother was terribly worried. Her father was mystified about the good girl with good grades who had suddenly fallen to pieces.

When she was fifteen her boyfriend was killed in an accident. By this time Beth had effectively learned how to repress her honest feelings. Not wanting to show any emotion lest all the heartbreak about herself came tumbling out, she got quieter and quieter. She attempted suicide at the age of sixteen.

As an adult, she suffered from low self-esteem, bouts of depression, promiscuous sexual behavior, and years of alcohol and drug addiction. She broke off marital engagements three times.

And over the years she had a feeling that something was not right, but she did not know what to do to get rid of the feeling. She was afraid to tell what had happened with her grandfather, but at the same time she was not certain that what had happened was at all important. "I had no conflict. I just held feelings in and used a 'cheerful face.' Now I am dealing with feelings. I have good friends for support and a therapist to help me open up. I feel a need to talk out the incest through a group. . . . I am slowly learning to be more open."

Beth is a self-employed consultant. Her job requires her to be self-disciplined and responsible. She is drug- and alcohol-free, and is talking out her damage in an incest support group. On the other hand, she sometimes thinks it is too scary to find out her feelings, since she is afraid of feeling bad. She is inhibited sexually with men and has not yet established a meaningful relationship. She is not even thinking about forgiving her grandfather. "First I have to learn to forgive myself," she says.

Trust in herself is coming to Beth. She is beginning to like herself, and chuckles about her "list of assets" that she keeps taped to her bathroom mirror as a reminder that she is a valuable person. With courage and hard work, faith in others is coming as well.

• ✻ • ✻ •

TRUST is learned in different ways by different survivors. Some learn first to trust themselves, then to expand their views finally to include others. Roberta, by contrast, found in her therapist one other person to trust, then with work learned to trust herself, and is now gradually making new friends, although she doubts she will ever be what might be described as free and easy about the world.

Nor should she be. Survivors learn to achieve a balance between trust and distrust, for surely it is not sane to trust everyone and to assume that the world is always a safe place. It is not. But neither is it sane to assume that the world is hostile and evil. Being able to discriminate is everything. Barbara states this view particularly well:

> First of all the most important thing in learning to be a survivor has been learning that the world is not an evil place. I had to move out of the incestuous environment completely before that could happen. . . . There is evil there in the world. But I've learned a gradual process of trusting my insides to judge people. "This one I can trust," or "Stay away from that one!" I'm good at this. And different from before when I thought everyone was out to get me.

Most survivors have had to sit down and think through exactly how they feel about the world. Does it feel like a hostile place? If the answer is "yes," then they go back to sort through their childhood universe to see why they might have come to see it that way. They probably discover that their perceptions were not far from the mark. It was a garden full of weeds, or a scary wilderness with horrors behind every bush.

None of us has the option of going back to make the garden perfect, but we can start by pulling a few weeds to get a better look at things. Sometimes we see the noxious and the bad and the evil. But we can also pause to plant a few roses. We come to discern the good, the bright, and the beautiful, and we can create some of that goodness and beauty.

Trust of the world and of people in that world, and confidence in their own perceptions, both come slowly to survivors. But finally they can accept the fact that whereas people and situations can be safe or unsafe, trustworthy or not, they have the power within themselves to distinguish confidently which is which, and to make healthy choices for themselves using that information. That willingness to risk, to have courage, and to work hard is what it is to be an incest survivor. Nobody said it was easy, as all our case studies show and as multitudes of women already know.

CHAPTER

5

Powerlessness and Control

I HAD *no refuge or safe place when I was growing up. I did not have my own room, so I could not escape, lock the door, and feel secure for even a short period of time. Our house was small, so it was hard to find a place indoors to be away from everyone else. Even when I sat at the kitchen table doing homework I felt in the way, because my family walked around me and grumbled about my always having my "nose in a book" and complained about my homework spread over the table.*

During the school day I had something of a refuge, because I felt safe and was not in danger of abuse. It seems odd now to hear children and young people speak of feeling imprisoned or hassled to have to go to school. School was a great place for me, and I could have lived happily there with occasional meals brought in. But I could not linger there; in elementary school no one stayed at the two-room schoolhouse after hours unless they were being punished. We were all expected to start right away to make the trek homeward. And in high school I lived a twenty-mile bus ride from school, so I could not even stay after school for play practice or meetings, because there was no ride home after the bus left.

Once home I was trapped. My friends lived more than twenty miles away. There was no neighborhood, town or city, to escape to, even if I had been able. This was the country, remote from people and places that might provide refuge to a child needing it.

I had inward escapes, of course. A chair, a green stationary rocker, sat in the corner of the living room, and there I sat, legs curled under me, reading for as long as people would let me. I read about faraway lands and fascinating and worldly people. Books and daydreams took me out of my surroundings and provided a haven I could find no place else. No one had yet found a way to intrude upon my mind and imagination.

But there were no fences around that green chair, and it was not posted with "no trespassing" signs. The metaphor comes naturally to me now that I am an adult and see what was happening to me. This part of the country was known as hunting and fishing territory. There was a hunting season for the wildlife, which meant that the deer, antelope, and elk could be legally hunted only a few weeks out of the year and were otherwise protected. There were no legal boundaries or posted territory around me whatsoever. It was always open season for my father to invade my body and to make whatever sexual demand he wanted, wherever he wanted (since I had no private place to call my own), pretty much whenever he wanted if no one else was around — and even when he could get me into a corner when people were around but not watching. I was also open season for my mother's appeals for work, usually a silent signal sent as she stood before the green chair, broom in hand, indicating it was time to give up the warm safe cave I had made with my mind and my book.

When hunting season did come for the deer and antelope, our whole family went out on the excursions. Both my parents bagged their game each year, and although I never carried a gun, I was expected to be part of that hunting party. It was required. Numerous times I watched my father aim at an unknowing animal that had paused looking up from its grazing or its rest. I watched my father carefully get the bead on the most vulnerable part of its anatomy, then squeeze the trigger on the high-powered rifle. He was an excellent shot; the animal inevitably either fell to the earth or was soon hunted down and killed. My father was a conscientious sportsman. He never let wounded animals limp off and die. He tracked them down and killed them to put them out of their misery.

I remember approaching with dragging and reluctant steps the spot where an animal lay and looking down into its soft, dying eyes. Then I watched my father slit its throat, open its abdomen, take out the insides, save the liver and heart, wrap them in a large red kerchief, hand the package to me, then grab the animal's back legs to pull it across the snow, leaving a trail of blood and hair on the white earth.

The hunting excursion had its effect on me. There was no escape. My father could pick off an antelope racing across a sagebrush plain at a great distance. He had a "scope" mounted on the high-powered rifle that could fix an animal in its crosshairs and kill it, even an animal as camouflaged, small, and fast as an antelope. What chance would I have had if he had decided to destroy me?

My fear was great. And I had so little territory to call my own and so little power to defend such fragile boundaries as did exist on my tiny island. My desert island was a green chair, an afternoon under a tree looking at the clouds, a quiet library where finally the bell would ring and the doors close. I withdrew deep inside myself into a tiny mental room guarded by a tight little smile, which I can still see in the photographs taken of me at the time.

In later years I came to love articles that "post" a name: spoons with initials, engraved brass door knockers, monogrammed linens, bookplates that say "This book belongs to —" and that show a tranquil, solitary person reading under a leafy tree. As a child I had inscribed the few books I owned over and over in a careful, ornate script, as if to seal for once and all something that could truly be mine.

I love houses with many comfortable rooms, each with a place to sit quietly and read undisturbed. And I have a room of my own, a cozy room with shelves of books, overstuffed chairs, and paint-

ings and photographs by friends, crayoned pictures by children, lace curtains, and plants on the windowsill.

And the doors have many locks. I have never been one to lament the passing of the good old days when no one ever had to lock their doors. I like knowing that there is a good lock on the door and that it is safe and beautiful and warm inside.

· ✳ · ✳ ·

IN Chapter 3 we saw that when the adult survivor of incest recognizes that she has lost her childhood forever, she weeps over it and gives it up as lost. She has, of course, a right to anger and resentment at never having had the tender nurturing that every child should be able to expect from her parents, and that would build the self-trust she needs as an adult. But being a survivor of incest is not a business of expecting to have gotten what was fair and reasonable: the harsh reality is that what was decent, reasonable, life-giving, and loving simply did not happen to this woman.

After raging about that fact and confronting it head-on, she learns to accept that she can nurture herself as an adult, having missed out on nurturing as a child.

But she also needs to remember that a paradox lay at the heart of this childhood role reversal. The girl who became a "little mother" was given a full dose of adult responsibility without any adult power to accompany it. Where there was ongoing incest in childhood, there was powerlessness. It is that simple — and that complicated. She had few choices but to comply with the demands made upon her, however burdensome and heavy those demands were.

Children, all children, begin with very few choices. Responsible parents will try to make available as many choices as they can for the child while she grows older so that she may learn responsibility. Effective parenting has as its goal a young person who knows her own power and its limitations. But an incestuous family wants no such thing. In incest the whole dynamic is power, power of the offender over the victim, and in such a family others are rendered powerless for the offender's convenience and his self-aggrandizement.

If a father wants, for example, to obtain sexual gratification outside marriage, he is in most cases free to do so. Illicit sex is neither so expensive nor so unobtainable that the offender could not readily find it. But he *chooses* to obtain it from an under-age child — "his" child.

The perpetrator is not likely to recognize that he needs power; his reasons are much more subtle, of course. He may rationalize by saying, "It would be wrong if I did this to someone else, but it's okay if we keep it in the family. That way we won't hurt mother." Or, "I'm older and going to protect you. You wouldn't want to do this with people your own age because they might hurt you. But I know what I'm doing and I love you." The perpetrator exerts power over a powerless person and manipulates her emotionally to satisfy his own needs. He may also manipulate the rest of the family to secure permission for his actions.

Violation of Boundaries

Once again, we need to distinguish what in this situation makes the child of an incestuous family different from other children. All children are powerless. To be a child is to be told what to do and, quite as seriously, to chafe and rebel at those restraints. Children begin their lives with little control over their bodies. Most children are taught gradually to be responsible for their physical, then their mental and emotional, selves. As adults they treat their bodies with care and respect. The religious concept of the body as the temple of the spirit is an excellent description of how this task, undertaken by responsible parents, can help create a healthy sense of esteem.

For the victim of incest, the temple has been destroyed. In incest, the physically intact self, the body that a child comes to know first as the real self, is someone else's territory, to be intruded upon at his will, without her permission. If she does "give permission" as a child, it is a travesty of what the word means. It is at most the child's pathetic attempt to gain some little power, but it can in no sense constitute real adult permission, freely given without duress. The truth is that the child does not have enough power to barter herself away. The perpetrator will get what he wants; the enterprising child may give herself some shred of dignity by exacting promises in return for the sexual favors she is forced to perform. But the legal concept of "informed consent" has no meaning in the context of powerless child and offending adult.

Since the child's body is violated regularly at someone else's will, she is unable to establish meaningful boundaries. One way children establish boundaries is to require privacy. Every parent knows there is a stage at which "no trespassing" and "top secret — keep out" signs appear on bedroom doors and dresser drawers; locked diaries become the order of the day. It is natural — and desirable — for a child to have the sense of self that draws a line against others, a line saying, "Here you cannot come in; this is just for me."

Violation of this normal desire for privacy has incalculable effects on the incest survivor. Nothing is truly hers. Accompanying this violation of physical boundaries is another violation far worse and far more difficult to explain: it is the violation of her *mind*. She begins to believe that she has no power, whether or not in fact she does. The authority figure who can lord it over her physically as a child also can have emotional power over her well into adulthood. This phenomenon is often puzzling to partners or spouses of survivors or people involved in close relationships with the adult incest survivor. Most survivors have heard a comment such as, "Why did you let it go on for so long? I mean, I know it was not your fault, but why didn't you stop it?" Or possibly a spouse complains that after twenty years of marriage, with the perpetrator now dead, the wife still admits that she sees her father in their bedroom during lovemaking. The husband in this situation may be angry and resentful that his wife cannot get rid of the ghost, and confused about why it lingers.

The incest survivor is probably puzzled too, and frustrated as well. After all, she is an adult now, and the fears that terrorized her as a child no longer apply. We heard numberless vignettes along these lines. Diana, at age twenty-five, with a good job, could not seem to move out of the house where she had been abused all her life. Marie, engaged at age twenty-seven, could not tell her fiance that her two older brothers had routinely violated her; shame and guilt overwhelmed her. Many women report the continuing influence of their dead fathers. Roberta thinks that he can hear her talking, even though he is dead. Carol found that she could not write about the enormities done her in her childhood without fearing that somehow she would be punished or even killed by her dead father.

These instances exemplify power, real power, of a sort quite different from the sheer brute authority of a large adult over a small child. It can mean lifelong slavery to an idea, to a master who may even be dead. Where does this incredible power come from?

The Power of "The Secret"

The source of this power game is the secret: the victim is handed a secret, and she is told that she now has the power to destroy others if she reveals it. This secret is explosive and destructive; it is like a hand grenade she is asked to cradle under her garments. If it goes off, she or someone she loves will be destroyed. When women reach adulthood, they often realize that in fact the sky would not have fallen had they told the secret, that the bad things threatened might not have happened at all. Then they feel guilty that they did not figure out they were being led on and deceived.

But again, it is the child's *perception* that counts here: *she thought she must keep the secret at the time.* Adult reality is another matter. The distortion about what is going on and what she thinks is going on is a clue to the confused sense of reality most survivors take out of their incestuous childhood.

In a nonincestuous family there may be similar confusions about power. A good example comes from the new and rather thorough literature on grief. We now know that young children often feel responsible for a death in the family. Perhaps Susie got mad at Johnny once and thought to herself that she wished he would die; when Johnny dies in an accident later, Susie feels stricken that her wishing had caused his death.

A responsible parent will assure the child that he or she has no power to cause the death of another simply by wishing it. But the father who is an incest offender, *by definition an irresponsible parent,* will give that child's illusion of power authenticity rather than discouragement, since that illusion serves his purpose better. More than one survivor has heard her father say, "Look what you made me do!" as he ejaculates. Or as he beats or slaps her he says, "You're asking for it; if you weren't so bad, I wouldn't have to do this." She seems to have power to make him abuse her, although she is not sure what it is or how it works. This is the beginning of the distortion of the notion of power that proves so enduring and so confusing to the adult survivor.

Threats and Power Games

The secret is a powerful weapon and the perpetrator uses it to frighten the child into never telling anyone that she is being hurt. Offenders use threats ranging from brutal promises of death on the one hand to subtle emotional manipulation on the other. And children on the whole take threats seriously. Many are told that mother will be killed if they tell; some that they will themselves be killed or punished. If in addition a pet is killed or a favorite doll is mutilated (or, in the case of the co-author of this book, wild game animals are killed), the child gets a clear confirmation of her fear that she or people she loves could be hurt or even destroyed by her telling.

Not all threats are so brutal. Some are quite subtle. Many fathers who are offenders involve the victim in physical activities in which the child learns she is his inferior in physical strength. Lillian's father was a strong, muscular man who often engaged his children in arm wrestling. Occasionally he let them win so that they would stay piqued enough for the games to continue, but the chief effect was the reminder that he was physically more powerful than they.

Tickling, and not of the gentle, amusing variety, is a tactic often employed not just for its eroticism, but as a way to exemplify power. Georgia would get into "tickle fights" with her father at his insistence, only to find him on top of her tickling her in places that made her uncomfortable and embarrassed, but she had no authority to stop the "fun." Backrubs can have the same effect: being asked to rub Daddy's back is a commonplace among incest survivors, although the nuances vary. Survivors are often summoned to rub the father's back even if the mother is near. Even without any sexual innuendo, such a service is questionable because it is calculated to make the child think of herself as a servant who must perform or else.

The power of the perpetrator is further enforced by threats that do not involve physical brutality or power struggles. These are forms of emotional manipulation, and they all start with the phrase, *"If you tell what we are doing"*:

— "it will break your mother's heart" or "your mother will have a nervous breakdown and will have to be sent away"

— "I will be sent to jail, and how will the family be supported?"

— "no one will believe you" (and the subtext here is, "You're just a kid, and I, after all, am a judge, a social worker, a police officer, a minister"; we have seen perpetrators in each category)

— "you will destroy the family."

These threats are so common that nearly every incest survivor can fill in the blank to complete the sentence.

Humiliation

Other survivors remember not just verbal threats but humiliation, browbeating, or physical assault that enforces the power of the abuser. Many girls suffered *both* physical and sexual abuse, while at the same time severe emotional abuse hung in the background. They were slapped, beaten, and hit; they were sexually abused; and all the while they were made to feel guilty and ashamed that any of these things was happening to them. Adults should try to consider the outrage and humiliation they would feel if a near relative even *hit* them; they might begin to understand how devastating is the burden of shame, guilt, and hurt that the incest victim carries into her adult life because of the way she was treated.

The child is often shamed and humiliated into submission. Lillian, at age fourteen, was first of all embarrassed that her father felt no compunction about coming into the bathroom when she was taking a bath, but she was humiliated as he stood at the door and sneered, "What do you think you've got that I haven't seen before?" Rhonda's father humiliated her and her sister by walking around downstairs in his jockey shorts while the rest of the family was fully dressed; as he strode around he questioned her about her dates, and then made fun of the boys she had gone out with. Rebecca's father refused to let her invite anyone home. If a friend came to the door, he turned his back and began muttering swear words. Rebecca was humiliated at her father's antisocial behavior and met her friends outside the door.

Humiliation of the victim becomes a family game in many cases. The victim becomes the object of abuse for the rest of this dysfunctional family; she is a scapegoat, a "garbage person." Suzanne was an honor student and a fine athlete; it was hard to find something about her to criticize, so her family settled on her physique and made references to her "piano legs" and her big feet. Cecily's father was a therapist. Even so, her brother was permitted to tease her unmercifully; on occasion he would take the plate of food from in front of her when she sat down to eat and call her a "pig." The brother was considered "behavior-disordered" and given therapy because of his actions, while Cecily, despite the many symptoms of the incest she was suffering from her father, was left untreated and was told that she "instigated" the abuse her brother was giving her.

The abuse that comes to a girl when she is a family scapegoat only helps to reinforce her feelings of powerlessness. The perpetrator can physically threaten her and emotionally manipulate her; her family can scapegoat her. She stands alone, holding the powerful secret, told that she will destroy herself and others if she reveals it. It is little wonder that with this confusion and despair, most incest victims contemplate suicide.

Adult Stigmatization and Guilt

Such despair is compounded in adulthood by guilt. When the survivor finally wakes up to what was happening to her as a child, she sees clearly how unfair it was. She was told she was inferior and treated badly; she was threatened with more abuse if she told; she was forced to submit to something she did not want. "Why?" she asks herself. "Why did I put up with it? I must have been crazy."

As an adult, she may suffer additional stigmatization if people find out that she was a victim of incest. This is a pervasive and strong element in our culture, which probably stems from denial. People don't want to think about sexual abuse of children, so they deny that it happens; and if assured by an adult woman that it did happen, many further deny that she can ever be healthy or "normal." Many survivors stay quiet about the incest because people — even people who love them — are likely to say, "Boy, if that happened to you, you must be a wreck! How could you ever get your life together after that?" Survivors are widely stigmatized, or branded as permanently abnormal, even when their auditor is sympathetic.

Professionals themselves may stigmatize survivors. Lillian's first psychiatrist was a Freudian and a male. After eighteen months of therapy, when she began to talk about the incest, he put it to her gently that, of course, she would have to accept someday the fact that she had sexually desired her father. His strict adherence to the concept of the Oedipal complex (the sexual desire of a child for the parent of the opposite sex) not only blinded this psychiatrist; he also reaffirmed to Lillian what her father had said: "See, you asked for it." So Lillian was twice branded because two "authority figures" had told her she was guilty.

Clergy have often reaffirmed the victim's "guilt." Not only is she asked to forgive her abuser, but she may also be asked to consider her own part in the offense, the ways she contributed to the "sin." One survivor when she was eighteen years old told a priest in the confessional that her father was having sex with her. The priest pondered awhile, then said reassuringly, "At least he is keeping it in the family." As the facts of incest become better known, clergy will perhaps learn to understand the needs of survivors, but our case studies show that some have been party more to stigmatizing than healing.

When the survivor begins to doubt her motives, and when she is further stigmatized by people she respects or loves, guilt rushes in. Maybe she still thinks she was responsible for the pile of accusations made against her. If she could have destroyed the family, she may wonder why she didn't opt to do exactly that and expose what was hurting her by reporting what was going on and thus saving herself. She feels crazier and crazier.

But a survivor is not being reasonable and realistic if she thinks she had power as a child and could ever have been held responsible for the incest. Many women still think, however, that they "asked for it," a message fortified by a society that has, until recently, thought that rape victims were also "asking for it." As an adult, she may still believe the message, "You must have asked for it."

She grows up feeling responsible for the incest and guilty for not having seized the power to stop it. It is no surprise, therefore, that power and control become major issues for her. If as a child you were powerless, but were told you were powerful, as an adult you will surely be confused. If as a child you were told that your feelings were wrong or did not matter, you will grow up without healthy or legitimate ways to express your feelings, or even be uncertain of their nature. If as a child you were encouraged to take responsibility for something you were not responsible for, you are likely to have guilt about what you do and what you choose not to do. And finally, if when you are an adult those childhood messages are confirmed by others, you may become defensive, angry, repressed, edgy, manipulative, depressed.

Marie is a woman in her thirties, attractive and capable, but there is something in her manner that turns people off. She walks, talks, and acts like someone who has a big chip on her shoulder. When asked about the fact that she has even lost jobs because of her personality, she retorts defiantly, "No one is going to tell me what to do with my life."

Marie's history explains her swagger. When she was six or eight years old, her older brother, then sixteen, told her that he wanted to perform a "science experiment." He gained her sexual compliance for years with that line, and finally her other brother, also older, joined in. By the time she figured out that this was no science experiment but, in fact, sexual abuse, Marie was humiliated at what she thought was her stupidity. She also felt guilty because it looked as though she had condoned the activity and was thus partly responsible for it. She thought she could never tell; her lips were sealed — conveniently enough for her brothers.

She grew up keeping the secret. Her acute sense of powerlessness as a child led her to become a defiant and defensive adult. Marie often found herself in situations in which she felt victimized again, she became angry at herself for letting it happen, and she responded with more defiance: "As I look at life, I see that it is filled with people who betray, frighten, and abandon me. They often trap me in a maze and force me to do things I don't want to do."

She is not permitted the most rudimentary boundaries over her body, the power to say "no" to unwelcome advances or even to things that hurt her physically. Her mind is being controlled as well, because if she does object, she will let "the secret" out, and she has been brainwashed to think that if she tells, someone else will suffer or she will be hurt or killed.

It is little wonder that adult survivors of incest often show confusion over the issue of power and control. Many manifest the problem by needing to take strict control over every aspect of their lives, making themselves into superwomen who still end up feeling cheated. Others have difficulty figuring out how to gain any sense of influence over what happens in the adult world; they remain passive and paralyzed when it is action and decision that may be required.

It is significant that so many of the women we interviewed were "caretakers": social workers, nurses, teachers, doctors. Some survivors entered the helping professions trying to change the world, to have some control over eliminating pain and suffering. The cause is noble, but frustrating as well, since pain and suffering are not readily amenable to being removed or relieved.

Not every woman tries to control her own life by taking care of others, of course. Each woman responds to the history of her own sexual assaults in a creative way, a way often directly related to what happened to her in childhood. Once again we witness adult survivors of incest struggling, often courageously against terrific odds, to get their lives in order and under some control. Before we move to case studies, we need to examine some of the ways women can respond to childhood powerlessness.

Control Through Perfectionism

Many survivors of incest become perfectionists as adults. They feel a need to control events and environments so that they are "just so," a state of mind that can create real problems for the people around them. They need to control what other people think of them, possibly in order to convince themselves that they deserve love or esteem. They may set impossibly high demands for themselves as a way of proving that they are valuable.

It is perhaps unfortunate for the incest survivors of the last two decades that they have had to coexist with the era of the Modern Superwoman. When the new feminism swept America in the 1960s, closely following in its wake was a "you-can-have-it-all" philosophy that has been especially hard on achieving women. Its symbol might be one of those Indian goddesses with arms coming out in all directions. A superwoman is like a goddess with eight arms, all busy at once: one carries the briefcase, one vacuums the carpet, one holds the baby, one holds a book, while yet others stir the *cordon bleu* sauce, mulch the roses, stroke the husband or lover to orgasm.

A woman who also happens to be an adult survivor of incest fits well into this crazy picture. She may welcome every possible way she can affirm that she is worth something. And she also needs to repeat and affirm endlessly that she is *powerful enough* to do so much so well. She needs to succeed again and again in every sphere, so that she is thereby proven to be good.

The perfectionist mode is an especially exhausting route to self-annihilation, however, since all the success in the world will never convince this woman that she is good and valuable unless she believes it herself. In fact, that solid wall of accomplishment may eventually shut out the light. As she does more and more and does it successfully, she may come to sense that people do not love and esteem her for her real self. That real self, frustrated in childhood because she had so little defense, may be a fragile and tentative person indeed. All the accomplishments may feel like a high wall, and the higher it gets, the more frightened she is to pull it down, for she feels so small and fragile inside. The more facade she creates, the more facade she has to keep in place.

Inside she may quiver; outside she may appear competent, even aggressive, and she becomes more isolated from her real feelings. A clear sign of the sense of powerlessness is her inability to express those feelings. As a child the incest victim became a fortified castle, and she defended herself most frequently by shutting off her real feelings. If a feeling threatened, never mind. She simply threw together another battlement, another line of defense, in order to keep from being hurt.

In her adulthood, these defenses against emotion keep her busy, particularly if they are carried on in conjunction with the super-woman activities. Not only is she to do everything well; if she fails, she must not show any emotion about it — no anger that she is having to do all this, no resentment about thinking these crazy expectations are normal, no exhaustion at having to carry it off well. And finally, she cannot even feel much pride or self-satisfaction at having done it all so well, because there is always the lingering, haunting sense that it could be done better, along with the exhausting knowledge that she will have to keep doing it over and over, repeating excellence to affirm that she really exists.

These pent-up feelings frequently lead to the therapist's office, where the survivor can finally spill her feelings of agony, inadequacy, and often simple exhaustion, since it is hard work keeping all the pieces in place. We have seen that these women in fact often make excellent progress in therapy, because they know how to work hard to achieve goals. They finally can learn to nourish that small, perhaps tender and vulnerable true self that has lain inside the seemingly competent exterior.

Eating Disorders

This strong urge to control or manipulate one's environment, which comes out of childhood powerlessness, also shows up in eating and other disorders that have their origin in childhood but persist into adulthood. Anorexia is controlling what, if any, food goes into the body as a way of seizing control of that larger environment. Bulimia (regular forced vomiting ordinarily preceded by binge-eating) is a way of controlling what goes in and out of the body, as is the excessive use of laxatives. Body image obsessiveness reveals itself in compulsive exercise and dieting as well. All these disorders occur with some frequency in adult survivors of incest.

Fitness seems to be the reigning fashion among Americans at the moment, so it is a bit difficult to explain how exercise regimens can be construed as "sick" behavior in an adult survivor of incest. Certainly no one would judge it wrong to get enough physical activity to stay healthy and fit. And watching one's diet is the better part of mental as well as physical health.

But jogging can be an obsession, and dieting can be destructive. Lauren, an attractive, outdoorsy woman of twenty-eight, made her fitness regimen into a full-time job. Daily she did Jane Fonda's videotaped workout, then jogged several miles after taking enough laxatives to rid her body of the skimpy amount of food she had ingested the previous day. After an hour of racquetball, she rode her bicycle for five miles. Lauren was at the same time bulimic, so she was vomiting ten, fifteen, and sometimes twenty times a day.

Just as many superwomen come to realize that their accomplishments, while valuable, may be a sign of maladjustment, so do many survivors of incest come to realize that obsessively trying to make their bodies perfect is itself a problem. A fundamental feeling underlies their unceasing attempts to improve: they think their bodies are dirty and ugly, just as they had thought in childhood, and they must work all the time to control their appearance lest they show the *real self,* which they take to be unattractive or unacceptable.

Many of the women who feel that they cannot reveal their "real" physical selves at any cost are, in fact, attractive women to an outside observer. Some of the compulsion to control their body configurations comes from the childhood experience of having been told, sometimes by words as well as by actions, that they were not pretty or good or valuable. It also comes from the inner belief that the forced sexual activities in childhood left their bodies dirty, shameful, unattractive, and loathsome. Their beliefs about their bodies frequently range from disgust to feelings of being rotten to the core and damaged forever. And the most beautifully shaped body in the world is worth nothing to its possessor unless she herself is convinced of its beauty.

Alcohol and Drug Dependency

Alcohol and drug abuse are commonplace among survivors of incest, and occur at a frequency higher than is experienced in the general population. Let us first look at the way Marilyn describes her use of alcohol and drugs to "control" the way she felt:

> I first began using [drugs and alcohol] to adjust my moods. I was in high school. I had no recollection of the incest at that time, but all I knew was that I felt different, lonely, and generally pretty shitty. I discovered that a few drinks would loosen me up, ease me into social situations, and generally help me to forget about what a travesty my life had become.
>
> But these things changed. Rather than [my] using drugs to control my moods, the drugs themselves *took* control of my life, and *I* no longer had control over them.

Finally, when she was twenty-six, life became unmanageable. It was in her sixth week at an inpatient alcohol treatment center that Marilyn began recalling the incest. At first she thought the flashbacks she was experiencing were somehow related to her newly found sobriety. But when she discussed them with her alcoholism counselor, she was quickly referred to a therapist specializing in the treatment of adult survivors of incest. There, she allowed herself to look at the flashbacks and to learn how her incestuous past was interfering with her functioning. Slowly, she learned to express her feelings clearly, rather than anesthetize them with drugs. Ironically, by *surrendering* she was able to regain the control of her moods and behavior she had previously lost to alcohol and drugs.

She still attends three Alcoholics Anonymous meetings each week, and is enjoying her seventh year of sobriety. She has re-entered therapy to try to gain a better understanding of her childhood abuse and its effect on her life today.

Marilyn feels that the abuse is a part of her that will always influence her way of looking at the world and of reacting to what she sees. She says, "The abuse comes up each time I make a major change in my life, but now I don't let the memories control me. I allow them to surface, I explore them, I experience them, then I let them go."

Marilyn no longer struggles against the fact that the incest gravely affected her and that her family was not what every child deserves. She accepts these facts, and is beginning to enjoy a life where "control" no longer dominates every move she makes.

Illness as Power

The other side of the coin from an obsessive and perfectionist striving to make the body beautiful is the use of illness and lack of physical well-being to control events. In childhood a rather common practice is to use illness to control the offender. Marianna had kidney infections frequently as a result of her abuse, but she also invented illnesses to garner attention and protection. Carol had long and painful menstrual periods, and she made them even longer than nature intended because her father would not touch her when she was menstruating, and her mother did not force her to do housework when she was having cramps. Sick headaches are common; hospitalizations come up frequently in the memories of survivors. And some survivors report that they "acted crazy" to get admitted to mental institutions, a safer haven for them than home.

When the ruses did not work it was because the offender was not a sensitive and nurturant person who could so easily be appealed to; most are not deterred by the temporary indisposition of their victims. Nonetheless many women tried to plead illness or physical incapacity to control the offender, often with some degree of success, especially if the illness took them to the hospital.

And if it worked in childhood, the adult at first feels comfortable with the same method of operating as an adult. A survivor finds herself pleading a sick headache to avoid sex. Or perhaps it is a chronic back ailment which incapacitates her. She finds that she cannot go out and look for a job or plan a career — an event that would add to her self-esteem and would nourish the fragile true self inside her.

Gerri is an example here. She has suffered chronic back pain for nearly all her married years, and even after therapy insists that she is too physically incapacitated to pursue her career. Back pain is real, and psychosomatic pain is real as well. And Gerri continues to suffer, from both the real physical pain and the situation she has created for herself, because she does not think she can ever escape. She is a doormat in her marriage and takes physical abuse from her husband, because she is convinced that her ill health would prevent her from ever holding a job and becoming self-sufficient. She must keep her marriage at all costs — even the cost of physical brutality. Gerri's way of controlling events as an adult is to make herself physically unable to handle that which she is mentally unprepared to face. What if in fact Gerri found out that supporting herself is beyond her capabilities? Then her worst fears would be confirmed — that she is a worthless, incompetent person.

Such psychosomatic illnesses are a form of emotional manipulation, attempting to "fix" people and events in a way that will prove satisfying to the survivor. These "control issues" are an extremely common form of neurotic behavior, so common in fact that it is difficult to discuss them only with reference to the survivor of incest. Anyone who has been a victim of a manipulative person — whether a mother-in-law, a job supervisor, or a spoiled two-year-old — knows how difficult it is to get out of the clutches of that control. Nothing, absolutely nothing will do but that one do things exactly as the manipulator wants.

Many adult survivors of incest we talked to were master manipulators until they began to recognize it in themselves. When they could focus on that behavior, they began to achieve legitimate power and control over themselves instead of manipulating others. This is often a difficult and lengthy process.

Manipulation Through Sex

Manipulation runs the gamut of human experience; it takes place almost anywhere. Take the case of Pat. She is a young, single, very attractive secretary, now training to be an interior designer. She experienced sexual abuse from her father nightly for nearly a year between the ages of twelve and thirteen. Her father is now dead; she has confronted her mother about it, and together they have worked with a therapist.

Pat is in pretty good shape. But the problem that has been hardest for her to eradicate is her resort to manipulation. The "incest message" Pat received was particularly pernicious because it seemed so "loving" and was cloaked in such subtle terms. Pat's father was gentle and persuasive when he told her that what he was doing was okay and normal and that he was showing her all that she needed to know about men. "He said to me, 'This is what you have to do to make a man happy, and if you do this well, he will love you,'" she recalls. "This message became a habit for me."

Passively accepting her father's embraces and message in childhood, she used sex as an adult to manipulate others. She spent her college years sleepwalking through her classes, steering one man after another into her bed. She never thought of affection or trust as reciprocal for long-term love. She manipulated men, and herself, into a sexual situation so that she could get back the assurance that she would be loved.

It took Pat a long time to confront her behavior and realize that she was neither feeling loved nor making herself happy. She had battened down her emotions as the inhabitants of a submarine batten down the hatches to survive under water. Her sexual control of men had been leaving her cold, mechanical, and very, very lonely.

Sexual manipulation is only one of many varieties of control that the adult survivor can use, but it is an especially damaging one because it carries so many feelings with it. Several of the women we interviewed had been prostitutes. They described their pleasure in "mastering past events." They were finally in a position to grant permission for sex, to exercise power over exactly what would be done to them, and to exact money for the privilege.

When Nicole was eleven years old, her mother's boyfriend came to molest her when her mother was not around and she was "sleeping." While she pretended to sleep, he began by fondling her breasts; then, in order to keep him from touching her breasts, she began to pull up into the fetal position, pretending all the while to be asleep. He then forced anal sex, making all of Nicole's attempts at control and self-protection futile.

As an adult Nicole engaged in prostitution for a few years, and she commanded large sums of money by performing anal sex acts. She could choose her partner, her own time schedule, and her price. And performing anal sex as an adult for money restored for a time the sense of control she had missed in her childhood. Nicole learned finally in therapy to face the reality that prostitution was, for her, revictimization, not power.

Joan was a high-priced call girl in California for a time. She was very clear about what she was doing: "Every time I screwed one of these guys, I thought of screwing my father but this time on *my* terms." She claims to have enjoyed her "jobs." When she came back to her apartment afterwards, she and her roommate (who shared the same profession and was also a survivor of childhood sexual abuse) howled in laughter over how they had taken advantage of their clients, all for a substantial financial reward. The idea was to turn the tables, to regain the control lost in childhood.

Joan also learned that her profession was not a healthy way to power. She married, had a child, divorced, and then sought a career. She now has a degree in hotel management and sees her career as a legitimate way to power. She is devoted to her small son, so devoted that she did not stay in her marriage to a physically and emotionally abusive spouse once she realized how damaging the situation had become for her boy.

As the cases of Nicole and Joan show, achieving legitimate power is a complicated issue for the adult survivor. When as a child she sees that there are no boundaries, that it makes no difference whether she says "no," and that she will be punished if she tries to resist, she learns powerlessness. As an adult she is apt to attempt to seize the reins, to her own detriment and that of others. She must learn that there are spheres of quite legitimate responsibility and control, but that there is also much that is beyond her power. She needs to learn the difference.

Early in their recovery, most survivors learn to grapple with "black and white" thinking, the dichotomy they learned in childhood. Either they were bad or good, responsible or not, beautiful or ugly. The world is far more complex than that, of course, and survivors need to learn the intermediate shades of gray.

And so there are some things they can control — a very short list and based on their own behavior — and much larger regions they cannot control and must learn to accept. They achieve the wisdom and discernment to tell the difference between real and false notions of power and control.

Three case studies offer more detail on the relationship of power and control in individual lives.

The Case of Linda

Linda is a thirty-year-old married woman with no children. She comes from a family of two older sisters and two younger. It is a hard-working upper-middle-class family. After a highly successful college career and several years of work, which were not so successful, she returned to school for a graduate degree; it was there that she met her husband. She works as an account executive for a large corporation, has risen rapidly in management, and commands a substantial salary.

Linda is articulate, attractive, and aloof in the way that a highly competitive, achieving young professional can often be. But her story is a complex one, and even as she tells it, she sees what she wants to change and the wholeness of feeling and legitimate self-control that she hopes will be hers.

Her father began to molest her somewhere between the ages of four and six. The abuse continued until after her first menstrual period, at age thirteen or fourteen.

> The first time was midday on a weekend, and my mother was home. He told me to get into the house and get undressed and into his bed. We had sex, and I was not to tell anyone and not to do it with any other men. I could only think of one other man in my life, my grand-father, so I said, "Not even Papa?" and he said, "No." I did not know what was going on.

Like most child victims, Linda did not have the right to question what was happening. "I grew up thinking he was Stalin," she says. It was a household where the children did as they were told or were punished severely. So she obeyed when she was summoned to perform.

Even though she had sisters, Linda remained convinced that only she suffered the sexual abuse. She did witness the intense emotional abuse that her siblings experienced from a severely authoritarian father. "Still, I did not believe they were sexually abused," she says, "because when I was with my father, no one else was, and when I was not with him, I was with my sisters." Linda felt secure, therefore, in her belief that she had all the exits covered.

It is no surprise that with such a stern father Linda was well behaved as a child, seldom drawing attention to herself at home or at school. As a teenager she led a routine and work-filled life. She did not date in high school and preferred to stay home and do her homework.

She continued to avoid socializing in college. "I was friendly with the guys on the floor in the dorm," she says, "but I really didn't date. On Friday nights I studied or went to movies or concerts by myself."

By her sophomore year Linda was experiencing painful cramps that left her feeling debilitated and ill. The campus medical center prescribed birth control pills which, of course, gave her the chance to become sexually active, although it had never been an issue before. Now she wonders whether she invented the ailment in order to get the prescription.

So she became sexually, though not romantically, involved with a number of men. None of the relationships "crossed the line into being romantic or intimate," she says.

She had "run away eight hundred miles to college," she says, and she moved quickly to establish financial independence. She abhorred the idea of not being in control of her own destiny:

> When I was in college I had no money. I took heavy loads so I could graduate and get a job sooner. I worked at summer jobs. I would sell my books from last term rather than ask for money from my family. And I was a hoarder. I would get checks for gifts and save them for necessities. I worked at a bank during the day and as a waitress at night during the summers so that I would have enough for the school year.

All of this to hurry through and become financially independent.

During her college and early work years, Linda made no close friends, so intent was she on establishing her financial and professional security.

> I have very few close female friends and they are not nearby now. I keep up with letters. They are the closest friends I have, but they are really not close. I was often lonely and depressed, but I never said so to my friends. Some of them never realized I was depressed or unhappy. They confided in me, however. I tended to be quiet and a good listener.

Linda continues, somewhat defensively, "Besides, what help could *someone else* be? If I lost my job, I could always be a waitress." Her comment indicates her biggest fear: that of being disabled or unable to work. She had not consciously missed close friendships or family. Even as an adult beginning therapy she felt good about her ability not to need others, never understanding what the lack of intimate connections spelled for her as a person.

And such distancing finally proved to be a professional infirmity as well. In her first job as an assistant bank manager, she began to thrive. Soon she found herself in a position few women had occupied, a job that involved fiscal analysis and no "people skills." Linda was on top of the world.

Her boss thought she was terrific, and she was then promoted to branch manager, a tremendous professional leap for a woman. Not more than six months into the job she started slipping, however. "I began to lose control and feel panicky. I kept coming to work late, and I took long lunches. At home I began to drink at night, and I slept a lot." What had happened? "I was fine in my office using my analytical skills," she admits, "but I had a hard time with social skills, saying, 'Hi, how are ya?' at business meetings and conferences." The more she failed, the less she tried, and the more remote she became. She could never admit to her boss what the trouble was: she could not relate to people.

Finally she was fired. Linda's eyes fill with tears as she talks about the humiliation of losing her job. She only told two people that she had been fired, never admitted it to her family, and only confessed the fact to her fiance after months of being engaged.

She took the opportunity to advance her education by getting a graduate degree in a field where few women excel. It is also a field in which she can in the future be self-employed. "I am comfortable now working because I know I can quit any time and get another job. I can even work at home if I need to. I know I don't have to tolerate environments full of nonsense. I have put up with enough of that." She has never seen herself as a victim, save of "circumstance." When we first talked to Linda, she was getting ready, after several months of therapy, to tell her mother and older sister about the incest. "It might be the impetus my mother needs to clear the slate," she said, anxious for her mother to leave a now faltering marriage.

Since that time, she has started to face the control issues in her life. She gave up the idea of needing to control her mother's behavior when her mother heard about the incest. She decided to "tell it like it was," without the secret agenda of urging her mother into a divorce. At the confrontation her mother, while shocked at the news, proved loving, supportive, and angry at the father. Her response was a great support to Linda, who has gained at least one parent's love and understanding.

When she told the secret to her siblings she found that two of her sisters had also been abused. Linda's confidence that she had been the only one to suffer had to be cast away. She discovered she never really had any control over her father's activities with the other girls. She also began to realize that she was farther along the road of self-discovery than her sisters, both of whom are still denying their pain. Her sisters have their own timetable; Linda cannot control what they will do.

She told the secret to some friends and found out in the process that for years they had been uncomfortable that Linda never talked about herself. While she had considered herself "a good listener," her friends wanted reciprocity and sharing, not one-sided listening. She decided to renew an acquaintance with a college roommate. Before long she found herself confiding the story of the incest, and to her relief her old friend was warm and supportive. Linda felt that she had become human. She saw that her need to be in control had led to loneliness and isolation. As Linda continues to address the power issue, her marriage is improving because now she communicates her feelings more openly.

Few are the areas of life where control will not be an issue. In a job environment, those who need to take control may chafe at the authority of superiors. Those who fear taking control may become doormats in the workplace. In the family, a controlling woman may manipulate everyone to get her needs met, even to the point of coercing her children to grow up to fulfill her dreams. The woman who has abdicated control over her life, on the other hand, may become chief servant to everyone in her family. And of course, power is a major issue in developing a healthy sex life.

Linda's self-examination and efforts to change have been fairly complete. She is a reformed "superwoman" who approached therapy and life determined to wrest livable solutions from confusion and unhappiness.

Control issues can also elude solution. They can be so subtly interwoven in a woman's life that she cannot catch hold of them. Our next two case studies show women who are having a harder time than Linda identifying what is wrong and doing something about it.

The Case of Dora

Dora is in her late twenties, an attractively tall and slender blonde with green eyes. When she called for the initial interview to begin therapy, she reported that she would not be able to come to the office by herself, since she did not drive and was too frightened to come alone.

Dora arrived accompanied by a cousin. While physically attractive, Dora soon proved herself an insecure and unhappy individual. She stuttered when she talked; most often she tried not to talk. She would not make eye contact. Her gaze focused on the floor as she was being addressed, and when she had to reply, her eyes wandered to the corner of the ceiling or the plant on the coffee table rather than to her listener.

Dora's family consists of an older brother, a younger sister, and her mother; her father died when Dora was five. Both girls in the family had been abused by the older brother. When Dora found him abusing her younger sister Pamela, she felt a surge of protectiveness toward her sister. She talked to Pamela privately, and together they confronted her mother. The brother subsequently was arrested, charged, and found guilty. He was ordered to move out of the house after serving a jail term.

Her mother still holds Dora responsible. "You sent him to jail," she says. This is a familiar pattern to Dora. As a child she had always been the family scapegoat. Although she was passive and obedient, her mother found every occasion possible to blame Dora for anything that went wrong. If the housework was not done and the meal cooked when the mother came home from work, for example, it ended up being Dora's fault.

There was a subtle belief in Dora's family that the male members were more important; therefore, they were not required to do anything around the house. After her father's death, Dora's older brother became a little dictator. And when he came often to Dora's bed and held his hand over her mouth and raped her, she accepted his behavior because she felt powerless and deserving of nothing better.

Problems came up in many areas of her life. In high school she began using drugs and alcohol. She attempted suicide when she was sixteen, and it was at that point that her mother sought out a small private school for her. This decision may have saved Dora's life, for at the school she met warm and accepting people. One male counselor especially listened to her, encouraged her, and developed a protective, nonabusive bond with her.

Once graduated and in the working world, Dora found new problems cropping up. She had a range of stress-related illnesses: stomach pains that indicated a pre-ulcerous condition, headaches, backaches, exhaustion to the point of lethargy.

Her social life held the worst problems for her. Because she was so attractive, she had no trouble getting dates, but she chose a sexual liaison with an abusive young man. It soon became customary for him to call her from a local bar where he was having drinks with the boys and say, "I'm coming over; you'd better be ready." And Dora would meekly take a bath and dress herself beautifully to be ready for his sexual advances. On one occasion she was at the bar with him. He wanted to spend time with his buddies, so he gave her a twenty-dollar bill, sent her home in a cab, and told her to be ready for him when he got there. She did as he commanded because, again, she felt powerless and without options.

When her boyfriend went away to college, he never wrote to Dora, nor did he send birthday and holiday gifts. Before he was due home for vacation, Dora would receive a postcard which said, "I'm coming home for break. Be ready for me."

During an argument that ensued after this kind of treatment, the young man hit Dora. *She* apologized to *him*. It never occurred to her to call the police. She thought she must have done something to incur his anger.

After two years of this kind of dating, Dora met another young man who said to her, when she explained about her boyfriend, "Why did you let him treat you that way?"

Dora replied, *"What* way?"

She began dating her new friend Dan because he seemed so kind, the first man she had found who cared about what *she* wanted. She waited for him to abuse her, but he has not done so. And now it is beginning to occur to her that not all relationships have to be hurtful and that perhaps she can be loved for the person she is. Dan drives her to therapy when she feels she is not strong enough to find her own way now, and he sometimes waits for her outside with a red rose, a gift to tell her how strong he thinks she is becoming as she confronts herself.

Other people are not as supportive as Dan. Her mother found out that Dora had entered therapy, and commented, "Well, what's wrong with that therapist? You still stutter, so she must not be helping you. You're wasting your money and time."

Dora is nonetheless still trying to win her mother's approval. She takes her to expensive restaurants for her birthday, restaurants that Dora cannot afford on her salary. Her mother remarks on the poor service or the lousy food, and comments later to the brother (who is now free after serving his term) that Dora had tried to entertain her, but that the restaurant was "really tacky."

Bosses ask Dora to work overtime without pay, and she complies. She still does not see her mother and brother for the people they are. She tries hard to make her family fit into a pattern of regularity and normalcy. And in order to make *them* perfect, she must make *herself* bad; it was her badness, for example, that made her brother "go astray," she says. She thinks it is perhaps her physical appearance that causes men to want to take advantage of her.

Dora is working hard in therapy and has made a lot of changes. There are times when she is assertive enough at work to stand up for herself. She has accepted the fact that her mother may never be supportive and may not be capable of being so. And she is now able to develop relationships with people who will not be abusive to her.

The Case of Jane

Jane is a study in control. At forty-six, she gives off an air of sturdy efficiency and a no-nonsense, businesslike approach to the world. Her hair is graying; she says it suits her perfectly because she wants to look her age. Her stride is athletic and vigorous, her blue eyes engaging and direct. Even upon first meeting, an observer would be likely to pick Jane as a dependable woman to carry out a task — whether it be organizing a church supper or a professional conference.

Shortly into an interview it becomes clear that Jane's calm and efficient appearance covers an uncomfortable truth: she has never been able to keep a job for very long. Despite all her intelligence, efficiency, and level-headed capability, she has bounced from career to career, job to job, role to role, stopping long enough in each area to organize a few things cleanly and clearly, then to move on.

She has never had therapy for her incest-related problems. She consulted a professional therapist once because she had been fired from her job. The therapy lasted for a year, and incest never came up.

In fact, she speaks as if her childhood sexual relationship with her father is of no present consequence to her. "He's dead now, of course," she says, "but I think of him as an unhappy, sad man. I feel sorry for him. It wasn't really his fault, and I just don't waste time blaming him."

What exactly happened to her as a child?

I don't really know when it began; I was probably very small, from whenever you can begin to remember things. And it lasted probably until pre-adolescence, ten-ish. It was basically my father touching my genitals. My father worked the night shift, and he was not around a lot. So it wasn't always daily by any means; it was once a week or so, and always when my mother was out of the house. I'm sure that it probably felt good, since I'm a normal human being. I know that it was not uncomfortable; it didn't hurt or anything like that. My father was not sadistic in any way.

He also fondled the foster girl who lived with us; the two of us shared a bedroom. And my father would come in at night to bid us good night when my mother was at a meeting or whatever, since she was fairly active in the community.

She was out one night (when I was about five), and when she returned, or possibly the next day, we talked about the fact that our father had slept with us. He hadn't slept with us — just gotten into bed with us. And she had a fit about it. I don't know whether that had anything to do with previous experience or whether she was aware of what was going on or whether she gave my father just a general "you shouldn't do that" or what. But that was one of the early experiences, and from then on, I didn't talk to my mother about it at all, because it was obviously very upsetting to her, and I was stuck in the middle of this thing.

Jane describes herself as an enthusiastic, saucy, cute child who shone in school. When she reached high school, she continued to excel in academic subjects and athletics. But she was never "date material" and was completely left out of the social scene. "I'm still not someone people have on their list to invite to dinner," she says. She thinks she was simply not good at the coquetry required to be a popular girl: "Well, that was just me and my fate. . . . I was regarded as a real good egg. I didn't care in the least about coquetry and I still don't, which, I think, infuriates my husband. He's often said to me, 'You're a great person, but you're not like a wife.' I don't make much effort to do that stuff."

Jane delayed marriage until she was thirty, although she says, "I was always strongly inclined to be married." She thinks she picked a husband like her father, a passive man whom she is not sure she respects. She delayed having children because she felt she was immature and would not be a good mother. She now has one child, a son aged four, and she does not plan more children.

Meanwhile, she has pursued her careers. Her interests had been in physical education and music, but her mother tried to push her into a career in nursing: "She thought there would be a job for me. She was very ambitious for me."

In her first job Jane failed to get tenure as an assistant professor in the small college where she had been teaching. Rather than continue her teaching career and try at another school, Jane decided to go into the business writing world. She landed a job as an assistant editor and was responsible for generating ideas and for a range of editing and proofreading tasks.

She liked her job but soon found her boss to be "a young twerp who knew nothing about the field," and she quit in disgust after eighteen months. She had developed ties to the company, however, and when she went to the president to announce her resignation, he asked whether she would be willing to move to another division, even though there were no titles scheduled for publication requiring her expertise.

Jane busily set about learning her new job, and she thinks she was reasonably happy for a year, when a company shakeup necessitated the trimming of her division. Jane was horrified to learn that her editor was letting her go. When she went to demand the reason, the editor made it clear that she had to trim staff and was keeping only two of the most congenial on board; Jane, she said, had too many ideas of her own and was hard to work with.

Since then Jane has done freelance editorial work at home,

where she has no real boss. A year ago she hired on as a consultant for a local supermarket chain to help the company put together its in-house hardware and housewares line. In six months she was fired because, she relates, her boss was too strong a personality and they did not hit it off.

As she talks, Jane begins to reveal that she feels defensive most of the time and has no close relationships at all. "I'm just incompetent in personal relationships. I'm great on the phone, but not face to face. I'm afraid I will face problems with my son, and that worries me a lot."

When asked about the surprising number of jobs she has held, Jane gives a thoughtful reply: "My thing is control. Absolute control of myself at all times, and I want to control others. I control my husband, there is no doubt in my mind about that, and probably my son. . . . I cannot share responsibility. When I'm not in control and subject to someone else's control, I'm unhappy. I am immobilized by authority."

She concludes the interview thoughtfully, quietly, wondering if she is ruining everything for herself, her husband, and son. She is not sure of the reason, only the effects. "I thought the incest and my background were a forgotten thing. . . . There is a penchant I have for intellectualizing and verbalizing everything away. I never got to feelings. Now that I think back to my relationship with my husband, I drown him with words."

She stops and sits in silence.

· ✳ · ✳ ·

SINCE that interview, Jane has moved a long way toward understanding how she has been dealing with her world. For years she denied that the incest had ever had any effect on her, insisted that it was not serious, and refused to see any link between her childhood problems and her adult failures. Jane has not chosen either to undertake therapy or to join an incest survivors' group, but she has begun to work by herself to remember, to confront her feelings, and to put together the links between the child and adult in her own history.

The issue of control is initially difficult for the survivor because it is so pervasive. She may be grasping at all kinds of things, as Jane did, to make her life appear to be under control, while in fact it is careening toward disaster.

But somewhere along the line Jane saw — and other survivors see — that the kind of control that manipulates others and forces love from them, and that takes so much energy and yields so little happiness, is no good. When she surrenders that idea of control, paradoxically the survivor is able to *take* control of the things over which she does have some influence. And she learns that it is vain to try to control the other things in her life.

This familiar prayer has become a favorite of Jane's and is a useful one for survivors to remember: "God, grant me the serenity to accept things I cannot change, the courage to change things I can, and the wisdom to know the difference."

Sexuality and Intimacy

SCRABBLE *was one of the games I loved when I was growing up, and we played a lot of it in our family. But even my favorite game got infected with the toxin of incest.*

One wintry Sunday afternoon, my father, my mother, and I had been playing Scrabble as a threesome; in the middle of the game my mother had to go on an errand. She gave up her place and put her letters back into the alphabet pool, upside down, as the regulations required. She put on her coat and hat and went outside and got into the car to drive away.

I began to panic as I always did when she left the house. Even while the car was warming up in the driveway, I looked across the card table and saw "the look" on my father's face. It was the sappy, soft look of sexual desire.

Before the car was out of the driveway, he had taken his turn at the Scrabble board and spelled a lewd term for a portion of the female anatomy. Horrified, I looked across the table and saw his immense sexual pleasure in the act. Then he reached over and pinched me.

Nothing more happened on that particular afternoon. But how can I describe the horror of it? He was, first of all, spoiling words. I love words, and there are so many of them in the English lan-

guage that it shows a real poverty of mind to choose a crude word instead of a colorful or exact or amusing one. He also was spoiling play. He ruined a perfectly good game and made it into perverted sex. He had been doing that for as long as I could remember.

The worst horror was the subtlest: the look of sexual desire on his face that preceded the act of spelling the words on the board. Anything could be poisoned by that look, even my favorite game.

It is hard to describe exactly what this "look" is, but I have experienced it since that Scrabble game in my childhood many times, including numerous occasions in my adult life. One afternoon about a year ago as I was standing across from my husband at the kitchen counter and he was looking at me with great devotion and desire, I caught the connection between his look and my father's. I understood finally the hollowness in the pit of my stomach. I was able to tell him about my feeling and he understood. I cannot say that "the look" no longer occurs between us, but I can say that whenever I am uncomfortable as a result of it, I tell him.

All this is a small indication of the problem that sexuality has been for me as an adult. In the past, being an incest survivor has meant feeling odd or different. But after time, work, love, and courage, I now feel and think of myself as a "normal" person.

Except in the area of sexuality. As a sexual being I feel — and wonder if I will always feel — out of step, just not quite normal. Just not like other people. Can anyone but an incest survivor understand how threatening "the look" can be, for example?

I do not know whether my experience duplicates that of other incest survivors, but I think that even if I emerge as a healthy sexual creature, capable of love and intimacy, my road there has veered miles away from that of the person who has not experienced incest. I got there by a different route entirely. None of it came "naturally." And while I may be wrong about this notion, I think that most people who did not experience incest had a pretty fair shake at discovering sex "naturally."

So what has it been like to be "unnatural" or even "abnormal"?

Most of my adult life as a sexual being I have felt like a skier buried under an avalanche. I huddle under the massive block of cold snow, cut off from expressing — or even knowing — my feelings, unable to move even my frostbitten fingers. But at the same time I am the rescuer, standing on the outside, shoveling off the snow to get over to the small, curled-up victim inside the cold, arctic bank. I am both rescued and rescuer. No one else can do for me the main task of rescuing. That is important.

Although the shoveling has been my job, I have been blessed with a partner to help me. Sometimes my partner and I have decided to avoid problems for the moment. Sometimes the pain and the effort are simply too much, and it doesn't seem worth it to climb the mountain. Better to take the pragmatic path around the crest and forget the noble challenge of climbing it.

And yet I am a sexual being, and sex is subtly interwoven into the fabric of my daily life. It still does not seem "natural" to me. There is a song from Irving Berlin's Annie Get Your Gun *called "Doin' What Comes Natur'lly." I hated that song as a child and I hate it now. I thought then that "doin' what comes natur'lly" was what was happening to me. As an adult I sometimes wonder whether acting on "natural" sex impulses might mean fondling and raping children. If "natural" means succumbing to unrestrained, unthinking reactions to sexual stimuli, give me nothing of "natural" sex.*

That response is not the only one that makes me feel moralistic, cranky, and slightly out of step with the rest of the world. I have described the fleeting glance, the look of sexual desire that most people in our culture think is an erotic moment profound enough to write a poem or song about. For my part, "the look" directed at me makes me sick at my stomach. It's a look I saw a million times, and it always meant rape. I cannot connect it with something desirable.

Do I then just turn out the lights so that I won't see something that disturbs me? No, because that bothers me too. A lot of molestation happened in the dark. And with the lights out, I am far more likely to provide a face and form of a victimizer than the familiar and loving features of the man I care for.

Because sex is undeniably part of me, I have had to redefine it to suit me. I have had to reinvent a part of myself that other more fortunate people never even have to think about.

And I try as hard as I can not to think about what those other people know or feel, because their experiences are not like mine. I don't have to take their word for it if they say something is "fun" or "sexy." Maybe it's not to me. Sex, after all, was used to hurt me, to give me physical pain and a wretched idea of my own worth. If I am to reclaim that physical and emotional territory for fun and sex, I have to be sure that there is no pain connected.

I do it each day in little ways. If a smile or touch feels good, I let myself feel warmth. If an intimate, warm exchange occurs with someone I have learned to trust, I call it sensual. If my lover and I discover a route to pleasure that suits us, that's good sex and intimacy.

I am having to walk my own way here. Yes, it's sometimes lonely, but it's the only path before me.

• ✳ • ✳ •

TO interested observers who are not themselves survivors of incest, sexuality might seem to be the most obvious and pressing issue to be addressed in a book about adults sexually abused as children. After all, incest is a sex crime. Sexual dysfunction in adulthood would be a probable effect of such childhood abuse.

We are placing the problem nearer the middle of the book because it was necessary first to grapple with those issues of control and trust that are so much a part of sex. And we add a crucial second word to the chapter title: intimacy. There are solid reasons for both decisions.

First of all, issues of sexuality are tremendously complicated. Perhaps no subject is more examined and investigated in contemporary culture — and remains less understood after being put under the microscope. Chain bookstores would have to close *en masse* if suddenly the subject were proscribed and no one were allowed to write about it. Media psychologists would have to pare down their air time without the deluge of questions about sex. And who knows how many magazines would have to cease operating without the main fare that sustains readership?

And yet, how much do we know, even with all the media saturation? C. S. Lewis, the popular religious writer and Cambridge don, thought that openness about sex does not necessarily assure problem-free sex:

> We have been told, till one is sick of hearing it, that sexual desire is in the same state as any of our other natural desires and that if only we abandon the silly old Victorian idea of hushing it up, everything in the garden will be lovely. It is not true. . . . They tell us sex has become a mess because it was hushed up. But for the last twenty years it has not been hushed up. It has been chattered about all day long. Yet it is still in a mess. If hushing it up had been the cause of the trouble, ventilation would have set it right. But it has not.

One reason for delaying this discussion of sexuality is that answers are hard to find. Incest survivors aside, problems about what constitutes a good sexual relationship plague the ordinary mortal of either gender. We seem obsessed with finding "love" and with it sex, happily and easily, and we are told that we can achieve it. Our divorce rate in America, now approaching 50 percent of all marriages, tells us otherwise. Clearly, sex is a "mess" for a lot of people, and they are not finding ways to live healthy sex lives.

Another part of the confusion is that sex is hard to define. "Machine sex," pushing the right buttons to achieve physical gratification, is one thing. Being enveloped in a warm, trusting, sensual, physical, and perhaps even spiritual relationship with another human being is something else. Reconciling the differences between these two notions might account for all the "how-to" books that prove such a boon to publishers.

Plain push-button sex seems fairly easy; animals do it with a remarkable rate of success. So do humans, but many find that that is not quite enough. Both men and women seem to be seeking something more than a single unvarying physical act, repeated over and over for years. The divorce rate and the high level of dissatisfaction reported by American women about their sex lives suggest that there is more to sex than the sex act. Sensuality, trust, play, and reciprocity, which are so much a part of intimacy, are the aim of the person who is striving to integrate her sexuality into her whole self. Hence the second part of our chapter title.

So sex is a problem that bedevils the ordinary person. Unhealthy sexual choices are very common in our culture. Women, in particular, are continually struggling to understand how to achieve satisfaction in sexual relationships.

But, as has been the case in every area we have examined thus far, the incest survivor brings to the subject of sex a set of difficulties that makes her problem more severe. Sensible people would have to agree that damaged children from unhealthy and dysfunctional families, such as those in which incest can flourish, are not good candidates for an effortless, healthy sexual relationship. The incest survivor must confront and resolve a host of difficulties that "normal" people may not have. By no means are we saying that she cannot achieve a healthy sexuality. Survivors are doing that every day. But she must realize that sex is not an easy issue and that she will have to be patient with herself.

Another reason we have delayed the discussion of sexuality for a survivor is that it is a composite of other issues. Difficulty with sex indicates difficulty elsewhere. Because problems with sex can be severe, they are often the catalyst that sends a woman into professional help — either individual counseling or group therapy. Sexual dysfunction can be the indicator of the state of the rest of her psyche.

Only after a woman begins to resolve the spin-off issues that come from incest will her sexual relationships become more healthy. "Healthy" sex for the incest survivor means the same thing it does for everyone else: trust, openness, vulnerability, closeness, intimacy, and reciprocity. Her road to achieve those goals may be longer and more circuitous than the road of the adult woman without incest in her past.

Sexuality is like a prism for the incest survivor. A prism is a clear, angled piece of glass that breaks a ray of light into its many segments on the color spectrum. Held up to the sunshine, a clear prism will cast a rainbow upon the floor — beautiful violet, blue, green, yellow, orange, and red. Within the shape and configuration of the prism lies the potential for the pure, beautiful colors.

Sexuality can scarcely be considered without reference to all the other issues in an incest survivor's life: trusting, owning her own feelings, realizing legitimate control, recapturing childlike delight and humor, and viewing herself with respect and esteem. Sexuality contains all these subjects. As women discuss sex, control comes up again and again, as does self-respect. Sexual dissatisfaction clarifies other issues. It is for that reason that sexual adjustment is such a good test of dysfunction; it is a clue to problems in other areas of life.

It is nearly always a mistake for an incest survivor to think that if she can "fix sex," she can resolve all her problems. One incest survivor wondered if she could get over her utter terror of intercourse with a man by becoming a surrogate in a sex research clinic. As she thought about it she realized that that would be no solution at all, since it would address none of the real issues that keep her from men, such as basic trust. This terrified and uncertain woman might be devastated by such an experience and receive little more than the reassertion that she is a sex object — a kind of revictimization. And so "fixing sex" does not bring one to sexual adjustment.

The issue is a complex one and the conclusions few and hard to come by. Rather than attempting to provide solutions, we have chosen to lay out the subject in a way that will reveal its many facets. We have not tried to summarize any particular theories about the development of "normal" sexuality. They can be found in books readily available elsewhere.

The fact is that there is at present little information or hard data about the sexual functioning of the adult female survivor of incest. Our approach, therefore, has been eclectic and empirical. We are acting as reporters here. Emerging from the reportorial process are some of the techniques actual women have used to achieve what they are convinced will be a lasting and satisfying peace with sexual intimacy in their lives.

A Round-Table Discussion

One thing is clear to us as we study the sex lives of women who have experienced incest: the adult responses to it are unique to each woman, although the range of issues is, once again, common to many. Limiting ourselves to a few case studies would, we thought, restrict the wide range of responses experienced by survivors, and inevitably we would end up spending more time on childhood histories than on adult sexuality.

We decided, therefore, to interview a group of women, both to collect a sample of responses and to benefit from the women's responses to each other. This group of incest survivors had been working together for ten weeks, long enough to know and be comfortable with each other. We have edited the interview only slightly. These responses were spontaneous and unrehearsed, a fact which shows how unerringly these women went to the heart of the issues and how present and immediate those issues are to them.

QUESTION: We feel that the issues of sexuality and intimacy are important ones for most incest survivors. Karen just came back from a conference on incest that lasted three days and had all kinds of workshops and keynote speakers, excellent people. Would you like to guess how many sessions were devoted to sexuality for survivors? The answer is zero. And yet the adult survivors we talk to are very concerned about this subject. Is there anyone here who has never had an issue with sexuality or intimacy?

(Silence)

QUESTION: What are the big problems?

LIBBY: Society. I didn't date until my twenties, and the men I went out with just didn't realize what I was going through, even if they knew I was an incest victim. They didn't give me the time or attention I needed to achieve orgasm or whatever. That really didn't happen until I met my husband, who took time with me. A lot of men, I think, feel that their egos are being tested through the sex act. I mean, if you don't have an orgasm, they feel hurt, and if they have to work on it with you, they feel hurt. The fact that I was having some dysfunction was coupled with the way men are in our society, with egos easily shattered in sexual situations. Also, looking back on it, a lot of the men I was with had problems — dysfunctions of their own. Attracting men who have problems of their own is another area, definitely.

QUESTION: What kinds of problems?

LIBBY: Competitive issues. They were impotent — well, not totally — but they thought that other men were able to get it up four or five times, and they weren't, so something was wrong with them. Or they had drinking problems, or guilt from earlier life, like divorce. A lot of them were looking for a mother figure, a savior; and I would just cuddle them and tell them it would be all right.

QUESTION: So you think incest survivors attract men who have problems?

LIBBY: I don't know if we exactly send out signals, but I *know* we are more accommodating in dealing with somebody who has problems.

LAUREN: I think we have more tolerance for pain — emotional pain, physical pain. Most healthier women in a dysfunctional relationship would get out of it quick, where we are able to be in it longer.

QUESTION: And thereby continue the abuse by not protecting yourselves?

SUE: We just know how to take more abuse.

QUESTION: So the chief problem is what men bring to you?

SUE: I haven't found that to be true, as far as sexuality is concerned. The more I think about it, the more a part of me wants to deny I have any sexuality, that I am a sexual being. . . . I like to be attractive, to my husband and to other men, although I have never considered myself a flirt. But not in a situation where it could possibly lead to sex. That's where I say, "I don't want to be attractive anymore" — if someone is going to look at me as a sexual being.

LIBBY: Yes, I still get the feelings, "How dare you look at me as a sexual being? How dare you consider me *just* a sexual being?"

ALICE: How would a normal person react? I mean, because of what happened to us — I know it seems normal to want to be attractive, but when they get into our space, it's like we back away. How would a normal person react?

PEGGY: We don't know. There are none here. (Laughter)

KAREN: Well, I'm the only one here who is not an incest survivor, and perhaps I can only speak for myself, but I see one huge difference between my own sexual development and that of survivors. As much as Carol hates the song about "doin' what comes natur'lly," I see my sexual maturation in that way. I had my first boyfriend at the usual age, and we did the usual things. It seemed so easy and without lots of complications. It was like learning to walk before I ran. No one ever forced me into sexual activities, and the preliminaries to adult sexual functioning were enjoyable and positive. But for all of you, it was different. You were forced to run before you could even crawl, let alone walk. And I think there is a fear of failure for a lot of survivors I meet.

KRIS: I don't think of the problem as sexual failures. I feel like when I have sex I'm certainly adequate and have orgasms. It's *getting to the point of having sex* that's the problem. Yes. There's something about someone looking at me — I mean if someone goes by and beeps, I get so enraged, and I don't get enraged very often. Sure I want to feel attractive and be attractive, but something about that steps over that boundary. It's a violation.

SUE: I agree. I don't see the problem as failure. I don't feel dysfunction per se. Only, when I think of myself as attractive, I think of myself as being a woman; but when I think of myself sexually, I think of myself as a sex object. Even with my husband. When things get, you know, hot and heavy, and he *looks* at me and is getting turned on . . . I just don't like that.

MARIANNA: I've felt the same way. I can really love my husband, but when it comes down to being in a sexual situation, and he's looking at me, and he thinks it's the most *loving* thing in the world, the most complimentary way to be relating to me, I hate him. I mean, I can't stand for my husband to look at me that way. It makes me sick at my stomach, and there's no way that I can have an orgasm. It just ruins things. And it is contradictory. For normal people that would be perfect . . . it's very confusing.

LIBBY: I don't really have that problem, and I have a satisfying sexual relationship with my husband. But sometimes I get upset because I have very low self-esteem, and I can't believe he finds me attractive. It's that I have an image problem. My only sexual dysfunction has been that I couldn't achieve orgasm vaginally. And I think now that that came about because when my stepfather was forcing sex upon me, I would dissociate myself from the situation and float up to the ceiling and do multiplication tables. I had orgasms then, and I felt guilty because I experienced mechanical pleasure. Later on, maybe I was still just dissociating myself. Maybe that memory was still there. But I don't have that anymore.

QUESTION: Do any of you experience flashbacks?

MARIANNA: I experience flashbacks, but it isn't anywhere near the problem it used to be. It seems like the longer I go, the older I get, the less intense they are.

QUESTION: You say they are getting less intense. So how did you come to this point?

MARIANNA: I haven't really resolved it yet. I've always tried to block it out, and I guess it's getting not as strong as it used to be. It's losing its power over me as I become stronger and healthier in therapy.

QUESTION: Has anyone here ever felt like swearing off men? (General laughter and groans of, "Oh, yes!")

LAUREN: I've never wanted to swear off men, completely. I think sometimes of swearing off having an intimate relationship but just keeping them around for sex. (Laughter)

LAUREN: Sex for sex's sake has no intimacy. I've just found out in the last year that I'm fearful of intimacy. I've never wanted to admit that.

QUESTION: Has anyone ever thought that a relationship with a woman might be easier?

KRIS: I think the boundaries for a sexual relationship might be fewer. I've never had a sexual relationship with a woman, but what I have had is a close friend since high school, and we have gone in and out of discussing whether we wanted a sexual relationship. I think for her it would be a lot easier because her mom is a lesbian. It would be easier for her than me because I probably conform to social pressures more. It just seems like you'd know what each other wanted and needed. It would be easier to understand each other.

QUESTION: Do you think it is possible to be a healthy sexual being and be celibate?

SUE: No question. I know a lot of people who do not engage in sex but they are very healthy emotionally. Maybe they do not have their sexual needs fulfilled, but I think they have the right attitude about it. They are not doing it to run away from sexuality; sex is not an issue for them. If I chose to be celibate, it would be because I have a lot of problems with it, so I would be running away from something.

QUESTION: I think we all have an idea of what a normal well-adjusted sexual person is supposed to look like, whether it comes from material you've read or TV or other people. When you think of that ideal, what is keeping *you* from being there?

ALICE: Self-esteem. Because of the incest — not necessarily the act itself, but the way people reacted to it; it became a situation where what I thought about it didn't matter. It was how everyone else reacted and how they perceived the situation and they put those values on me, and then I turned away from my own feelings and stopped trusting myself and started believing what everybody else said about other situations as well.

QUESTION: So lack of self-esteem is your big stumbling block?

ALICE: I visualize this normal healthy woman as being someone who has great self-esteem and who is really self-assured.

QUESTION: What's the big stumbling block for the rest of you?

SUE: Fear.

QUESTION: Of what?

SUE: Of everything. (Laughter)

SUE: Fear of intimacy, of trust. Fear of losing control. Fear of being controlled.

LIBBY: I'm still concerned that I feel self-conscious. I'm more assured in sex than in other areas of my life, because I know my husband loves me, but I have a general poor self-image that carries over into other areas of my life. I'd love to be like one of those women who is big and fat and they don't care and their husband loves them. And they waddle around and they're not self-conscious at all. I mean 350-pound women, and they have varicose veins, and they still have a good time. I'd like to be as unself-conscious as that. I want to be where I don't care what I look like or how I smell or if my hair is disheveled.

LAUREN: I think my stumbling block is the fear of being controlled. I don't like anyone controlling me in sex. Or the fear of intimacy. If I'm intimate, I get more vulnerable; I let down my guard and let someone get that much closer. I mean when I'm talking about good sex, I'm talking about emotional sex. You know, when you're in love with someone, it's like a drug: you think about it all the time. I don't like anything having that power over me. Incest had that power over me too.

KRIS: I agree about trust. If my entire sex life were to be masturbation, I would have a *wonderful* time. When you have a partner and you have to partake in being a fully sexual being, I don't trust that at all. I cannot comprehend how that would be.

This group of incest survivors in a short period of time brought up nearly every issue pertaining to sexuality that we have heard from other survivors. Perhaps this fact is predictable, given the issues that are reflected in healthy sexual functioning for a woman. If trust is an issue — if she cannot trust the veracity of her own feelings, not to mention the reliability of a partner — sex will reflect the problem. If she does not feel assured and confident that she is a good and valuable person, sex will reflect the problem. If control and a sense of boundaries concern her, the issue is sure to be present in her sexual functioning. Sex filters all these other issues. The clearer the issues, the better that filter, the brighter and healthier her intimate life.

Each woman's history dictates that some issues, and thus problems with sex, will be more difficult than others, and some will loom larger at different periods in her life. Check with these women in ten years, and their individual concerns will have changed; but any random interview with survivors might still echo the problems these women have as they try to untie the knot of sex and intimacy in their adult lives.

The only aberration in the interview is that no one mentions being inorgasmic. The inability to reach sexual climax is a common problem for survivors. Most of the women in the interview feel capable of sexual functioning technically defined; i.e., they are able to achieve orgasm either by masturbation or with a partner. Yet none of them would say that sex is not a major problem for her, despite that narrow definition of success. Most feel they are missing something.

Their broadest concern is that something is just not right; and although they identify several problem areas, there is a more general concern that sex has been spoiled for them. Concern with good sex may be a problem for these modern Western women' in a way that it was not for incest survivors in past times. One hesitates to be so arrogant as to judge what women felt in previous generations, but it seems possible that our foremothers were not quite as burdened with missing "sexual success" as we are, although without any shadow of a doubt they experienced incest in vast numbers, and their victimization was compounded by the low status of women in society. If sexual pleasure were the domain of men and childbearing that of women, there might have been less preoccupation with "good sex." These women in the 1980s know that they are missing good sex, and they are keenly aware that the incest in their past is creating the difficulty.

The Language of Sex and "The Look"

The most fundamental reason adult women survivors of incest feel that there is something wrong with their sex lives is that they are speaking a language different from everyone else's. Most people speak the universal sign language of sex, a kind of language where nothing need be said and which goes beyond linguistic and geographic barriers. It is by this subtle language that a woman traveling in Italy knows she is being eyed lasciviously or that a GI in Vietnam brings home a bride who speaks not a word of English.

The survivor receives the signs and cues of this language differently from others. Because of what happened to her as a child, because her first sex experiences had the content they did, she is changed forever. Communication — the "sex message" system — has been distorted for her. She sees and responds to the language differently.

This is a broad and sweeping statement, and we mean it to be, because it is the only explanation for why many women survivors feel weird, confused, and distraught on this issue. Language systems (which are not just confined to linguistic forms) are the most basic components of human culture. If a large human group is taught that A stands for B, but a certain select few are enculturated with the message that A stands for C, the subgroup is not in tune with the dominant culture. To meddle with something as basic as language systems is to work the most pervasive and thorough-going change possible for a human. And this is what many women feel: they are getting a message about love and sex distorted through the lens of childhood abuse and rape.

The best description of this anomaly comes up in the interview as women talk about "the look," the expressions and body language one person uses to send another the information that she is desirable sexually, whether or not there is any overt act (and in most cases there is not). Women grow up knowing "the look." They are culturally conditioned to it by adulthood. When they see *Gone with the Wind,* and Rhett Butler carries Scarlett up the crimson stairs in his arms, he has "the look" in his face. On the TV soap opera it is that glance across the room that first begins the clandestine affair. And of course eye contact and body language are the signals that begin the liaison in a singles bar.

The nonabused co-author of this book gives her account of "the look":

> A while ago, I ran into an old high-school flame. He invited me to have a cup of coffee, and as we sat at a café, reminiscing about old times, I caught "the look." Even though it only lasted a moment. I can fix his blue eyes in my mind at this very minute. It's nice to find that someone other than my spouse finds me sexually attractive. "The look" doesn't frighten me; it's appealing, because the memories connected with it are pleasurable. I can enjoy "the look" solely because I know that nothing more need materialize.

Karen expresses a view commonly held by nonabused women for whom "the look" can be seductive and pleasant. In fact, a woman without a history of sexual abuse may initiate the interchange that leads to "the look." But to some survivors "the look" is threatening; for others, it results in abject terror. Because they are so sensitive to it, survivors probably know this look more acutely than does the rest of the female population. Many say that they can catch a sex signal a mile away. Some are so adept at seeing the clue that they may surprise their lovers by being able to predict sex desire almost before the partners know they are giving the signal.

There is good reason for this adeptness. In childhood most women learned to discern "the look" very quickly because *their very survival depended upon detecting it*. If they could see what was coming, they might be able to get out of the way. If they were not lucky and had to stay and submit, they could at least ready themselves by bracing against the hurt that was coming.

When the incest victim grows up, "the look" does not remind her of healthy anticipated pleasure. Marianna described her feelings about it in the interview by saying that "the look" made her "sick at [her] stomach." The reason Marianna feels queasy and turned off sexually is that in her childhood that same look from her father meant that she was trapped and forced to perform. She is still shackled to her childhood signal system. Even though she is now an adult and her husband does not want to abuse her, "the look" does not spell pleasure for her.

Marianna knows she is responding differently from most women in this situation. Her last statement is telling: "And it is contradictory. For normal people that would be perfect." Not only is she a stranger to "normal sex" communication; she *knows* that she is a stranger. For Marianna and the survivors like her, sexual messages split her in two. She feels one way and yet is completely aware that she ought to feel another way.

This is a wearing business for the woman translating sexual language into what she thinks she ought to feel. It is so difficult and confusing that survivors may find ways to avoid this kind of communication altogether. Some become social hermits, never mixing with others long enough at any one time to bring about sexual messages. Others make themselves so unattractive by being overweight, unkempt, or ill clad that no one is likely to notice them; being attractive carries a risk.

Many women rigidly avoid eye contact in order to reject any sexual overtures. "In college a friend pointed out to me that I always walked with my head down, staring at the pavement," says one survivor. "That way I didn't have to look at anyone." Another woman who works in a suburban mall has to open the store early in the morning, when no one is there except male security guards. She assiduously avoids eye contact with them, for fear that that would make her uncomfortable.

By such demeanor a woman survivor is giving out another signal loud and clear, and that is, "I am not looking at you because I am afraid." Her body language broadcasts the message that she is a helpless victim, frightened even to exchange glances with a man. Perhaps it is this very message that accounts for the excessive number of reports of rape and sexual revictimization in adult survivors. Sex offenders are less intimidated and more likely to pursue a "victim" who appears to be an easy mark.

In most situations "the look" leads nowhere; it is only an appreciative glance that says, "I find you attractive." But if the situation is such that further erotic involvement is possible or even likely, the survivor's apprehension grows, and she may want to flee, just as she wanted when she was a child. "If my husband comes home from work and is very affectionate and begins to look at me in that kind of way," reports one survivor, "I begin to get uptight and maybe give back the message that I'm not available, that I'm going to bed early because I don't feel well."

The "Erotic Interlude"

The "normal" population might find erotic excitement in the tension that grows from an initial look and concludes in full love-making. The survivor, on the other hand, is apprehensive and likely to give back a negative signal to cut off the erotic interlude. The anticipatory time before a sexual encounter is far from pleasant for her. Kris is saying this in the interview when she states, "It's *getting to the point* of having sex that's the problem."

There is ample reason for the apprehension. Like "the look," the erotic interlude means something different for the survivor from what it does for others. In fact, as a child the survivor may not have had the opportunity to see "the look" at all if the abuse happened in the dark. In that case, other signals became important for her. Many a woman lay awake as a child listening for the footfall, the creaky stair, or the sound of the hand on the doorknob that meant he was coming to abuse her.

Marie's two older brothers abused her, so she became adept at distinguishing the sounds of their approach when they came in late at night after she was in bed. She could instantly identify each member of her family by the way he came up the stairs:

> I knew exactly which stairs creaked, so I would know how far away he was. I knew which man in the house grabbed hold of the bannister rail at what point. I knew my father would go first to his bedroom, then to the bathroom, but my brothers would go to the bathroom first, so when I heard my father go to his room I was so relieved because he never abused me. I knew every night sound, and I lay there with the covers up to my chin, half awake, but very alert waiting for something dreadful to happen.

This "waiting for something dreadful to happen" is what takes the place of the erotic interlude in adulthood. For these women as children, there was nothing playful or pleasant about waiting for sex to take place. For the surviving adult, "foreplay" was distorted in childhood. The erotic interlude became a time to expect and prepare for physical pain, shame, and guilt.

Sexual Message Incest

All incest survivors know about these sexual message problems, for the message, of one kind or another, preceded the actual sexual abuse. For some women, this "sexual message" was all that the incest entailed; it constituted the entire abuse. As we have seen, the sexual message system is pervasive and complicated, and it is not the case that women who "only" experienced the message did not really experience incest.

This kind of "sexual message incest" includes a great deal. A father may watch his daughter dress or undress. Many women knew they were being spied on as they showered or bathed, and fathers often invaded their daughters' privacy in the bathroom. Extreme jealousy about boyfriends and inordinate interest in intimate details of the daughter's dates are another form of this kind of incest, as is perverted interest in her growing body. We spoke in Chapter 4 of the survivor whose father insisted she lie spread-eagled on her bed after her first menstrual period so he could examine her "to make sure everything was O.K."

Finally, a man can send a sexual message by strutting or posturing. He walks around the house with few clothes on to show off his physique or rubs his genitals under the guise of scratching himself. Perhaps he stands and urinates boldly with the bathroom door open so that the girl passing by can see him.

The reason this kind of incest "message" can be so damaging is that it is covert, continual, and often terribly confusing. It tells the daughter that she is the object of her father's sexual desires, even if he does not choose to use her in a physical way. As such, it distorts "sexual messages" she receives in adulthood, so that she might see herself as the object of a sexual gambit when, in fact, many such messages are not invitations to sex. But the survivor has trouble, perhaps, even with something as benign as a compliment. Her antennae have been warped by years of getting abuse messages.

Rhonda is a professional woman in her early thirties who is happily married and the mother of two children. Although she does not consider herself an incest survivor, she was the object of exactly this kind of covert "incest message." When his daughters were teenagers, her father walked around downstairs in the otherwise all-female household clad only in his jockey shorts. He objected to all of Rhonda's dates and ridiculed the young men by calling them demeaning names behind their backs. And when she went to her junior-senior prom and had her hair beautifully arranged for the occasion, he became enraged and began pulling at it and calling Rhonda a slut.

"That was all that really ever happened," she says. Her father, now in his late fifties, has divorced and married a woman younger than his youngest daughter. Though Rhonda is a liberal and sophisticated woman who understands that May-December weddings are not unusual, she feels uncomfortable viewing the sexual look between her father and his new wife: "I have trouble watching my father caressing her. It seems inappropriate in terms of age. I see myself there."

Those distorted messages she got when she was a girl affect Rhonda as a parent, and she thinks hard about the messages she may be sending her son. "My seven-year-old is interested in Mommy's body now, but he's at that age that I don't know what to do. I'm afraid if I take his hand away from my breast, he'll stop cuddling. I suspect this is a problem for every mother with a son this age, but is a little more heightened for me because of the way my father treated me."

Being a "Sex Object"

There is yet one more confusing element in the "sexual message" system for the incest survivor as she compares herself with the rest of the population. This has to do with the fear of being attractive lest she communicate that she wants to be sexual. The women in the interview want to separate "attractive" and "sexual." When we look back to the interview, we see Sue saying, "When I think of myself as attractive, I think of myself as being a woman; but when I think of myself sexually, I think of myself as a sex object." She had said earlier, "I like to be attractive, to my husband and to other men, although I have never considered myself a flirt. But not in a situation where it could possibly lead to sex. That's where I say 'I don't want to be attractive anymore' if someone is going to look at me as a sexual being." Libby says, "I still get the feelings, 'How dare you look at me as a sexual being? How dare you consider me *just* a sexual being?'" To be perceived as sexual is not a desirable thing for Libby. It is too painful a reminder of the abuse. Kris adds, "There's something about someone looking at me — I mean if someone goes by and beeps, I get so enraged, and I don't get enraged very often. Sure I want to feel attractive and be attractive, but something about that steps over that boundary. It's a violation."

Plenty of women find whistles and catcalls from construction workers or random passers-by demeaning and angering. But there seems to be more here than feminist ire. "I get enraged," says Kris, who speaks of a "boundary" being violated. Sue puts "attractive" and "sexual" in watertight compartments: to be attractive is to feel like a woman, but to be sexual is to be an object. Libby says, "How *dare* you?"

This issue excites more than ordinary emotion. None of the three attempts to give a reason for her feeling, perhaps because these women themselves do not know where the anger is coming from. A couple of hypotheses are possible. One is that incest survivors suffer guilt about being attractive if it leads to sex. Another related hypothesis is that they need to reject the idea that women want to be a sexual lure by being attractive, because it sounds too much as if they are "asking for it."

The survivor knows that as a child she did not ask for it, but she got it anyhow. Still, it is the rare incest victim who as a child did not think she was doing something to cause Daddy to act this way; she just didn't know what it was she was doing. Many thought their looks or manner must have been the cause, and they took steps to make themselves plain or fat or unattractive. But despite their efforts to be unattractive, they still seemed to be turning him on. So the adult survivor may feel insecure about what signals she is giving out if she has by chance turned someone on.

Take the case of Rebecca, who suffered digital and oral rape on a regular basis from her father from age five until she left home at eighteen to go to college. She was not at all sure what she was doing to draw her father's consistent attention over all those years:

> It was awful. It was like I was giving out signals, like the high note only dogs can hear. Except that I couldn't hear them either, so I didn't know what I was doing to bring it on. I was a cute child, but by the time I was a teenager I got overweight and stayed that way. I took a lot of abuse from everyone in my family about how "round and firm and fully packed" I was. That was an ad for cigarettes, I think. So I knew I was plain and fat and brainy and all sorts of unattractive things, but he still kept coming on to me, even as he abused me verbally about my ugliness.

Rebecca's grandfather and uncles also made passes at her. She began to believe that she was hopelessly sexual and just drove men wild, when a priest at a Catholic college she attended attempted to seduce her:

> I was in his theology class, but he said I was so good that he wanted to tutor me privately. It sounds dumb, but I thought he meant it, so we met alone over a period of time, and he made comments about my losing weight and even brought me a calorie chart. He always tried to kiss me as I left, and one time he pursued me around the table before I finally escaped. I didn't know why he did that if he also found me in need of a calorie counter.

Rebecca was almost surprised not to receive attentions with sexual overtones from her summer employment when she worked for an accountant. After four years of college, she went on to graduate school, where she was often the victim of sexual harassment:

> Now I am older I can look back on it and say they were a creepy bunch, horny old academics, who would make a sex joke and then leer at the girls in their class or chortle under their breath. But they weren't all old. One young professor when I came in to talk about my term paper was soon beside me on the sofa he had in his office and was looking at my legs and looking me up and down with ab-

solutely anything else on his mind but the term paper which I was trying to talk about.

Rebecca reports that she had lost weight and become attractive in college and had many dates with men her own age. She had no trouble with them, and stayed out of sexual entanglements just by saying "no." It was the older men in authority — the priests and professors — who seemed to pick up a signal from her. Did the years of incest condition her to giving out the message that she was willing to be a victim again?

Rebecca, and many women like her, are not sure of the answer. But she is fearful that she may unknowingly give the same message again to a male authority figure. That fear makes her stay away from professional and social situations where she might meet a man who would ask something of her; she cannot trust what she might be telling him by her response.

Finally, if to be attractive is to offer a sexual lure, survivors often want nothing of it. Many women in society at large think that a woman makes herself attractive in order to be a lure, as a bright spinner is to a lake bass. They are flattered by such attention, even if they decide to reject its source. They know that an "I find you attractive" message does not mean that the sender of the message necessarily has to end up in bed with her. She has the right to say "no." And that person has the right to be telling her she is beautiful without necessarily wanting any sexual outcome at all.

Such sexual teasing is often foreign to the incest survivor. She has no such elasticity. It is scary to have her hair done and buy a new dress and then to have someone make a pass at her at a party. Some women might laugh and say, "Isn't that wonderful? Guess who made a pass at me." The survivor, on the other hand, may feel angry, indignant, or confused.

Even if a woman is aware (as are most of the women in the interview) that she is looking at a potential sex situation differently from a woman who did not experience incest, she still has to live and function with that knowledge. It is like a wraith or ghost that never leaves her side, for often in the look of a person who is supposed to love her — her husband or lover — she still sees and responds to the look of the man who first victimized her. The old message from childhood forces her to feel trapped, scared, and powerless again. Unless she works very hard at getting a new message, sex in her adulthood will continue to turn her into a small, quivering, cornered victim.

Flashbacks

Nearly any survivor working at these problems will say that the hardest to deal with are flashbacks of the original sexual assault, which often occur during sex. They are hell to live through. If we consider the trauma the adult rape victim — who usually is raped only once — must live through as she tries to get her life back to normal, we have some idea of how hard it is for the incest survivor to keep reliving numerous episodes of incest as a child.

In the interview only Marianna mentioned flashbacks as a problem, but we encountered it often in the women we talked with. There seem to be several kinds of flashbacks. "Emotional flashbacks" create a feeling but are not necessarily accompanied by a full rerun in technicolor of former sexual abuse. Emotional flashbacks are commonly associated with sex; just enough discomfort or sorrow occurs to ruin the sexual occasion at hand. The sexual functioning of many a survivor has been crippled because of them.

Flashbacks can be triggered by any number of stimuli. The body often seems to remember what the mind does not. So even a touch by a lover that seems harmless on the face of it can trigger a flood of feelings, sometimes accompanied by vivid memories of the incest. The sense of smell, such a rich part of sexual functioning, is also a frequent catalyst for memories. And it is not only body smells that bring back memories. Many women had fathers who were alcoholic, and the instant they smell alcohol on their lover's breath, they are turned off sexually.

Taste is another catalyst, of course, for the woman who as a child was subjected to oral sexual abuse. Even sound, the last of the senses one might expect to be associated with problems, can trigger memories. If sex abuse happened in the car with a radio blaring loud rock music, then that kind of music may cause sexual discomfort.

Most women report that these flashbacks are so intense that they momentarily dissociate from the present situation and feel themselves back in the original abusive one. Even if they are able to repress the memories, the sexual experience still feels traumatic. "I used to burst into uncontrollable sobs after intercourse," says one survivor, "no matter how gentle or thoughtful my husband had been, because the whole idea of sex was so sorrowful to me."

Getting rid of flashbacks does not just happen; it must be worked at, *hard*. As in nearly every other issue faced by the adult survivor of incest, a woman must stop denying and recognize the problem, facing it head-on. She needs to confront the actual memory triggered by sex and live through all the pain and anger that it brings her. Then she can internalize the fact that she is now an adult with choices. Although it may take a long time, she can learn to choose to experience the present rather than the past.

A good example here is Kathleen Marie, first mentioned in Chapter 2. After her mother's death when she was twelve, her stepfather raped her; then she went to live with an aunt and uncle. There she was repeatedly assaulted by her uncle until she tried to leave for a convent at age eighteen. Her parish priest would not recommend her for the disciplined religious life because he sensed she was running away from something rather than embracing God.

As a teenager Kathleen Marie was "petrified on dates," and was shy in school because she was always afraid she would be raped. These two facts show how the sexual messages she had gotten from her uncle and stepfather had reduced her to the fear that *any sex* could equal rape. She was continually fearful as a teenager, a time when any attractive girl is bombarded with sexual looks from boys, not to mention men. Kathleen Marie translated such messages into rape signals. Imagine the abject terror of that kind of life for a child and young woman. An appreciative look or wink which says, "I find you attractive," is received by the victim as, "I want to rape you right here and now."

In her early twenties Kathleen Marie found a gentle man who did not threaten her, and she fell in love and married him. Everything seemed to be going well until her husband asked her to perform oral sex, which he enjoyed and hoped she would as well. She began to experience paralyzing flashbacks which frightened her because she had not previously recalled the incest.

Kathleen Marie found that in her marriage she could avoid oral sex and thus the flashbacks, but she desired a full range of sexual expression with the man she loved. She entered therapy and worked through all the memories and pain. At the end she wrote a letter and made a phone call to her policeman-uncle who had raped her for so many years.

The letter is a classic of its kind. In violent language to match her angry feelings, she purged herself of the horror he had caused in her life, and threw him out of it forever. Having confronted all the pain, *not just the flashbacks,* she had the strength to distance herself from her entire childhood. She directed her anger at the appropriate objects — her own abusers and abusers in general: "I think laws should be stronger," she says. "Mutilation of these men is okay, and prison is too good for them." Having put her uncle in his place, she was able to turn to the enjoyment of her own sexuality along with someone who did not intend to harm her, her husband.

The Sexual Maze

Kathleen Marie's story ends hopefully. Not all do. The flashbacks, the overlay of past memory on present sexual functioning, the confusion between being sexual and being attractive, and the tremendous distortion of the world that incest survivors must live through make sexual intimacy an intricate maze, confusing in its twists, turns, and blind alleys.

Some women try to escape the maze by denying or deferring their own sexual needs. It may be a relief to take care of a troubled partner, to concentrate on making him or her "well," in order to take the spotlight off herself. Libby mentioned this response in the interview as she discussed the possibility that incest survivors attract "problem men." She argued that incest survivors are drawn to men who have problems — such as alcoholism, impotence, unresolved divorce issues, or emotional insecurity. Libby adds later, "A lot of them were looking for a mother figure, a savior; and I would just cuddle them and tell them it will be all right." These women will be more "accommodating" to problem men.

The women in the interview were not unaware of what they were doing. Lauren says, "I think we have more tolerance for pain — emotional pain, physical pain. Most healthier women in a dysfunctional relationship would get out of it quick, where we are able to be in it longer."

Add to this tolerance for pain a willingness to take care of men and a good dose of powerlessness, and the result is a toxic combination. Experts who study abused people — from battered wives to rape victims to physically abused people — note that this segment of the population can be revictimized in more than one way; that is, once abused, they often become targets for other kinds of abuse and often linger in painful, damaging life situations. Such seeming perversity has led some healthy people who watch this cycle to remark cynically, "They seem to bring it on themselves."

If they do, they do not always know it. Libby says in the interview, "I don't know if we exactly send out signals, but I *know* we are more accommodating in dealing with somebody who has problems." And Sue says, "We just know how to take more abuse." Both are talking about the combination of feeling powerless and feeling fragmented. The former is a direct result of child sexual abuse: cornered, overpowered, given no choices, the child submits to abuse and humiliation. As an adult she continues to survive a sexual situation by doing what she may have done as a child, splitting herself apart so that she will not have to feel.

This fragmentation seems greatest for women who felt sexual pleasure when their bodies were being manipulated in childhood. Libby spoke about dissociating and "float[ing] up to the ceiling [to] do multiplication tables" as her stepfather abused her. She felt tremendous guilt that her body experienced pleasure. Libby and other survivors like her who may have felt their bodies lubricating against their will or experienced an orgasm over which they had no control recoil at the repeat experience. The bodies that conspired against them once are certainly not to be trusted now.

In fact, many survivors feel that they don't own their bodies at all. They have been an object, a place where things happened, where others came to get pleasure and then abandoned them, only to return to repeat the cycle again and again.

Many feel that they live by stepping outside themselves. They are like actors, walking through their various roles, reading the script handed to them, waiting for others to tell them how to feel and act.

The Lesbian Choice

A word here about lesbianism. The traditional view is that sexually abused people are unable to function, that they are society's losers. That stereotype is occasionally amplified by the equally pernicious perception that women abused by men can never deal with them again; when they refuse to capitulate to "the look" they turn to women instead. Hence, according to this line of reasoning, most incest survivors are (or are likely to become) lesbians.

Our sample was small, so we cannot predict accurately what the incidence of lesbianism is among incest survivors. It seemed to us that the lesbian choice occurred at about the same rate that it does for the rest of the population; by no means was it the choice of the majority. More important, the women who chose that lifestyle did so less as a reaction against men than as a positive sexual choice for themselves. They still had to continue to deal with men in their professional or working lives and thus still faced many of the same issues heterosexual women face. They did not become hermits because they were lesbian.

At the Midwest Conference of V.O.I.C.E.S. (Victims of Incest Can Emerge Survivors) in November 1985, a well-attended panel on sexuality for survivors was led by two lesbians. One related that she had known her sexual orientation at an early age, possibly as early as age five. The other, a professional woman in her late forties, had had both heterosexual and homosexual experiences, and had decided on the latter as more satisfying. She also stated in a later interview that it is less her choice of partner than how she is feeling about herself that rules her sexual actions, even her fantasy life. Whatever the sexual lifestyle, of course, it is possible either to enjoy a genuinely reciprocal relationship or to feel victimized.

What Survivors Bring to Our Understanding of Sexuality

Human sexuality is complicated, and its study has not lent itself to easy conclusions. It would be false, therefore, to pretend that we are finished and done with the issue of sexuality for the incest survivor. What we can do is to leave the topic with a brief outline of what seem to be the major problems, even if the solutions are not forthcoming.

Larger questions of power and pleasure inevitably intrude into discussions of sexuality. As the authors talked about the issues in this chapter with people who had not been incest victims, it became clear that the struggle survivors face is shared by more women than just incest survivors. Many women in the general population see "the look" and with it the suggestion of a power differential between men and women that is far from natural — or desirable. This feminist reading of the situation can be found clearly stated in contemporary film criticism, where it has been said that the man is "the bearer of the look" and the woman its recipient. Scarlett O'Hara, assertive as she is, cannot disregard Rhett Butler's sexual power; she must give in. "The look" communicates this power imbalance, and incest survivors are just more canny than other women in sensing it because they have, in fact, been victims of male patriarchal power. They *know* what "the look" means, and it threatens them.

Some women who are not incest survivors, such as Karen Lison, the nonabused co-author of this book, think that this feminist reading of the power differential with which survivors can associate their feelings is a misreading of a harmless sexual message system. These women have never been threatened as children with unwanted sex from an adult relative, and they think that the sexual message is less one of power than of the pleasure in flirtation and teasing. Incest survivors, because of their early experiences, would naturally not know about this message system. "Listen," says one young, attractive, and intelligent woman — a wife and mother of two — "I do it all the time. I think *I* often give the first message to the man, and I *enjoy* him looking back at me in a way that says I am attractive. It has nothing to do with heavy sex. It's harmless flirting, and I enjoy it." She was never abused as a child and has a warm and close relationship with her father now that she is an adult.

It is not possible to say which view is closer to reality: the real question is, *whose* reality? But the incest survivor has a unique light to shed on this murky controversy. Hers is obviously a sensitive reading of how it feels to be an adult woman who was hurt as a child by male sexual power. And her challenge as an adult is to seek out a healthy sexual identity despite her history. She must find her answers in a culture obsessed with sexual satisfaction and pleasure but short on how to attain them.

Survivors can learn to say clearly to themselves and to others exactly what hurts and what feels good; that is a solid way to build honest relationships. They discover that intimacy is made up of small attentions, friendship, and quiet trust. In intimate settings, these elements are as individual as the survivors and as unique as the lovers. Each survivor must write her own agenda, make her own way, attack her own issues in the way that makes most sense to her.

Finally, incest survivors have less likelihood than many for falling into the erroneous belief that sexual behavior exists in a vacuum. They feel — and know that they feel — that every other issue they face rushes in when sexuality and intimacy come into play. Sexuality is the distillate of all those other issues, the pure essence. How we feel *in toto* about ourselves comes out when we are sexually intimate with another person. Perhaps that perception is as close as we can get to a central truth here. And perhaps, because of her sometimes horrific and damaging experiences, the survivor has something to teach the rest of us about the abuses of sexual power, and the complexity of true intimacy between two human beings.

7

The Healing Process

THERE *finally came a period in my adult life when everything ground to a halt. And then I knew — with a certainty that defies description — that I had to do something. I looked around me and saw for the first time that despite all my feverish attempts to keep everything together on all fronts, my house of cards was fast falling around me.*

It was May, the spring of the year, when I opened my eyes to the collapse. I looked at my children, then four and nine. For nearly a year my younger daughter had regularly been having a screaming, crying tantrum the minute we sat down to dinner. I had done everything for her — a good Montessori school, expensive day care after school until I got home from work, the right toys and books. But she was out of control; I thought I had a budding juvenile delinquent on my hands. And one night that spring I found myself spanking her in her bed after one of the tantrums, and I couldn't feel inside me that I was hurting her. I felt numb to the pain I was giving her, and that made me scared, because I had been beaten as a child and I have never forgotten the pain, both physical and emotional. Here I was humiliating my child in the same way and I had failed to connect it with myself. I felt empty.

Spanking had never been the issue with my older daughter. The single time I had punished her physically had been when she was a toddler and ran into a busy street. She was a gifted child, sensitive and bright, and she had begun the school year as usual with great promise. But two months into the first semester her teacher called me to a conference in the principal's office in alarm, because my child was failing all her subjects. And she left her lunch box at home nearly every day and often her boots and mittens stayed at school when she wandered home, seemingly oblivious to the weather.

I say "my" child because I took responsibility for everything that went wrong, including the fact that my marriage was giving me nothing. My husband had retreated deep into the tunnel of workaholism. When he did come home, exhausted, I tried to talk to him about what was going on at the office (as I was whipping up the wonderful dinner that my four-year-old was sure to interrupt with a tantrum). I tried to be a good wife and to listen, but I had no sympathy or feeling for his plight. My own agenda was crowding out anything he might have been saying. In fact, it seemed to me that he had few problems and almost no reason for complaint, next to all that I had to do and to bear. When we were together alone, which was rare enough, he was thinking about his work and I about the seventy things I had to get done before bed. We had no problems with our sex life because we had no sex life.

I was drinking too much each evening before dinner, and I always felt guilty about it at the same time that I kept reassuring myself that I deserved a drink for having put up with all that I did each day. That alcohol treat seemed to make the rest of the day bearable.

I had changed careers as an adult, since Ph.D.s in English literature were in oversupply and the demand was ludicrously low in my specialty. I was angry about the swarms of older men who sat comfortably in tenured positions and did nothing to deserve them, while younger scholars — more and more of them female — were edged out of ever having a stable academic career.

But I claimed it would not deter me, and I set out to find some-

thing to do. It was an enormous effort (partly because I was carrying so much bitterness about having to change careers at all), but I finally found a job, one in which I was quickly promoted to a position of leadership. But what I see as challenge now, felt like a burden then.

My job required some travel. I dreaded being alone in a strange city, so I feared trips. I felt paralyzed and inflexible: I wanted routine, predictability, safety — along with recognition, of course, and higher wages and promotions. I was loath to work overtime in the evening lest I neglect my family, so I arrived at work early in the morning and then made my later-arriving colleagues know that they were lazier than I.

I finally snapped, as a result of the long hours, the demands that I be creative, the problems with my co-workers. So one morning I went in and told off my boss, reading him a sermon from a hastily scratched outline I held in my shaking hands. I got personal and told him what I thought of his abilities and how he was ruining our projects. He was stunned with the rush of accusations and pent-up anger. I gave thirty days' notice and walked out, ignoring an invitation to come back on a part-time basis. I vowed that I wanted to see my employers come to such ruin that they would have to sell pencils on the street corner.

I was not giving notice to my boss as much as I was giving notice to myself. The message said, "I can go on no longer with this hurt and pain. It has to stop or I will die."

I quit the job in May. I spent the summer with the children and gave great attention to my vegetable garden. Meanwhile, I checked with friends and associates about therapists; I had been moved to do so after an article about incest had appeared in the Chicago Tribune. *I drew up a list of ten psychiatrists, psychotherapists, and social workers and decided to interview them. I was sure that incest lay at the bottom of my troubles: I decided to put it up front with any therapist I talked to.*

In September I began to interview, and the second woman I met was a psychologist in an office full of plants and warm brown and gold furniture. I looked across the small comfortable room into the eyes of a woman who, it seemed to me, was not about to turn her back on me no matter what I told her of myself. There was such kindness and understanding in her eyes, and at last I knew that I had found a safe place.

So I began.

• ✳ • ✳ •

EACH survivor goes through phases on her healing journey. Each one has to do with a change in perceptions or in attitudes — ways of looking at herself, others, and the world around her.

The steps are not always so clear as they are outlined below, but by the end of the journey, as the healing is well under way, all fourteen steps have been taken in some form. They do not follow the same order for each individual. But they always begin with the recognition that the pain has become unmanageable, and they always conclude with a sense of hope for the future and satisfaction in the present.

Let us first outline the fourteen steps, then take each one at more length.

The Fourteen Steps of Growth for Survivors of Incest

1. I cannot manage my pain alone. I must seek help.
2. I acknowledge that something terrible happened. I know it is not my imagination; I was a victim of childhood sexual assault.
3. I begin to recognize my feelings. There may be sadness, anger, fear, guilt, and shame. I allow myself to experience them all.
4. I discuss the abuse thoroughly with my therapist. I completely re-experience and begin to deal with feelings appropriate for each incident of abuse that I can recall. I share feelings of shame with my survivors' group.
5. I begin to realize that I was probably acting *appropriately* at

the time the abuse occurred. (That is, my reactions were appropriate; the abuse was not!)

6. If there was a part of the molestation that was pleasurable to me, I am coming to terms with the fact of that pleasure and I am dealing with the guilt surrounding it.

7. I perceive the connection between my molestation and my current behavioral patterns and relationships. I am beginning to develop some control over that connection.

8. I recognize that I have a choice as to whether or not I confront my perpetrator(s).

9. I am beginning to understand what I desire from relationships, as I learn to trust my perceptions.

10. I am able to enjoy intimacy.

11. I develop a sense of self and my self-esteem has increased.

12. My resistance to talking about the abuse (although not necessarily the details of it) has diminished.

13. I realize that I have a choice as to whether or not I forgive my perpetrator. I *have* forgiven *myself*.

14. I am in touch with past anger, but detached from it so that it is not a constant part of my feelings and a negative influence on my other emotions, my functioning, and my relationships with others. I no longer live in the past. I live in the present and welcome the future with all its fears, imperfections, and unpredictabilities.

Step 1: I cannot manage my pain alone. I must seek help.

The first step is the longest.

The process of healing must begin by taking account of the years of denial. Beginning to acknowledge that there is a problem is a distance down the road from the cure. But the beginning of the cure is always a result of realizing that, in some way, life has become unmanageable. A woman may experience unwarranted fears about harm coming to herself or to her children, bouts of crying over seemingly minor events, anger or rage without being able to pinpoint the source.

Years have been spent surviving and denying. Most of the women seeking help for incest in their adult lives do not enter therapy until their thirties. Of course, many have had previous therapy without addressing the incest: either they were unaware that they had been violated or, if they knew, they were unaware of its importance. Often their therapists were as uncomfortable as they were discussing it.

What have these women been doing in these years of denial? Most were treating *symptoms,* circling round and round in a pattern of discomfort and complaint, occasionally getting help, but more often than not having one symptom clear up only to have two others take its place. Among the array of symptoms and treatments that a woman may have been through are the following:

PHYSICAL ILLNESSES.   Headaches, stomach and bowel disorders, heart palpitations — all result from the stress of keeping in her feelings and protecting the secret she carries.

EATING DISORDERS.   The relatively new programs designed to treat anorexia and bulimia are filled with incest survivors. The woman may have attended such a program. Closely related are problems with obesity, or the victim's perception that she has weight problems. This is endemic among survivors and arises from the distorted body image that they grew up with. The woman has perhaps tried crash diets and intense exercise regimens.

ANXIETY, DEPRESSION, PANIC ATTACKS.   These have possibly been treated by medication. Mood-adjusting medications or antidepressant drugs can be helpful when they are taken with the advice and under the care of a physician. Many survivors could not get through the day without them. But these medications treat only the symptoms, not the core issues, and it is possible to be treated for depression with medication and still stay sick.

SUBSTANCE ABUSE, EITHER OF DRUGS OR OF ALCOHOL.   Here programs are well established and effective. The issue of sexual abuse, however, may not come up, although the program perhaps does a perfectly good job of helping the survivor deal with the substance abuse. Likewise, survivors may have gotten into other so-called "Twelve-Step" programs, such as Overeaters Anonymous, Emotions Anonymous, or Al-Anon, a program that helps people learn to deal with an alcoholic family member or friend. Again, these are all effective programs, but nonetheless they are not designed to confront the deeper problem of sexual abuse.

SEXUAL DYSFUNCTION. Rampant among women in our country, this is the companion of the incest survivor. To help herself be orgasmic she may have tried everything from a vibrator to a sex clinic with her spouse.

SELF-MUTILATION. The cutting, burning, or other injuring of her own body, or the desire to mutilate herself, is an illness that is increasingly coming out into the open and being discussed. The correlation between self-mutilation and childhood sexual abuse is very high, according to experts in the field. Pioneering attempts are going on in different parts of the country to treat self-mutilators. If the victim has been fortunate, she may have located specialized help.

None of this is to say that what the survivor of incest has done to preserve and help herself has been in vain. On the contrary, protecting and nurturing herself in such ways helps her to survive: the truth will not come out until she can deal with the pain, and these other techniques are ways of tending to herself, albeit in a surface way by treating symptoms rather than core issues.

Some of the subtler ways of overcoming this pain may, in fact, be quite positive on the face of it. Many survivors have become frenetically involved in their children's school or with community projects, by way of compensating for their own lost childhood. This involvement lets a woman say, "I am a good person; look how well I take care of my children," and in fact school, child, and community benefit as well. But this volunteer work does not substitute for an honest enjoyment of children for their own sakes, and can often blur the distinction between duty and love.

A survivor may make a career choice that comes out of the desire to understand what happened to her and to nurture others. A large number of survivors have chosen the helping professions — nursing, social work, teaching, medicine. Unquestionably these women bring to their calling a quality of understanding and of mercy that is rare, and their professions are glad to have them. Even though the incest experience often contributes qualities of empathy and gentleness to a survivor who enters the caring professions, she can find herself running dry in her work if she has not ever been able to resolve her own issues. A woman who gets a Ph.D. in psychology to understand others but has not yet confronted the damage done to her own self by the incest she suffered in childhood has a lot of work to do.

A survivor may have sought solace in religion and, unfortunately, been more hurt than helped by it. Many religions teach the value of resignation; the incest survivor is a sitting duck for that message. She falls in quickly with the line that says, "This is just my cross to bear, and the more I can do what is expected of me without ever complaining, the better and more virtuous I will be." There are other truisms: "God will never give you more to bear than you can stand," or "Don't question God's will or you will go to hell."

The clergy (often unwittingly) play this game too, when they preach forgiveness without understanding the depth of the sin and wrong that the abused woman feels. In fact, clergy are a crucial link if they hold the power to forgive; a woman may feel she can bypass feeling the legitimate anger and simply say, "I forgive him because he did not know what he was doing."

These techniques may help in the short term. None will substitute forever for a genuine understanding of what has happened to her. Finally, she will have to admit that she is hurting and that she needs help. Then the healing can begin.

GETTING OFF DEAD CENTER

So there she is: *stuck* in the midst of her pain. The process of healing and change in the life of the survivor can begin ignominiously enough with a feeling of being stuck, unable to move. Life has become uncomfortable at best, intolerable at worst. She does not want to be where she is, although she may not be able to verbalize that about herself. That information comes with hindsight.

She may be immobilized for a long time, because even though her status is painful, it is at least familiar. Change, the first step in healing, may still be a long way in the distance. Many survivors stay in situations that can strike other, healthier people as ridiculously difficult or even hopelessly abusive. The reason is that a former victim of sexual abuse may not know when she is being mistreated as an adult, and she may not yet know that there is any other way to live. But healing begins when she *knows* she is hurting and decides no longer to be a passive victim.

What moves her out of this unhappiness and inertia? Sometimes it is a jolt, a lightning bolt, as it were: the loss of a job, the death of a family member, a divorce or severed love affair, or a severe illness or injury. The catalyst can be less dramatic, a seeming piece of happenstance. Perhaps she sees a flyer in the public library about a group meeting for adult survivors of child abuse and decides to attend. Or she picks up a book about incest or finds herself talking to a friend about her childhood or having her first flashback. It may be a trip to a physician because she is depressed or cannot sleep or thinks she is afflicted with PMS (premenstrual syndrome). But, somehow, each woman beginning the healing process recognizes the subtle but unmistakable feeling that she needs to change.

We do not want to give the impression that the healing process is a smooth affair where any part is predictable or easy. The survivor may not understand until years later, for example, that the life jolt that got her off dead center made her sit up and confront the fact that she was sexually abused. Often she does not recognize that jolt as important, and she is not even aware that her reaction to it has meant change. What she probably knows at the time is that she has migraines or that she feels out of control of her life. She feels guilty about sex and her lover or husband is complaining. She is lonely and cannot make friends. She finds herself short-tempered or screaming at her children. She knows only that she is miserable.

Women usually do not make an immediate incest connection. They may not recall for years that the incest occurred: memories have an uncanny way of coming only when the survivor can deal with them. The psyche has tremendous abilities to protect itself from pain.

At first she may feel like a pressure cooker about to explode. All the years she has held anger in, biting her tongue or feeling like a doormat or trying to be perfect. Now that pattern begins to fray. There are little explosions and big ones. The woman who had been a good girl, then a good wife, accommodating to her husband and children, finds herself talking back to her doctor or refusing to placate her husband or to serve her children. The good and steady employee at work may decide finally to tell off her boss or even change jobs or quit and go on unemployment. One woman described her discontent surfacing this way: "I knew that life was not fair, but what I was having to take suddenly seemed ridiculous. I knew I deserved more than this and I got angry."

THE "YES . . . BUT" TWO-STEP

At some point the survivor decides she must do something. *Deciding* to do something is not the same as *actually doing* something, of course, although it may be a step in the direction of action. And if there is one predictable thing about change, it is that it will be scary and uncomfortable. That knowledge is enough to immobilize many survivors for a long time. The new ways will be unfamiliar and difficult; the old ways are easier, and it is the familiar groove that appeals.

This is the stage we refer to as the *"Yes . . . but"* two-step, the dance that keeps a woman going in circles, never advancing. "Yes, I would like some improvement . . . but not quite yet." Or "Yes, I know I have incest back there . . . but it's not affecting me that badly," or "Yes, I know I need help . . . but I'm waiting for time/money/the children to grow up/my father to die." Almost any excuse will do for the second step of the two-step.

And the stages overlap: she steps forward one pace toward change, and she falls back two, or progresses two paces toward recognizing anger and retreats one. The woman who wakes up one morning saying she can no longer bear the pain in her life might wake up the very next morning content to leave well enough alone.

This kind of indecisiveness is borne out by the experience of therapists who cooperate with emergency hotlines. Every time an incest program is aired on television or radio, counselors specializing in abuse are deluged with calls after the program. But when they return the phone calls a day — or even hours — later, they are as likely as not to hear an excuse or be assured that nothing is wrong that the victim can't handle. "Oh, it's really not a problem," or "You must have gotten the wrong number," are clear signs to experienced counselors that the person in fact has a problem but is not ready to deal with it. Many continue in this limbo for months, even years, wavering between action and inaction, with bouts of the "Yes . . . but" two-step in between.

THE STEP INTO THERAPY

Every woman's experience is different, and not all will be able or willing to find professional help. For our part, we have never found a survivor functioning well who had not reached out, whether it was to an individual therapist, a therapy group, or a self-help band of survivors. There are no doubt people who manage to heal themselves with reading, self-discipline, possibly even prayer or meditation. Although these devices are helpful as supplements to the main task of healing, we have never seen a woman who used them as her only path to recovery.

A woman entering therapy after lingering for some period of time in the "Yes . . . but" two-step will encounter the experience in her own unique way. First of all, not many women bring up incest immediately as the "presenting problem," that specific complaint that brought her to the therapist in the first place. She may know that she has a deep, dark secret someplace in her history and may even remember something of the incest, but she usually feels that there are too many other pressing issues that she must deal with first: her life seems to be falling apart.

The perceptive therapist sees incest as the central fact and the other issues as spin-offs. In fact, a woman and her therapist may see the same body of facts from totally different perspectives. The client is frustrated that things are not perfect. The therapist takes a note about why anyone would expect that life could ever be perfect. The woman complains that she feels as though she is caretaker to the world; the therapist asks who appointed her to the job anyhow? And why should she continue buying into relationships that give her so little in return? The woman says she should be angry, but she cannot *get* angry. The therapist nods and makes a note about guilt or repression. The woman was once a child, perhaps, who was punished if she showed anger or any emotion, and she has learned to deny any angry responses.

Mostly her self-esteem is so low, her confidence in her value as a person so fragile, that she believes she has no right to be happy anyway. If, as we have said earlier, sex is the prism of the *issues* brought about by incest, self-esteem is the prism of the *emotions*. It is the injury to that core of herself, what she believes her worth to be, that probably focuses all the problems in the therapist's office. And of course low self-esteem is a predictable characteristic in the adult who has suffered through childhood abuse: how can a girl grow up feeling good about herself when she was physically *used* for another's pleasure, emotionally *abused* at the same time, and often neglected by other members of the family and told she did not count? She has been devalued in the closest relationships we can have in this world — in her family.

We have outlined the reasons that a woman faces emotional problems as an adult, emotional problems that can lead to physical ones as well. The question now is how does she purge herself of the hurt? How does she put her life together on a new footing? How does she get over the shame she feels that all this happened to her? If healing is to occur, the emotions must come out. The anger must be confronted, re-enacted, and accepted. The guilt must be confessed and examined. The feelings of worthlessness must be seen as a picture in a distorted mirror, the mirror held up to her in her childhood, which is no longer a faithful reproduction of who she is. The feelings of isolation must be lifted by sharing them with another person or persons and by reading and learning about others who have been there too.

Step 2: I acknowledge that something terrible happened. I know it is not my imagination; I was a victim of childhood sexual assault.

The next hard step in therapy is to acknowledge that the abuse took place and to learn to make the connection between the present pain and the assault that occurred in childhood. Even if the survivor knows that the hurt she is feeling right now has something to do with the incest, she must go back and re-experience some of that pain.

This is a tall order. Many women do not remember the incest; how are they then to connect adult problems with childhood pain? Some women remember incest and some of the events but cannot for a long time connect it with the person they are now. It seems to have happened to someone else (not at all surprising, given how practiced many survivors become at dissociation). Finally, even if she remembers events and details, her feelings about those events — whether she was responsible, whether or not it was right, whether she asked for it — may still need to be straightened out.

And the flood of new emotions never felt before are terribly frightening.

One woman reported a dream that showed she was on the verge of this major breakthrough:

> I remember standing on a bridge watching a little girl ice skate on the frozen river below. The ice was crystal clear and I could see through it perfectly at my vantage point, but the little girl, being so close to the ice, could not see what lurked below. As I watched in horror, I desperately tried to warn the child that monsters and snakes with large mouths were making their way through the ice to devour her. I felt frightened by what I saw and powerless that I could not warn the innocent child of what was coming.

A few days later this woman began remembering her incestuous childhood. She started feeling safer letting her memories surface, knowing that she had a trusted relationship with a therapist and a survivor's group that would understand and accept her. The memories began to flow.

However the blockage is removed, the survivor begins to remember. Chunks of time previously unrecalled begin to take form. The memories are terrifying. Cold sweats, panic attacks, or stoic silences may occur. Slowly, the survivor acknowledges that something terrible has happened — she was a victim of child sexual abuse.

It took Janice nearly a year in therapy to remember the pain her father had given her for most of the years she was growing up. She recalled that he came to her bed every night when her mother was away at work, forced his fingers inside her vagina, and pinched and fondled her breasts. But she felt no outrage. Her moment of breakthrough came when she heard herself telling her therapist that she was at least partly guilty because she had never told him to stop, and for the first time she heard her therapist saying, "Nonetheless, *he had no right*. You were a child, and he was an adult, and *he had no right* to come and hurt you." To a nonabused adult the therapist's observation may have been self-evident, but to Janice it meant understanding for the first time that her father had been in control over her and had chosen to hurt her, despite her having loved him (she thought) devotedly over the years. At that point she began to connect with the little girl who had been punished for something she never did, and her rage began.

Ruth began therapy remembering the incest, at least in large outline. Her mother was not "all there," as Ruth puts it, and spent whatever mothering time she had with Ruth's ill younger brother, often accompanying him to the hospital or out of town for cures. The father, meanwhile, spent his time in a bar, and it became Ruth's responsibility to go fetch him from there for dinner. After dinner Ruth put him to bed, since he was too drunk to do so himself.

Ruth thought that she must have seduced her father. In fact, she could even call up behavior that would prove it, because in order to get her father's attention away from his cronies in the bar, she found herself doing tricks and acting "seductively," attracting attention from the other men as well as her father. Obviously, she felt, she was guilty of what subsequently happened to her.

The adult Ruth is an enterprising and ambitious career woman. She needed to think that she had always possessed power, even as a child. She finally confronted the incest when she saw that her father was using her, that he could have come home from the bar and put himself to bed or, in fact, not have been in the bar in the first place. She had resisted the truth because she thought that if her father had used her, she must have been weak or crazy to allow it. Being weak meant being like the mother she despised, a possibility she could not accept.

Making the connection to childhood takes time, and the subtle distinction between what happened and what might have happened had things not been so wrong and distorted is far from a matter of automatic knowledge. The process of recovering childhood memories is one of the most painful a woman can experience. Many people become so frightened at this point that they back out of therapy; they fear the pain of remembering, and if they do begin to remember, they feel that this pain will last forever and that the cure could not possibly be worth it. The tendency to emotional numbing or to dissociation — the separation of feelings from present functioning — increases during this painful period. Just holding a job or living through one's domestic chores can be difficult.

Part of the pain comes from looking at one's childhood. To sit and remember can be hard, but the suffering seems to worsen when therapists or groups recommend going back to old albums for pictures of the survivors as children. Photos that show the victim with her abuser are especially painful — and most useful, because the woman may suddenly have a rush of memories as she looks at that former self. At its annual meeting, V.O.I.C.E.S. (Victims of Incest Can Emerge Survivors) asks delegates to bring pictures of themselves as children. These are posted on a large bulletin board festooned with yellow ribbons, symbol of hope for those who have been held hostage by the past.

Most women launching into therapy as adult incest survivors find themselves reading whatever they can get their hands on about the subject in an attempt to understand what happened to them. At present, confessional first-person accounts make up most of the available material on incest. These agonizing stories have a clear use. They confirm the woman's experience and let her see that she is not alone. To immerse oneself in this kind of material, however, is something akin to reading about the Holocaust. The sheer weight and terror of the stories depress and discourage one.

Keeping track of dreams is useful at this point as well — and, once again, disturbing. Some of the dreams at the beginning of therapy re-create in some form the original abuse. Sleep disturbances can be common at this period: nightmares, awaking screaming or shaking, fear of going to bed, fear of turning out the light, sleepwalking, grinding the teeth in sleep. But even though they can be expected, they are dreadful to live through, not just

because of the memories they call up but because sleep disturbances make the woman in her waking hours more tired and tense
than she was before she began therapy.

This is strong medicine to prescribe: you *must be* "stirred up"
in order to remember vividly enough to be healed. Who wants
willingly to take on such a heavy burden? Still, it can and must be
lived through. These experiences, once remembered and relived,
finally become the ancient history they deserve to be.

Gradually the pieces fall into place. When the inquiry into incest
first begins, women are likely to feel that they have been carrying
around five hundred pieces to a puzzle that has never been put
together. They have nothing but questions: "Why did this happen
to me?" "Why wasn't I protected?" "What role did I play?" "Was
I at all responsible?" "Does this happen to other people?" "What
does all this have to do with me now?"

In time and with work the facts begin to interlock, as understanding finally comes. Many seemingly unrelated events form
the background until the whole landscape becomes clear. One
woman, for example, cherished her pet dog and cat and obsessively protected them from harm. When she came to examine why
she treasured her animals so, she recalled that her perpetrator had
threatened to kill her childhood pet to make her comply. She had
forgotten that detail, and remembering made her understand her
adult self better.

Women need to recognize that this memory dredging can be dis-
orienting, even dangerous. For many, it is not wise to drive after a
therapy session because they experience dissociation for a period
of time after the intense memory they have experienced. It might
be wise not to schedule an important business meeting or a critical
work task right after such sessions.

Each woman discovers what she needs to do to nurture herself
through this period. It is important to remember that she has in
fact been taking a peek over the brink of hell, and it is only natural
that she should be feeling disconnected, angry, fearful, anxious, or
a host of other emotions. It helps her to know that she can ap-

proach that brink again and again to remember and still survive! This gives her confidence that she will live through this dreadful period of remembering.

She will find even more resources inside herself as she lives through the flashbacks that are likely to occur at this point. These are like flashbacks in film when the camera interrupts the flow of the narrative and jumps backward in time to show a scene from the past. Looking at photographs or reading material related to incest is a conscious attempt that can be started up or stopped at will. When the depths begin to be plumbed, however, unconscious memories begin to emerge, and these flashes can be startling. Something the woman encounters in her daily life jogs her memory in such a way that she gets a feeling — or even a full, technicolor rerun — of an event or time in her previous abuse. Because these flashbacks are so common, they need to be understood, so let us break them down into more manageable categories.

Olfactory stimuli seem to awaken especially strong flashbacks; that is, perhaps, one of the reasons that so many flashbacks occur during intercourse. Many survivors cannot bear the smell of semen; it calls up the image of abuse and horror too vividly for them to continue lovemaking.

But it may be a less obvious odor that triggers a flashback. Martha was at a family gathering when a brother-in-law came out of the bathroom having just put on some after-shave lotion. Martha recounts that she had an instant picture when she smelled the lotion: she felt herself as a child curled up in bed naked and she saw coming toward her a pair of blue shorts with something wiggling inside. She did not know what it was or whether it was alive. The picture startled Martha as an adult, and she could connect in that short moment with the confusion and fear she felt as a child waiting for her father to get to the bed where she lay. It is possible that as the abuse began Martha dissociated and so never really felt the pain as much as she did the confusion and fear of the unknown thing coming toward her in the boxer shorts, with the smell of after-shave in the air.

Tactile stimuli can trigger flashbacks, and occur often in an erotic context. Several women reported discomfort at being approached from the back. Paulette was standing at her desk when her husband came up and kissed the back of her neck. Without a moment's thought she circled and slapped him on the face. Luckily, she was able to remember that she had been abused from the back and trapped at her desk, and she could tell her startled husband that he had just taught her an important lesson about flashbacks.

Ellen and her lover enjoyed a playful and happy time together. Their mutual affection helped her to restore her lost childhood. One afternoon as they were romping on her bed, she looked over at him and suddenly his face became her father's. She screamed.

The lover or husband of a woman who is living through flashbacks needs to understand that she has no control over when they will come, and often her reaction seems senseless and surprising. Even apparently irrational preferences begin to make sense if she lets herself delve deep into her feelings. Some women cannot lie on their backs in bed, sleep in the nude, or feel any weight on their chests. Night terrors of any kind — threatening shadows and sounds; dreams that result in waking up screaming or sweating; talking and even walking in sleep — these are all events to examine carefully.

In the daytime flashbacks can be triggered from seemingly harmless sources, such as music. One survivor remembers being abused in a car with country-western music in the background. Since then, she has not been able to tolerate country-western music, and innocent Hank Snow is anathema to her.

Hard though the counsel is, a woman faced with this rush of emotion, whatever the source, must stay with the emotion and focus on its origin. "Focusing" as a technique has been much explored as a way of understanding a range of feelings and actions. In the special case of incest memory, however, it can even be sharpened and refined. Focusing is like using a telescopic lens to come closer and closer to the subject: at first the survivor has a foggy, confused feeling with perhaps a dim mental image, like a blurred photograph. Focusing then lets her draw the image up closer; as she readjusts the mental "lens" she finally can see the entire picture clearly. She can also back off if the picture becomes too painful.

Step 3: I begin to recognize my feelings. There may be sadness, anger, fear, guilt, and shame. I allow myself to experience them all.

For years she has stuffed away her feelings. Imagine continuing to deny reality and keep a secret for thirty years for fear that no one will believe you, or, if they do, feeling that they will hate you for it and find you culpable of horrendous deeds. None of this allows for open expression of emotions.

The survivor first comes to recognize and begin to deal with the feelings of shame, of being "contaminated" or "damaged." She will then feel angry about being used and abused by the perpetrator and will experience rage also at the nonprotecting parent (usually the mother).

It has been necessary for most survivors to become "feeling avoiders" to survive the childhood abuse. We all know "feeling avoiders." They are the people who have difficulty talking about themselves except on a very superficial level. Many are adept at chitchat, but the weather and their flower gardens are their only topics of conversation. Other "feeling avoiders" talk little, and they leave us to wonder what they are thinking or feeling.

As the woman dredging up her incestuous childhood begins to heal, she experiences all the feelings she repressed in childhood. Here are some examples of how these feelings manifest themselves and how the survivor learns to listen to her body.

SADNESS

Few adult survivors of incest are able to cry when they begin therapy. One woman said that she could not open the floodgate even an inch or she would certainly drown. She was certain that if she let just one tear fall, she would never be able to stop.

Many women have stopped tears so long that they do not know how to cry. To get through brutal canings in the public schools, English schoolboys used to hold their breath and even hyperventilate. Eventually the effect is to deprive the brain of oxygen and cause lightheadedness. Many survivors do much the same; they have a hard time letting go in the diaphragm area so that a sob can come out. It is physically impossible to weep when you cannot breathe. Yoga exercises or other relaxing techniques help women learn to cry.

Once women learn to weep, they seem to lose control over *when* they weep. Carol found herself sobbing helplessly as she walked down the sidewalk, and she was certain passers-by thought she was crazy. It is common for women to well up tearfully just watching television ads in which children are laughing and playing innocently. At first it is easier to weep at something else — an animal or a child — than it is to weep for oneself.

SHAME

Women experience feelings of being contaminated or damaged. "I am rotten to the very core of being" or "hopelessly imprinted with the stamp of incest" are examples of these statements of shame. One client told how she felt after hearing in the news about thirty-one hundred tons of garbage floating on a barge that had been rejected by six states and three countries. The woman said, "I felt I could identify with those tons of garbage. Who could possibly want anything to do with me if they knew what I did as a child? I was forced into inhuman acts, and that's how I feel now — inhuman. Like a pile of garbage."

ANGER, RAGE, AND FEAR

How could an adult survivor of incest *not* have anger and rage? Karen Lison reports that when she first began seeing clients with incest in their backgrounds, she did not understand why these feelings were mainly directed at the nonprotecting parent. She concluded that very often it felt safer to express anger at persons or objects *other than* the perpetrator, because his power is over-whelming. One client feared her father's rising from the dead and punishing her if she expressed the slightest degree of anger at him. These are powerful, paralyzing feelings, and the victim wants to avoid them.

GUILT

After looking back at her childhood and recognizing that the incest perhaps lasted several years, the adult survivor often asks herself why she didn't do something to *stop* the abuse when it was occurring. "Why didn't I tell someone?" is a frequent lament.

But she must remember that she is looking at her actions through an adult's eyes now. As a child, she was tricked, manipulated, and used. She was naive. She had to be: she was a child. Karen Lison offers clients twenty dollars for the name of each person they could have told who would have put an end to the abuse. She has never yet had to pay up.

Sometimes it helps clients to spend time with children who are approximately the same age as they were when the abuse began. It amazes them to see how naive and innocent they must have been and how unsophisticated children's thought processes are, compared to that of adults. Children see things differently from adults.

Karen Lison often asks clients if they hold the rapists or other sex offenders we see in the news media responsible for their behavior. Or do they see the victims as responsible? Most survivors readily find these unknown offenders to be responsible for their actions. "Then why," she asks, "do you think that you, as the victim, were guilty? And you were a minor, as well, protected by the law."

Step 4: I discuss the abuse thoroughly with my therapist. I completely re-experience and begin to deal with feelings appropriate for each incident of abuse that I can recall. I share feelings of shame with my survivors' group.

This is a scary, painful step for a survivor. It can also be scary, painful, or intolerable for the therapist. And this is why it is important, if possible, for a survivor to work with a therapist who is experienced in treating adult survivors of incest. Some therapists can honestly say, "I cannot deal with hearing the gruesome details of incest. I refer clients elsewhere." This decision must be respected. It is harder, however, to respect therapists who continue the treatment but downplay their client's need to talk about what happened because they are uncomfortable with the subject of incest. Talking about the gory details is a necessary step toward recovery. There is no going around it; the pain must be remembered and felt if the survivor is to get past it and put it behind her.

Some therapists recommend ways of reliving the memories to provide a new, more hopeful ending. This means that a memory is relived twice — first the way it happened, and second giving it a new ending. Just as in Step 2 some survivors wondered whether the pain would ever end, so in this step survivors wonder if they will have to relive the same memories over and over again. It is possible to live through *a memory* with a therapist who, together with the client, will help provide in the therapy session a new chosen ending to an old memory.

One survivor had had a dream of her family dressed in pioneer clothes in a wide field. The whole family was engaged in burying her alive. She and her therapist decided she could change that image and used a controversial technique. They put pillows together to represent her family, and using a tennis racket she was able to chop off the head of her perpetrator and soundly whack the other members of her family. She reported a sense of comfort and satisfaction after this exercise.

There are a number of other ways to begin the process of talking about and dealing with the incest. Because the experience evokes feelings of shame, clients sometimes ask if they can turn their chairs to the wall so that they need not make eye contact with their therapist. Others do better with writing out the memories and reading them aloud. Still others use poetry or art work to evoke their feelings.

Shameful feelings are difficult ones to verbalize. But if a survivor does not share them, the isolation and loneliness she experiences are harder to overcome.

Step 5: I begin to realize that I was probably acting appropriately *at the time the abuse occurred. (That is, my reactions were appropriate; the abuse was not!)*

Often women are confused about why they acted as they did during the incestuous years. They are better able to accept themselves when they begin to understand that behavior. One survivor recalls her delinquent adolescence:

> It's so much clearer to me now. I wasn't a rotten kid; I was reacting to the situation at home, hoping that *someone* would recognize that things were terribly out of whack. It's sort of like I desperately wanted someone to find out about the incest, but I couldn't come right out and tell. Of course, no one ever caught on. Then, by the time I was eighteen or nineteen they had me convinced that *I* was the bad one. And by then I had even forgotten why I started being a delinquent in the first place. I can see it clearly now.

The delinquent behavior was an understandable response and an appropriate one when the abuse was occurring, in that even criminal responses to abuse make sense. That level of hurt can result in an equally hurtful response, even though we rarely see that happen. In 1987 there was an overwhelming public outcry in favor of the Long Island, New York, girl who hired a hit man to kill her father when she learned that her sister was being incestuously violated, as she herself had been all her life. People in the general population seemed to understand such an extreme response.

As an adult, the survivor usually can accept her previous delinquent behavior as a survival skill she learned, a choice she made at a time when her choices were gravely limited. But she does not need to view herself in her juvenile days as "the bad one." There were reasons for the way she behaved then. If she had been an adult, such delinquent behavior would have been a full-blown criminal offense. When she was a minor being abused, her acting out was understandable, and she may be able forgive herself for it.

Step 6: If there was a part of the molestation that was pleasurable to me, I am coming to terms with the fact of that pleasure and I am dealing with the guilt surrounding it.

Many women spend years trying to deny that there was pleasure connected with their incestuous episodes, and then begin ever so slowly to get in touch with this realization. Not all abuse is pleasurable, of course, and many perpetrators do not care whether they hurt the child. Women who experienced pain or discomfort from the abuse may have a less complicated time getting rid of guilt than those who experienced pleasure.

Some perpetrators begin by caressing, touching, kissing, and gentle fondling. These produce pleasurable sensations. Add to this the fact that the child perhaps experiences little affection or attention from other family members, so the abuse becomes the only form of physical contact that the child receives. When the child begins to understand that this behavior from a trusted adult is inappropriate, she feels ashamed and at the same time responsible for the pleasure. After all, it is her body, isn't it? And she is asking for the pleasure, isn't she?

At some point in her healing the survivor begins to understand that, in some ways, it was *not* her body. She was not in control of her responses, even though these are responses we ordinarily think of as voluntary. *The orgasmic response in a child is not voluntary: that is the very point.* If it was important for the perpetrator that his victim be orgasmic for his own pleasure, then she was orgasmic. He physically manipulated and controlled her. She was a pawn to the perpetrator's sexual technique.

Getting in touch with "the little girl" inside is a helpful tool for dealing with the reality of that pleasure. When the survivor looks at the orgasmic response through adult eyes, she may misperceive and think that as a child she desired sex from the perpetrator because it felt good. But when she gets back in touch with the little girl she was then, she can see herself for what she was — a naive and helpless victim craving love and affection as all little girls do. And then she can understand her pleasurable responses as necessary and life saving.

Step 7: I perceive the connection between my molestation and my current behavioral patterns and relationships. I am beginning to develop some control over that connection.

There is a "point of no return" in healing. By this we mean that each survivor comes to a point where she begins to feel that her life is turning around and heading in the right direction, that she is moving toward complete recovery, and that she will never be quite the same. As one client put it, "I'm starting to see how I *allow* things to happen to me, at the same time that I blame the world for being unfair. I still *act* like a victim."

This is a powerful statement, because this woman is claiming the responsibility for her own actions. She is beginning to see that as a child, she was powerless against the abuse that was occurring, but that as an adult she has choices. As a child she could *not* have said, "So long, folks. I'm checking out of this rotten family and finding myself a new one." But today she can say, "I will not allow myself to be treated cruelly. I will not accept inappropriate behavior. I will not let myself be victimized over and over again."

Step 8: I recognize that I have a choice as to whether or not I confront my perpetrator(s).

Before a survivor considers whether or not she will confront her perpetrator(s), it is extremely important for her to understand the purpose of such a confrontation. If her goal is revenge, or getting the perpetrator to respond in a particular manner, or controlling or influencing his behavior in any way, the confrontation will probably not be a satisfying one for the survivor.

The only certain satisfaction that can be gained from confrontation is the opportunity for the survivor openly to express her feelings — whatever they are. These feelings openly expressed can "lift the weight of the world" for many women. And communicating these feelings to the guilty party who caused them can yield positive effects for her self-image. "At last," said one survivor, "I was able to verbalize what I had kept bottled up, fermenting, for thirty-two years." She went on to say, "There's nothing better for one's self-image than finding the courage to free oneself from the bondage that secrecy and withheld feelings impose on us."

For many people, the response they get to their vented feelings can evoke new ones. Many women openly express their hurt and anger to their perpetrators only to have them respond with statements that are aimed at diminishing the importance of the incest and the emotions evoked by it.

Possible responses from the perpetrator include, "You shouldn't feel that way — it was a long time ago," or "You know I never really hurt you," or "You wanted it as bad as I did." The survivor needs to be healthy enough to disengage from these responses and refuse to allow them to cloud her own success — finally being able to release feelings she had kept repressed for years. A survivors' group can be a wonderful source of support at this difficult stage of growth for some women.

Because the perpetrator can still evoke fear in many adult women, being on neutral turf with an easy escape route is a must for such survivors. Many women benefit by carefully planning the physical setting and by providing support and protection for themselves. One woman planned the confrontation in a park where she could not easily be trapped and where her father could not escape into a room and lock the door behind him. She had stationed friends around the area who, to all intents and purposes, seemed to be random picnickers, but who in reality were watching out to come to her defense if her father became violent or if she needed help.

Most important, each survivor needs to believe that confrontation is a choice, *her* choice. Whether or not to confront is her option. It is not necessary for gaining health, but if she chooses to release her emotions in that way, she can choose a safe environment to do so. The yield can be increased self-esteem.

Step 9: I am beginning to understand what I desire from relationships, as I learn to trust my perceptions.

What she herself desires from a relationship may be an issue that the survivor has never considered. Too often survivors are more concerned about what the other person's desires may be. When women are asked to review how they meet their needs, the result is often a black or white response: either they are willing to accept totally inappropriate treatment in relationships or they expect unrealistic perfection.

Over time the survivor learns what feels good and can become for her an acceptable mode of behavior. One woman says,

> I'm finally stopping myself from putting everyone and everything into airtight compartments of good and bad, white and black. I see the entire range and I know that there is no way to rigidly compartmentalize. I accept others and myself complete with flaws, and I no longer search for perfection. My relationships have changed drastically since I began learning to do this. Other people seem to sense that I accept them, and they in turn accept me. It's the only way to live for me.

The survivor begins to equip herself with the skills she missed at an early stage of development. She practices learning to trust herself. That process might begin by learning to trust just one other person, possibly her therapist.

When one person can be proven trustworthy, the survivor expands her field to other more risky situations where perhaps she has never learned the ground rules. She may need to learn how to express anger at the office and still not lose her job. She may need to learn the kinds of interpersonal skills required in a social life that includes dating.

She finally learns that she has rights, that her feelings count, and that she can let people know who she is and still be accepted and even loved. That is a great step for her.

Step 10: I am able to enjoy intimacy.

It is the feeling of shame that isolates the survivor and proves to be the roadblock to intimacy. Shame creates a fear of exposure, an unwillingness to trust others, and deep anxiety because of the need to keep the secret. Because of these manifestations of shame, the adult survivor then feels different from other people: she fears she will be abandoned if her secret is exposed, and she therefore isolates her true self from other people. She is lonely, and the vicious cycle continues, propelling her into isolation, despondency, and even profound mental illness. The illustration explains this cycle.

The only way out of shame is also the only way toward intimacy: she learns to share feelings with others. She may begin, perhaps, with an individual therapist, then members of a survivor's support group who have all experienced similar abuse. But should those opportunities not exist in her community, she can start by confiding to a therapist, counselor, or trusted friend, and then take her secret into a small but trustworthy group of people who will understand and accept her. (For more information on how to begin this process, see letter "Z" for "Zero in on building a strong support system" in Chapter 8 and the list of Helpful Organizations at the end of the book.)

The lower circle in the diagram illustrates how sharing feelings can help to end the cycle of shame so that intimacy can develop. The survivor experiences a reduction of anxiety, feels accepted by others, recognizes the resultant increase in self-esteem, feels less lonely and isolated, and, finally, finds that intimacy is possible.

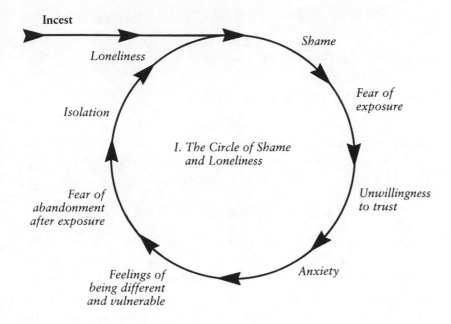

Incest

Loneliness

Shame

Isolation

Fear of
exposure

*I. The Circle of Shame
and Loneliness*

Fear of
abandonment
after exposure

Unwillingness
to trust

Feelings of
being different
and vulnerable

Anxiety

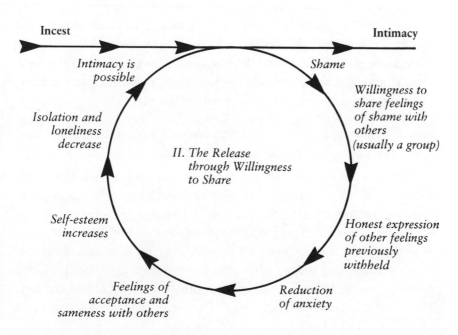

Incest

Intimacy

Intimacy is
possible

Shame

Isolation and
loneliness
decrease

Willingness to
share feelings
of shame with
others
(usually a group)

*II. The Release
through Willingness
to Share*

Self-esteem
increases

Honest expression
of other feelings
previously
withheld

Feelings of
acceptance and
sameness with others

Reduction
of anxiety

Step 11: I develop a sense of self and my self-esteem has increased.

Self-esteem cannot be gained in a vacuum. As women risk telling their stories and begin obtaining affirmation from others, their self-esteem increases.

One woman explained it this way:

> After telling my "secret" in my survivors' group, my initial response was fear and anxiety. I was certain everyone would be repulsed by me. But when I looked into the faces of my fellow group members and saw tears welling in some of their eyes, I knew they accepted me — in spite of what was done to me. Suddenly, I began to see it in those terms — the abuse was *done to me;* I did not *do* it.

Affirmations from others need follow-up by the survivor if she is to increase her self-esteem. The "doormat" perhaps needs to take an assertiveness training class. The "wimp" stands up for herself in an argument. The "victim" sets limits and boundaries. A good beginning rule is to say "no" out loud to someone or to some plan at least three times in one week. When women learn that they can say "no" to something they do not want, they learn that their feelings, their very selves count for something. They are no longer child victims who have few choices. They are adults who risk and take chances. This sense of courage leads a woman away from victimization and toward healthy self-esteem.

Step 12: My resistance to talking about the abuse (although not necessarily the details of it) has diminished.

Most survivors remember clearly the first time they told their secret. "My face turned blood red and my heart rate soared," is how many characterize the feeling of that initial revelation. But each time a woman trusts and carefully reveals her pain to appropriate, caring, and supportive people, the physical reactions become milder. Says one survivor, "I enjoy watching myself now. It's encouraging for me to see that I can talk about my abuse without all the pain I used to feel."

A kind of desensitization occurs. The survivor is no longer in the grip of shame, which formerly diminished and devalued her.

Step 13: I realize that I have a choice as to whether or not I forgive my perpetrator. I have forgiven myself.

Forgiveness is a complicated issue, however we look at it, whether psychologically or in terms of religion. It is also the one term thrown at survivors all the time, so that many come to hate and even reject the concept.

It may be useful to define what forgiveness is *not*. To forgive is not to forget, to sweep memory and anger under a rug and pretend that they never existed. Survivors should reject this simple-minded, but all too common, use of the word. In fact, a survivor can never truly forgive until she remembers the crimes done against her and until she experiences the rage and upset that she could not express at the time the incest happened.

Forgiveness is not passive and sweet. Here we are burdened with a much simplified notion of Christian forgiveness, that we must not judge and must be quick to forgive. People who cite the Bible can find all sorts of justifications, like "Judge not that ye be not judged"; "Cast not the first stone"; "Turn the other cheek"; and "Go the second mile."

Survivors who are Christian need not be put off by selectively chosen passages from Scripture that seem to equate meekness and passivity with forgiveness and goodness. The Jesus who emerges in the Gospels, after all, expresses anger at wrongdoing and as aggressively fights evil as He preaches love.

Nor can forgiveness be conferred — even by the clergy. Forgiveness comes inside each human heart, and there is no way a third party can pronounce a word and make it happen.

Forgiveness is, rather, an opportunity for maturation and growth for the survivor. After remembering and weeping and confessing to herself and others the hurt she has felt and how that hurt has made her act, a survivor is ready to forgive herself. She did not ask for the incest. She is not a bad person because it happened. She is innocent of that charge.

She does need to take responsibility for any wrongdoing she committed against others as an adult that may have happened because of the incest. Perhaps she hurt her children because she herself had been hurt, or she found herself unable to love and tried to give pain and injury to those who wanted to love her. She accepts what she has done, experiences remorse and anguish for those actions, and resolves to change.

She forgives herself by giving away her anger and pain and letting it go, probably to God, who, after all, is a much better judge of how the perpetrator ought to be punished than she is.

Forgiveness is really a matter of giving up a burden and being able to stand up straighter afterward.

Step 14: I am in touch with past anger, but detached from it so that it is not a constant part of my feelings and a negative influence on my other emotions, my functioning, and my relationships with others. I no longer live in the past. I live in the present and welcome the future with all its fears, imperfections, and unpredictabilities.

The cloud begins to lift. It has been such a long, slow process that it is hard to articulate an exact moment of change, but the weight of the world seems to fall from her shoulders. One woman expressed it this way:

> I see myself as being better able to accept the day-to-day difficulties that occur in my life. I used to fly off the handle, then regret it afterward. Now I can step outside myself and observe the discomfort building. Then I allow myself to feel it, and then, and only then, can I act to manage my feelings. My anger from the past doesn't interfere with today. I can separate the two and distinguish the difference between them. I can manage today without the burden of yesterday's pain.

Other women feel that a sort of grieving process has been completed at last. The past suffering has been put to rest. Only now can the survivor choose to let go of the pain. Only now can she accept life's imperfections and marvel at its beauty. Only now can she accept that fear is human, that life is unpredictable, and that she wants to go on living to feel both joy and sorrow.

8

Recovery: Reclaiming
Our Lives

I T WAS *a golden day in October when I terminated my therapy.
I had been at it, all told, six years.*

*It was also nearly Halloween, that short season of spooks and
ghosts and "things that go bump in the night." The calendar
seemed right. It was a time not to purge myself of fear but rather
to recognize it, name it, and celebrate it. Traditionally, "All Hal-
lows Eve" is the time that the dead come out of their graves, and
we have given the day sinister and frightening symbols that em-
body fear: bats screeching out of haunted houses, jagged-toothed
lanterns, black cats that make bad luck, ghouls that come back to
terrorize the living.*

*Yes, Halloween was a good time for me to memorialize fear, for
fear has been my life's companion, dark, heavy fear that rested like
a lump on my back. I have always lived with fear: fear that I
would be hurt, fear that if I stepped out of line I would be killed,
fear that I was not perfect, fear that if others saw me for what I
really was, they would despise me. Green, wretched fear that never
lifted.*

*I have, however, been at the business of naming my fears, and
when I see them face to face, I can see that they are Halloween
spooks, frightening in the dark, but really rather modest when
seen in the light of day. How had the fear lifted?*

For one thing, I had been confronting fears in therapy and beating them with a very large stick to make them smaller. Our children once had a book called Brian and the Terrible Whatsis, *in which a small boy is forced to confront the Whatsis, a hairy, horned monster who lives in the basement behind the furnace. One day the little boy misses his mother, and, fearing that she has been harmed by the beast, summons the courage to go to the basement and confront it. He finds it, ugly as sin, sitting on the washing machine, and he takes a broomstick and begins chasing and hitting it. The Whatsis cries for mercy, but the little boy persists, and the Whatsis gets smaller with every whack until it becomes so tiny and absurd that the little boy wonders why he was ever afraid of it. And he opens the basement door to find his mother picking flowers in the back yard.*

I have been beating my own Whatsis down to size. I have forced myself to confront fears. I have even put them into a book. Putting things down on paper and letting others read them is a way of putting them into perspective. The word is powerful in that respect.

But alongside the process of knocking fear down to size has been the job of building from within. The journey has been like that on the Yellow Brick Road, where Dorothy and her companions start out seeking a magical solution to their problems, then find along the road all they were searching for: the straw-stuffed Scarecrow gets brains by having to invent a route to the Emerald City, the heartless Tin Woodman gets a heart by exercising love, and the Cowardly Lion acquires courage by defending his friends. At the end of the film version, it only remains for the Wizard of Oz to pin a cardboard decoration on each. Not even the Great Oz can bestow spiritual gifts; they must be built out of what was already there.

At a certain point my journey became a building from within rather than a search for a magical solution. When I began therapy I felt much like a fortified castle with walls two feet thick protecting nothing inside but a void, a nothingness. I felt hollow, fright-

ened all the time. What lay within seemed a blank, a white place.

The change came when I confronted a little girl inside me and realized that I was not hollow. One day I was sobbing, remembering myself from a first-grade picture that I held in front of me. My therapist said gently, "And how does the little girl feel?"

"Cold," I sobbed, "cold and lonely."

Until that moment that little girl had been separate from me. I adopted her right then and there. I grabbed her as a mother would and hugged her until she became mine, until she became me.

And I nurtured the little girl who nestled inside my breast by trying to listen to her needs. My therapist suggested ways to warm us both, because finally the little girl and I had become the same and our needs were the same. I don't mean that I had become a six-year-old girl, only that her feelings became part of me, and I found myself responding to the world in the best possible way, through the eyes of a child. I was vulnerable and I could be hurt, but I could also see the world in its freshness.

Gradually I began to feel myself as solid, with a center.

I began keeping a spiritual journal during Advent, the beginning of the liturgical year and the season of preparation for Christmas four weeks later. I wrote what I felt, fear as well as joy, growth as well as setback. As I look over that journal now I see warm and cold as a theme, and I see how I began to achieve that inner warmth so necessary for survival. The Christmas story is the coming of light, hope, and good will into the world. Its emblems are a radiant child warmly wrapped, tended by a loving mother. Outside are angels and a star lighting up a dark sky.

I let the light and warmth glow and grow. Spring came. I am a gardener, and I see that the metaphors in the journal begin to turn to growth: seeds germinating in dark ground, reaching for light. Tender sprouts emerging, fragile at first and easy to trample and flatten, become strong plants under the summer sun. Oppressive heat and drought are gifts of their own, for they create deep roots, *the kind that come from any adversity; they are what distinguish the showy annual flowers from the deep-growing perennials that last through all seasons, even the cold of winter.*

My whole world was changing. And that was when the fear began to lift, although I did not notice it at the time.

My father was dead, had been for a decade. He was no longer able to kill me, although I had felt the weight of the dead hand from beyond a grave, a weight and a fear that said, "If you ever tell, you will be destroyed."

Finally, I decided to kill him — figuratively, of course, for the rest of the world thought he was dead. I wrote about my hurt; I told my secret to all my family; I shook my fist at him and called him names; I dreamt about him. In one memorable dream I was waiting in the alley at the back of my house with my local police officers in their orange and white squad cars to arrest him for his crime against me. Sure enough, up the alley came a blue sedan with my mother driving, and he got out looking small and timid, and his hands were manacled in front of him. The dream ended with my mother coming forward to argue with the officers that he should not be arrested.

I began to remember the good things about him. In my gray and grim childhood he was the only one who sang and played the harmonica. He spun yarns and told stories so riveting that I can hear them still. When I entered the spelling bee year after year, he was the one who coached me with long lists of words to spell aloud. When I won a contest and called home with the news, he wept over the phone. He loved me. A twisted, harmful, evil, and bizarre thing his love was, but he did love me. It felt okay to admit that.

My mother was a different matter. She was alive, and I had never had any desire to kill or hurt her, since she had not been the one abusing me. What I had always wanted from her was love, warmth, acceptance, motherly protection.

I finally realized I would never have those things from her. In a sense I forgave her, as I had forgiven my father. I speak only for myself, but for me forgiveness happened when I no longer gave them the power to hurt me. I decided not to ask any longer for the things she could not — or would not — provide. Why keep knocking at a locked door of an empty house?

I was not wrong to want love, warmth, acceptance, and protection. I had just been seeking it in the wrong places. So I began looking for mothering, nurturing elsewhere — a sort of composite mother made up of the gifts of many people. I belong to church groups where I have found rich mothering in the older church-women. I have a novelist friend who corrects my prose and calls me long distance to give encouragement. My children mother me without our acting out a role reversal: my older daughter takes me shopping and, with a teenager's energy and enthusiasm for clothes, leads me through the maze of racks and dressing rooms to find pretty things to wear. My younger daughter is the kind to slip her arm around my waist and kiss me on the nose for no reason at all — rather the way a mother would rumple a child's hair and smile a smile that says, "I love you just the way you are." Friends mother me, both male and female friends, by telling me I am funny or well organized or a good leader. And they take me to lunch and give me birthday gifts — I who never had a birthday cake at home and never had a party.

My husband does not so much mother me as befriend me. He is my companion day in and day out. From him I have finally learned some trust in men, and from him I am learning the depth and pleasure that a love between man and woman can offer. It has required patience and love on both our parts.

I have begun to trust the world and many of the people in it. When I have fear and hurt, I am usually able to discern whether and how it relates to the dreadful past. Reclaiming my life has meant putting past together with present, melding all the pieces of my life together into one, and accepting that person for what she was, is, and will be. For I must always remember that I carry within me a little girl who was hurt, humiliated, and abused. She will always be there, and she must be attended to as I move

*through the seasons and through the years, in times of mirth and
times of sorrow. That little girl and I are one.*

· ✳ · ✳ ·

WE conclude this story of adult survivors of incest with three vignettes, followed by a list of survival techniques gleaned from a
wide spectrum of survivors. Each of the following stories is real,
although names, dates, and places have been changed. Each shows
an adult woman who has put her life together after childhood incest. All are over the age of forty; all have long histories of abuse;
all have wrestled with the issues we have discussed in this book.
All have lived with their pain and learned finally how to integrate
it into the fabric of their lives, transmuting hurt into courage,
translating suffering into triumph.

Four Stories of Courage

Ruth has just ordered quiche and a salad for lunch. We have
met at a pleasant restaurant near the religious bookstore she tries
to visit whenever she has a day off. Today her browsing has
paid off, and she has picked up three little books for her new
nephew — one a "touch and feel" book, one a book of nursery
rhymes, and one a cloth book about animals. For herself she has
purchased a book about spiritual journeys, a modern *Pilgrim's
Progress*. She will begin reading it tomorrow, she says. Ruth reads
daily and meditates every morning to keep her mind straight and
her spiritual life in order.

In her remaining spare time she writes poetry and short stories.
She has limited spare time, however, because she holds a high
management post at a major corporation. Having been a responsible and capable employee over the years, she now finds herself
at age forty-eight with a healthy income, a secure future, and a
comfortable life.

She is learning to deal with the pain of her past. We have already
heard a part of her story. Ruth's mother abandoned her emotion-

ally to care for Ruth's younger brother, who was handicapped and required constant care and frequent hospitalizations. Ruth took care of her alcoholic father, going to the bar to bring him home for dinner, then putting him to bed before her mother returned home. He raped her violently when she was eleven. Ruth came out of poverty, degradation, a loveless and abusive environment.

And still she sits before us, smiling gently, her graying hair in an attractive cut, her jeans and shirt showing her relaxed mood on a day off. Her adult life has been no picnic. Her first marriage was to a man with whom she had two children. Routinely, after he had sex with Ruth he went to the bathroom to throw up. She thought it was because she was ugly; that is, until the day she came home from work and found him in bed with a man.

Her second marriage was to an alcoholic who rapidly went through the family's meager financial resources and hinted one day that Ruth could help the family income a bit if she would agree to sleep with an acquaintance of his for money. She agreed, for the family was in dire straits. The one-time favor became a habit, the habit became a profession, and her prostitution bought not only food for the family but a boat for the husband and plenty of booze. The marriage ended abruptly and dramatically when she learned that her second husband had sexually abused her then teenaged daughter. She left the marriage and refused to come back to the molesting stepfather even after he had gone through an alcoholic treatment program. He continued to harass her, however, often sitting in his car outside her apartment or calling her in the middle of the night to threaten her.

She raised her children. She got her education at night school, and finally got herself promoted to a job in which the pay was good and the advancement rapid. Then at age forty she went into therapy and began to put her past into perspective. She has had long-term lovers but wants no more of marriage.

And tonight she and a group of her friends from ACOA (Adult Children of Alcoholics), all her age, are planning a pajama party.

They are going to a nice hotel as a group — just "the girls" — and they are going to wear baby-doll pajamas and take teddy bears and have lots of Coca-Cola and chips and old teen music. They are looking forward to getting back a little of the lightheartedness of childhood that they missed.

• ✳ • ✳ •

THE two women sit in the beautifully decorated living room of a North Shore home. We are sipping apricot tea and nibbling Girl Scout cookies as we chat.

Charlene and Celeste have been friends for nearly two decades. Their husbands were business associates, so they saw each other often at parties and dinners. Celeste is a music teacher, and Charlene has come to her recitals for years. They have visited the Art Institute on a regular basis together and attended downtown concerts and chatted the afternoons away. Each is fifty-five years old, but it was only a year ago that Celeste had the courage to say to Charlene, "You know, my father molested me when I was a child." To which Charlene replied, "So did mine." And they hugged.

And now they are speaking about the effects of that molestation at length, for the first time, to each other in our presence. Their replies complement each other; they are refined, soft-spoken, educated, and literate women, and as they talk they are quietly courteous and show verbally and with smiles the support each feels for the other and the respect they have for their years of friendship.

Charlene's father was a con man; he spent time in prison for grand larceny, but was able to wangle a pardon. When he got out, he continued to dupe people, but he kept himself out of the hands of the law. It was when Charlene was ten, and he had been released and pardoned, that she went to live with him. He abused her whenever he could until her mother divorced him and took the children to live with her.

Her mother was an alcoholic, as Charlene now sees, and the outrageously dysfunctional behavior of both parents made her determined to live an absolutely "normal," morally upright, and prosperous life. She chose carefully a man who was able to give her money, privilege, and a good name.

But as an adult she was hounded by her past, even though she tried to deny it. "I faced confusion," she says. "Who do you tell? You don't tell. You pretend that you're a Middle Western housewife, practically a virgin, and you hold yourself together the best you can. In the meantime, I drank."

Eight years ago Charlene faced up to her drinking problem and joined Alcoholics Anonymous. The first time she admitted the incest was when she had reached the Fifth Step ("Admit to God, to ourselves, and to another human being the exact nature of our wrongs"). She went to an experienced priest to confess; the priest was himself a recovering alcoholic, and he was the one who told her that the incest was a major problem that she should confront in individual therapy.

In these eight years Charlene has realized that her years of smiling, acting pleasant, and pretending that nothing was wrong had also been a time in which she had let herself be betrayed, put upon, and victimized again and again. "I had been bottling it, stuffing it for years," she says. As she grows spiritually, she is able to resist revictimization.

Celeste understands and nods. Celeste's father was a member of a stern religious sect, so that she felt set apart as a young person both because of the incest and because her family was "unusual." The incest began when she was ten and continued until she was fourteen. "I finally was able to tell him to leave me alone, and he pretty much did," she says. She had learned that he was keeping a mistress, and threatened that she would disclose that fact to her mother if he continued to molest her. "My mother did learn, later, about the mistress, but not from me," she says, "but the point was that I was able to use that information to control him, and I did."

Celeste and her husband have raised four children. She has given music lessons and performed for various civic functions all her life; now she has begun to compose music. She has used her music as therapy, but she has also found a way to deal with the pain by way of religion and forgiveness. "I have prayed and tried to be kind to my father," she says. "It is part of my nature to be that way, although I can show anger too." Celeste's father, now dead, had tried to make a pass at one of Celeste's daughters. When her daughter told her about it, she went to her father, reprimanded him sharply, and then told her daughters never to be alone with the man.

Celeste has decided not to seek therapy. She believes she has managed the problem well all her adult life, and she is ready now for a life of quiet retirement and inner creativity. She says to women younger than she, "Accept yourself as a person God created and know that what happened was not your fault. Rid yourself of the feeling you were to blame, and remember that we all need forgiveness."

Charlene's advice is that of a woman who has been struggling with alcoholism for years. It is, "Go and get good help. Somebody you can trust. The turning point for me was getting it all out. If you start early, you don't need to bring all this to your later years, which should be happy ones."

· ✳ · ✳ ·

LOIS is a therapist. Before she undertook her therapy training she had a career in Christian education, having taken an advanced theological degree from a respected seminary many years ago. At age forty, her world came apart when she recalled that her father, himself a profoundly religious man and a respected mainstay of the church in her community, had sexually abused her.

Lois is a comfortable and friendly woman, attractive in a gentle and warm way. She smiles at the paradox of how her life has turned out. She left the church in anger nearly a decade ago, and now, after a struggle and complete turnabout, she finds herself running symposia and seminars for clergy about abused women. "I go to groups in churches, although I am not part of any organized religion, because I know how to help them," she says. "The clergy is a target market. They need to know about this, and they want to know."

If anyone could teach the clergy, it would be Lois. Not only her therapy degree and her theological study but her experience as a survivor has taught her a thing or two about healing. She was forty years old before she recalled the sexual abuse, and her father was by that time old and ill. Still, her rage was such that when she went home to be with her dying mother, she thought she might kill her father. She locked herself into her room that night, but she woke up frightened that she might have unconsciously gotten up in the night and strangled the old man.

Her parents died three and a half weeks apart, and Lois was left with her rage. "I wrote him letters," she says, "and I talked to him at the graveside. I wish I had been healed enough to confront him when he was alive." But she accepts that she was not and that she did the best she could to get the anger out.

She speaks of the biggest issues in her life. "It was the loss of my fantasy family that shook me up the most. Everyone came to our house to play. We were the perfect ones, the church-going 'normal' family. I finally had to accept that my family was not perfect."

She also had to learn to handle the rage and anger that ensued. "Anger was not acceptable at my house. And it certainly was not acceptable to be angry with God!" More recently, she has realized that her two brothers do not understand the depth of her rage and possibly never will.

Lois knows who she is and where she is, and that includes areas in which she definitely wants to see some improvement. "I am miles away from a sexual relationship," she says, although she is heartened that she is taking the first courageous steps in the direction she wants to go. She is joining singles groups where there are men serious about marriage and commitment, and she is beginning to date.

She had wanted children. Now she has accepted that she will never have them, but she has mourned her loss and done what she could to replace some of the pain. "I have my nieces and nephews and friends' children," she says, and she sees the relationships as good for the children. "I can listen to them about things that their parents can't hear," she says, "and they can come to my house and be themselves. I have decided to be a first-rate aunt."

She has learned that she is responsible for herself.

She has learned also that forgiving is a process. "I may have forgiven him, my father, I'm just not sure. What I do know is that it doesn't ruin my life any more, and that is a sign that forgiveness has taken place."

Lois is taking her message of healing to others who do not know as well as she how much it hurts, how the healing can happen, and how to accept the fact that life is not fair.

The ABCs of Recovery: Taking Care of Yourself

Accepting oneself as an incest survivor also means accepting that the wound left a scar that will always be with one. Survivors learn to live with that wound. When it begins to hurt, they accept where the hurt comes from and find the way to care for it.

We are not, by and large, talking about dramatic or earthshaking events. There are certainly periods of intense suffering in recovery that would be unbearable if they lasted a lifetime. But more likely we have to face the pain that comes in little ways, the daily fare of survival. And it is probably a lifelong process, this recognizing the hurt and learning to heal in specific ways. One incest survivor, now in her fifties, when asked what her main struggles were at this point in life, replied, "Stay tuned; they change every day."

It is unrealistic to expect that survivors will completely get over this hurt. What they learn to do is to live with it as its power over them diminishes with time. And as they live and practice courage, kindness, and hope, there are more or less helpful ways to look at life. We listened to survivors talk about what helps most and found that we had a list of recovery tips so basic that they were a veritable alphabet of how to live. So we have called them the ABCs.

These tips are not useful for everyone all the time. But they point to ways of coping gleaned from many women's lives, lives rebuilt and reclaimed after the devastation of incest. We offer them less in the spirit of prescription than of suggestion, less for cure than for optimism and hope. They come from the experts, incest survivors themselves.

A. Ask for what you want; say "no" to what you don't want.

The failure to say out loud exactly what we need is not a condition limited to survivors; many people expect to have their minds read. We think that relatives, friends, or co-workers can pick up brain waves, guess what we want, and provide it.

Determining what we want and need is, of course, the first issue. Survivors have had so much practice at denying, at putting others' needs ahead of their own, that it is often hard work for them to find out what they need.

And it is often even harder work to open their mouths and tell people exactly what they want — and what they don't want. But the rewards are manifest when they do. "Please don't touch me that way," says a wife to her startled husband, who perhaps never knew it made any difference. "I feel sensitive about that; I need more gentleness."

"I need some time alone right now" or "What I really want is a warm hug" is a request that helps establish the boundaries that either never existed or were consistently violated in the past. One statement says, "Stay away for now," and the other says, "Please come near." Both are valuable messages. And learning to say it — and to hear yourself say it — is the most valuable message of all.

B. Beauty — Open your eyes to it!

To open our eyes to beauty — whether it be a sunset, a painting, a beautifully decorated room, children at play — is to affirm goodness. Survivors were subjected to tawdry, brutal, ugly events during their childhoods. When they stand back from those humiliating, shame-giving episodes and look at beauty, they can see that the world is good. They feel more whole. Their lives need not be shadowed by the ugly past. If we let ourselves be surrounded by dirt and ugliness as adults, we say something about the way we feel ourselves and our bodies to be. If, on the other hand, we let in beauty, we are affirming something about our own essential beauty and goodness.

For many survivors, collecting or other hobbies help affirm their sense of beauty. Barbara likes antique furniture because, she explains, it has been chipped and damaged over time, but its beauty still shines through. It, too, has survived! Marguerite collects crystal because its fragility and purity appeal to her. She dusts it carefully and likes to watch the light gleam through it. Another survivor collects quilts because she thinks of the quilt's creator making block by block the colored squares, then stitching them all together. It reminds her of how she assembles her own life. Sometimes her life feels like a "crazy quilt," a jumble of color and fabric scraps, but she thinks that crazy quilts are beautiful too. An older survivor, a native of France, told us that when her life becomes too stressful, she returns to Paris where, she says, "I bathe myself in culture and beauty."

Beauty is where we find it — an iris in a vase, a trip to the art gallery, a walk in the woods. As we look and drink in beauty, we are nurtured, and that is strengthening and good.

C. Cry.

Survivors have a lot of grieving to do, and they need to cry. Tears, of course, express more than sorrow, and grief is a complex emotion with many stages. Behind tears can lie rage and anger, frustration and confusion, or just plain sadness that we never had a real childhood. All survivors experience these emotions at one time or another, and tears can be a good way to vent those feelings.

Some women choose the times and kinds of crying. Ruth found relief in crying and pounding on the earth of her father's grave when she visited it. Lillian dealt with much of her anger by going outside alone on her patio at night and shaking her fist at the sky, crying and calling her father obscene names.

But more than likely, the tears will be unbidden. In every survivors' group, tears come regularly and often without much apparent reason. They serve as a release, and we do not need always to understand rationally what is being relieved.

Many survivors find themselves embarrassed momentarily when they "mist over" or cry at movies, television shows, or some other event that seems to have little to do with incest. Perhaps the occasion is a portrayal of innocent childhood or perhaps it is some sorrow so hidden that the survivor herself cannot connect with it. But those of us who are survivors must be gentle with ourselves; we are mourning a lost childhood, and may need to feel sad at times. Just as you would not deny tears to a person who has just lost a loved one, neither should you deny yourself tears for a lost childhood — that grief, too, is real.

D. *"Do it scared."*

We speak a lot about having courage and taking risks — constant traveling companions of the survivor of incest. But courage actually lived out might better be described as "doing it scared," for that is a more accurate description of what happens.

It wouldn't be risk if the choice were obvious and easy. And so what survivors are trying is something new, and that is just plain scary; our fears are often legitimate because we fear revictimization. But we are not suggesting huge leaps that would only prove survivors to be foolhardy superwomen. What we are talking about is listening to our inner voice and carefully weighing the outcome of a situation first, and *then* deciding the course of action. We might ask ourselves, "What is the worst that could happen?" Then we plunge ahead, trembling and quaking. And when we have come to the end, we'll know we've survived again, and the next time will be a bit easier.

Sara was afraid of the city; she was secure enough on the streets in the suburban village where she lived and worked, but city streets and people sent terror into her heart. So she made herself call and get bus information. With map in hand, she rode to the downtown, disembarked, walked to the zoo, had lunch at a hot dog stand, visited a feminist bookstore, then rode home later in the afternoon. She conquered most of her fear, and had a wonderful day. She felt good about the sense of competency she experienced and next time the ride was easier.

Carol was fearful of fast expressway traffic, but she wanted mobility, and she needed to learn to manage this part of her life. So she made herself drive to all kinds of places in all kinds of weather, even though her husband was usually willing to transport her. What she now experiences is less fear than a healthy respect for traffic dangers.

The fears that bedevil most survivors are the minor phobias that hinder us from leading regular lives and keep us from enjoying life and having access to those growth experiences that could deepen our self-esteem.

To conquer those fears, nothing can beat "doing it scared."

E. Exercise.

We don't need a book about incest survivors to tell us that a program of regular physical exercise is good for the body. Everybody — from Cher to the AMA — is already telling us that.

So why are we bringing it up?

A big reason is that exercise for survivors can be the *wrong* kind and can put us at peril. Our society does not help us in this matter very well at all; we are shown starved and emaciated bodies as symbols of good health for women, and crazy, obsessive behavior labeled as "serious exercise."

Some survivors struggle with the notion of perfection — perfect bodies — and exert strict control over eating and exercise to obtain that image of thinness portrayed in our fat-obsessed media and advertising industry. Exercise regimens undertaken to reach physical perfection do us no good and may even be harmful to our overall sense of self.

Others are obese or have a hard time taking care of their physical selves, and the images of health and fitness seem such an impossible goal that they give up even trying, so distant does the end result appear.

We need to reject those messages that say "Burn, baby, burn," or "It has to hurt," or "No pain, no gain." Why should a survivor, whose whole life was filled with such pain, want to hook into messages such as these? There has been quite enough pain, thank you.

Survivors can send their own messages. Sensible goals include energy, vitality, good health, and physical and mental well-being. Physical exercise can be built into the daily regimen, but it must be the kind that offers pleasure, nurturing, and care. It might be a brisk walk each day, taking time to stop to smell the lilacs or watch the children play hopscotch. Walking or biking to work or deciding to take the stairs instead of the elevator are excellent choices. Working on an exercise bike can be made pleasant by watching television or even reading a book while doing it.

The benefits are many. We start to feel our bodies; just having aching muscles reminds us that we *have* bodies! As our bodies grow more "physical," we feel more attractive and our esteem grows as we know we are taking care of the "temples" that house our souls.

F. Food and healthy eating.

Like exercise, food is an issue for survivors that is complicated by the attitudes of society at large. What society shows us is only that thin is good; it does not address the issue of *how we get thin*. Abusing food is a way that we hurt rather than help ourselves. Many of us are less interested in the food itself and the wholesome good it can do us than we are in distraction from feelings we get from stuffing ourselves and then forcing vomiting. Adhering to a diet designed to make us thin as rails but lacking essential nutrients focuses more on control than on the benefits of food.

Again, survivors need to ignore the crazy standards of "thin is beautiful, no matter how you get there," and set out a nurturing way to achieve good health. Eating nutritious meals is a way of affirming that our bodies are worth attention. Evidence is all around that a high-fiber, low-fat diet helps secure maximum health and prevent disease. Jane Brody's *Good Food Book* is a sane and helpful discussion of the issue and provides wonderful recipes for a high-carbohydrate, satisfying form of eating.

But there are also "comfort foods," dishes that make us feel nurtured and that we can use for the times we want to connect food with love. One cookbook says about these foods, "There is food for the body and food for the soul. One keeps you alive, the other makes you happy. . . . These foods have magical healing properties that no doctor or chemist could concoct." One survivor's grandmother was the caring person her mother was not. When the young girl came to her grandmother's house, Grandma offered a big slice of homemade bread, cut fresh from a loaf she held to her ample bosom as she cut. She topped it with homemade butter and preserves. It should be no surprise that nothing comforts that woman, years later, like a slice of warm homemade bread.

The oldest standby in the comfort category is surely chicken soup. Its aroma and taste suggest a loving mother in the kitchen, tending her sick children with maternal tenderness — a far cry from how many survivors experienced their own mothers. But the soup calls up the image, and one can be comforted by it.

Homemade breads and muffins fall into this category as well and, as Jane Brody points out, can be highly nutritional. Custard, rice pudding, birthday cake and ice cream, hot cocoa — each survivor has her list, and she can indulge herself in that food when the situation calls for it; when she eats it, she will know she is being comforted.

Of course, desserts feel best of all to many of us, and there is absolutely no reason to punish ourselves by staying away from them entirely. What is life without an occasional hot fudge sundae or a slice of cheesecake? There are many worse things we can do to ourselves.

Our biggest foe can be mindless stuffing with fast food, tasting nothing, hoping to feel nothing, and sedating ourselves against our pain just as surely as if we were drinking alcohol or taking drugs. Being aware that food is a big issue, working at remembering that fact, and then setting about making wise and comfortable choices helps most of all.

G. Gray areas and how to accept them.

The healthier survivors become, the more they realize that the choices offered them are less often black or white than a deep rich shade of gray. There is right and wrong, good and evil in the world, but they come in mixed packages and deceptive wrappings.

Survivors are often confused in their feelings about the incest. If they could just dismiss all the acts of all the years as bad and their perpetrators as evil, it would be so much easier. It is ambiguity that is difficult. One can hate the incest and feel its hurt and, possibly at the same time, remember caring about the perpetrator. We shake our heads and say it cannot make sense, but in fact many survivors end up hating the sin and still feeling some love for the sinner.

How can we live with such split feelings? By doing some packaging of our own. We can wrap the bad feelings, evil actions, and clear wrongdoing into a garbage bag and put those feelings out to be thrown into the incinerator. But if there were any good feelings, kind actions, or affection, we need not throw those away into the same garbage bag.

Many women are convinced that, despite the incest, their perpetrators truly loved them. There is nothing to be gained by throwing away memories of true affection or genuine attentiveness and support if they occurred.

If your past is pure, unadulterated evil, feel free to call it that. But if you feel confusion about the presence of some good, why not keep and cherish those feelings? Many of us have precious few good feelings from our past, so being kind to ourselves means not throwing away anything positive that we can hold to our breasts and be glad about. And perhaps in dealing with our incestuous pasts in this manner, we can extend our understanding of the deep, rich shades of gray to other areas of our lives where previously we rigidly compartmentalized everything into black or white.

H. Hug.

There is nothing like a hug to communicate affection, warmth, and nurturing. It is the best nonthreatening way for survivors to assure themselves — and be assured *by* others — that they are good people, deserving of love.

Much has been written about the psychology of touch, and survivors moving toward health will be experimenting with what feels good and what feels bad. And they are learning to communicate with others about how touch affects them — from sexual touch to handholding to embraces.

But a hug is a lot less subtle than other touches. It is a whole-body affirmation to the other that we are glad she exists, that she is valuable and good, and that we like connecting with her.

Survivors may want to learn both to give hugs and to receive them. One survivor remarked after a television show about child abuse that she kept wanting the caseworker on television to give the child a hug. The survivor identified with the little girl and felt that the child needed to be hugged and told she was not a bad girl.

When we receive hugs, the child within responds. As children, our boundaries were trespassed all the time. Private places were exposed and hurt by the abuser; he or others may have hit or beat us; family members may have scapegoated us and called us names. Many survivors felt humiliated and ashamed themselves because of what *others* did.

What all children want is to be hugged and told they are wonderful, to be told they are loved no matter what. That didn't happen to many survivors when they were children. They can let it happen now as adults.

I. "I-language."

Survivors need to get in touch with their own feelings and at the same time to resist being told by others who they are and how they feel. "Owning our feelings" is a discipline learned over time, but survivors can help themselves along immensely by saying "I" when they mean their own selves.

"I-language" is harder than it sounds. It is so much easier to say "someone" or "a person" or even "you" when we mean to say "I." Here is an example. "I feel hurt by what you said" communicates something far different from "You are always saying such hurtful things." We all need to step inside our language, make it say what we mean, and then stand firmly behind it.

People around us may react with surprise or even displeasure. In our culture we have grown accustomed to language that evades the truth and points the finger away from ourselves. What, after all, would happen if people in business and politics began to practice brutal honesty and linguistic clarity? When we try to be more honest about ourselves, we will begin to observe how others use language to obscure the truth and to remove themselves from responsibility.

As children, many survivors were treated as if they didn't exist. Those of us who are survivors need to recapture our feelings, to stand up and say "I" when we mean our own selves. Then there is no longer any doubt that we exist and that we have feelings that we need and want to call our very own.

J. Journal keeping.

"Keeping a journal" sounds a little frightening to those of us for whom writing is a difficult chore. Some people do not communicate easily on the written page. To others, writing is easier than talking, and writing that is entirely private is one of the best therapies available.

What is so useful about actually writing things down, especially if it does not come easily? First of all, a journal is *written,* a record that you can go back to read. Dreams and flashbacks are both parts of the incest puzzle that come together more quickly when you record them. You can tie up loose ends, pick out important images and words, and, finally and most important, witness your own progress, day to day or week to week.

There is also the fact that writing can be cathartic. Since no one else is reading the journal, you can draw pictures, create poetry, even swear. For those who have trouble expressing anger verbally, a big "FUCK YOU" on the written page is immensely satisfying. It gets the anger out and doesn't hurt anyone.

In a fine film about child sexual abuse called *Breaking the Silence,* one of the survivors remembers writing "flowers, flowers, flowers!" in her journal. She was unable to understand why she was moved to write those words until she visited her parents' home and wandered into the bedroom where she saw the flowered wallpaper. As a child she had lost herself in the flowers on the wallpaper to escape the pain while her father abused her. It was the journal that helped provide the connection for her.

Another benefit needs to be mentioned. So-called "writer's block" is also usually a "feeling block." A person who cannot write may be having trouble expressing feelings. And conversely, making yourself write can help unclog those feelings and get the juices running again.

Journals help us recognize progress. Many survivors gain tremendous satisfaction by occasionally taking the time to read past entries in their journals. It becomes crystal clear how far they have come on their healing journey. One survivor reported that she felt terribly frustrated by the lack of progress she felt she was making. Upon reviewing her journals from past years, however, she was encouraged by the tremendous changes she had made. She had to look at the past to put her present state in such a positive light.

K. Kick a pillow.

Anger and rage are healthy responses to the way survivors were treated as children. They were subjected to outrageous adult behavior, absolutely unjustified on *any* grounds.

But most survivors have capped their anger for years, both by pretending that nothing had happened to them and by suppressing any anger they did feel until it became complete denial. As the curtain of the lie rises and the truth is revealed, survivors begin to feel that pent-up rage. What is to be done with all the anger? It should be directed where it belongs, but often the appropriate objects are not around or not safe; the perpetrator may even be dead, and the family members miles away. And if you take out your anger on new family and friends, you are being unfair, especially if you take it out on your own children.

So what can one do with all this unexpressed rage? One answer is to kick a pillow or hammer it with bare hands. In a safe place and away from people (especially children, who would not understand and might be upset), survivors can sob and bawl and whack an inanimate object until their rage is spent. One creative survivor purchased boxing gloves and punching bags; another bakes bread, but pounds the dough with all her might beforehand. (She tells us her bread is "the best!")

Does it feel like a tantrum? You bet! But survivors are owed more than a few tantrums for the unfairness they had to endure as children.

L. Laughter and lightheartedness.

It is said that the devil does not take jokes well and that hell is a place of high seriousness. Survivors often describe their childhoods as that hell. Nothing was funny — or fun — ever again after they were handed "the secret." There was no full-bodied, carefree laughter. Humor, like many other things in those dysfunctional families, was inappropriate. Perpetrators often laughed as they made fun of their victims — hardly humor — or they seemed to smirk as they talked about sex or "dirty" things.

How is it possible to come out of that distorted history and still find lightheartedness, gaiety, and laughter? Are survivors condemned to take themselves seriously all the time just because they bear such a burden of pain and sorrow?

As we grow to trust ourselves and accept the fact that we do not have to be perfect, it becomes easier to laugh, both at ourselves and at the world. It is wholesome and healthy to do so. In beginning to open our eyes to the creation around us — instead of focusing our gazes inward and finding guilt and shame — we discover ludicrous and delightful sights.

Much so-called humor around us is self-deprecating, dehumanizing, and cruel; it often has a victim. Survivors do not need to be amused at that kind of humor; they know what it feels like to be held up to ridicule and to be picked on. When we open our eyes and ears to creation, we see whimsy, caprice, and gaiety. And if we can tell a joke or laugh at our own lumbering selves, we scare the devil away and invite the angel of whimsy to take his place.

M. Music.

"Music soothes the savage breast," it is said. The glory of the musical idiom is that it reaches far beyond words to soothe, heal, and give joy. It is one of the most powerful tools we have to cure our frayed nerves and anxious souls.

The range of musical taste is as broad as survivors are numerous. We have heard many women mention as powerful and inspiring Whitney Houston's music, especially the song "The Greatest Love of All," which affirms the importance of self-love. For women in other generations, Helen Reddy sings the truth, and gospel singers who radiate faith and hope are favorites.

Classical music is a favorite with most of the women we interviewed, although choices of composers, selections, and musical periods were as individual as the women themselves. But few would gainsay the power of Bach or Mozart to collect the emotions and bring tranquillity to a harried day.

Several survivors were musicians, and they spoke of the power imparted to them by performing as well as listening to music.

Contemporary rock lyrics that are overtly or covertly sexual and violent are distasteful to many survivors. A piece of advice is relevant at this point. It is not uncommon for health and fitness or exercise groups to use contemporary music to supplement the exercises. Some of this music can be distracting — or possibly deeply disturbing — to incest survivors. Either the beat or the lyrics can remind the survivor of sex or even trigger a flashback. If she is doing floor exercises, she may be lying or sitting in a position in which she feels vulnerable, and this can increase her fear. We want to get in touch with our bodies, but if the lyrics speak of rape, abusive acts, or social mayhem, we may feel revictimized. The same could be true of male "crooners" or country-western singers who sing about sex in scarcely veiled terms.

In such a situation, do not be afraid to confront the group leader about the quality of the music. If she does not accept the criticism or if she sneers at your reasons, be aware that you have rights too. Taped and televised exercise programs that use only unobtrusive music are available. You may need the assurance that your sexuality is not being exploited in song as you are trying to integrate your physical, spiritual, and sexual self in exercise.

N. Nature.

Barbara, whose moving story of abuse so permeates this book, is a nature photographer. She especially enjoys taking pictures of ducks and geese. Even though she lives in a city, she can spend nearly all her free time on her hobby. Beginning in mid-March, she makes regular trips to the zoo to observe mating and nesting, which start in early spring. Then there are ducklings to watch; she photographs the life cycle through the whole summer of growth. In the fall she journeys to a wildlife preserve and camps out in the country to photograph migrations.

Many survivors go out of their way to glimpse the beauty of nature. Jane is a devoted gardener who spends all her spare time

either working in her many flower gardens or planning and order-
ing new plant material. She says, "Gardening helps me because I
leave all sense of time behind. That satisfaction of nurturing, that
side of me, comes out when I am in my garden. I work out con-
versations, feelings, problems in the garden. It's a receptacle for all
my troubles, and I come out calm, having left the world behind
for awhile."

Perhaps another's way of connecting with nature is less absorbing than Barbara's photography or Jane's gardening. Some survivors mention love for trees, leafy and strong bulwarks in summer,
bare skeletons of strength in winter. Trees seem reassuring. Other
survivors mention sunsets, thunderstorms, wildflowers, animals,
rainbows. In nature is the plenitude and fullness of life. When survivors witness the beauty of nature, they often feel reassured and
strong.

O. Open up to a higher power.

Some survivors are firm believers in Christianity, Judaism, or
another major religion; others do not name a divinity but depend
on a Supreme Power outside themselves. Many survivors list spirituality or a belief in God as the single most important element
that helps them to heal.

Nonbelievers might find this fact puzzling. After all, atheists and
agnostics often come to their positions out of the argument that
the prevalence of evil in the world proves that there is no God, or
if there is, it is not a benevolent one. And surely incest survivors
are aware of the evil and pain in the world, not to mention ugliness, injustice, and unfairness. One might expect that they would
be condemning God, not praising Him.

Why did most of the survivors we interviewed want to believe
in a Supreme Power?

We can only touch on a few reasons we have heard, but a couple
are common. In the case of those drawn to Christianity, one is the
power of the figure of Christ. Many survivors identify with His
suffering, His compassion for others, and His triumph over sin

and death. They are confident that He can understand their pain, having suffered the cross. There is nothing remote or cold about the figure of Jesus Christ.

Others put themselves into the hands of a power greater than themselves and let that power lead them one day at a time. They do not name that power or characterize it by sect or by sex; they know that when they show compassion toward themselves or others, they are experiencing that Other. Many survivors get in touch with that Other by way of daily meditation. Making their souls quiet, they listen for guidance. Some feel that they do not have to make this journey on their own and that the road of spiritual recovery, long as it seems to stretch before them, is the only road to follow.

P. Pets.

Cats and dogs, parakeets and finches abound in the households of survivors, who frequently love and spoil their animals, perhaps the way they wish they had been spoiled as children.

Tastes vary about the choice of animals for pets. It is even possible that the pet one chooses has something to do with the nature of her abuse. Roberta keeps a parakeet; not only does she have allergies, but she readily admits that she is not an emotionally demonstrative person. She would find that a cat wants to be stroked and a dog needs to be walked, and she knows those needs would annoy her. A bird expects just the kind and amount of care she is prepared to give. It does give something back; it obligingly hops on her finger or roosts on her shoulder and "kisses" and chatters when she has time for play. But she can also be remote if she wants, and the bird will do perfectly well in its cage.

Other survivors crave a comfortable fat cat that curls up in the bedclothes with them to sleep. Cats are rather like the teddy bears so cherished by survivors. They are usually comfortable and warm animals that provide solace and purring at nap or bedtime. They provide cuddling pleasure and an opportunity to stroke and pet.

Although some survivors love and cherish their canines, others were forced by their perpetrators into sexual acts with dogs, and find them anathema for reasons that are easy to understand. Some survivors like the security of a good watchdog. And yet others are like Carol Poston, who, while writing this, has her comfortable old dog at her feet. Her dog nurtures her with tail-wagging and soft, understanding eyes. It is the dog who persuades her to get out for the daily walk and who wags a tail in glee if she puts on gardening shoes. And she can confide anything to the dog's soft ears and bury her head in its fur and cry — and get devotion and dog kisses in return.

Q. Quit blaming yourself!

What could be more common — and more futile — than the phrases "if *only* I had . . ." and "if *only* I hadn't. . . ." These are pleas to go back in time or to adjust events so that they will turn out to our satisfaction. Short of Alley Oop's Time Machine we will never be able to go back in time to do anything, much less to "fix" things so that incest would not have happened.

Survivors need to accept the truth that the incest was *not* their fault. There is no "if only" about it. Adults, however, do bear responsibility for their behavior. When survivors go around morosely hating themselves for what happened in the past, they are choosing to punish themselves (and probably those around them) for something that can never be changed, no matter how much they may want to erase it.

More important, guilt about the incest can lead into revictimization. One survivor, aged fifty-five, looking back on years of pain over the incest, said, "It was like being born with one arm. I thought that something was wrong with me to attract this kind of attention, so I let myself be a victim again and again." Self-hatred and self-blame lead to little or no self-respect.

Survivors need to turn the equation around. If you quit blaming and hating yourself, self-respect and self-esteem will increase exponentially.

R. Read.

Most survivors find that the journey to self-understanding starts with books. Reading is a major component of healing. Because this subject is so important, we have included a list of titles at the end of the book (Recommended Readings) for people who want to find out more.

Here, however, we would like to point out that there are several categories of book that can prove useful. They include:

— First-person accounts about living through incest. They help you to understand that you are not alone, and the best of them help purge the emotions by the words and descriptions with which you can sympathize.

— Professional books, that is, books written *by* professionals in the field *for* other professionals. These are helpful when you are ready to try to understand treatment methods and you are working with a therapist. Many survivors feel that understanding their symptoms can help them understand themselves. These books often give an overview of incestuous families and describe the culture in relation to how we react to incest, how often it occurs, what kinds of things the culture permits, and the extent of societal taboos against incest, so they provide a helpful context for the survivor.

— Spiritual guides, an especially useful kind of book. Daily affirmations from ACOA (Adult Children of Alcoholics), books about healing the child within, and works on spiritual growth such as Scott Peck's *The Road Less Traveled* give much needed guidance about how life, though difficult at times, can be rewarding and fulfilling.

— Children's books. Many survivors are drawn to children's books, perhaps because they lost the childhood time of innocence and play in which to enjoy them. If you have children of your own, of course, it is easy to find the opportunity to satisfy this appetite. If you are childless, it takes some nerve to inquire about such literature at a bookstore or library, but the rewards are many. Besides, who needs to know that *The Velveteen Rabbit* or *Miss*

Jaster's Garden that you have just bought or borrowed is for you and not for a niece or nephew? And it is also surely true that children's literature is timeless, much of it classic, and if you feel like reading through all the Oz books just for fun you can tell yourself that you are filling a void in your education as well as enjoying yourself.

S. Say "thank you" to compliments.

Survivors often find compliments hard to handle. It takes practice to say a simple "thank you" when someone stops to praise us or when something nice and comforting comes our way.

Some feel compelled to minimize what they are or what they have done by explaining it away so that they get no credit. "What a beautiful job you did organizing this event," someone says to a survivor, who retorts, "Oh, it was nothing, really. People helped out, so I didn't have to do anything." Or if someone compliments her on how nice she looks, she finds herself saying, "Oh, *this* old thing!" or "Really? Do you like it? I got it on sale for fourteen ninety-five."

Wouldn't it be nice if she could just accept praise as a tribute to something good about her? One survivor tries to build her self-esteem by making herself repeat to herself, four times, any compliment she receives. She wants to be sure that she has heard the words and that she has integrated the fact of her worth into herself.

As a group, survivors generally are so self-effacing and humble that they do not need to worry about getting swelled heads or becoming braggarts by their acceptance of compliments. They were told so often in the past that they were ugly, no good, guilty, and at fault that for some it may take years of compliments to bring their feelings of self-worth up to par.

Those of us who are survivors need to let praise sink into our souls, to let ourselves feel valued, and to say a gracious "thank you" to any bringer of a compliment.

T. Take time to be patient with yourself.

Healing takes time, a lot of time, and you have to be ready to let yourself spend the time it takes to get better. You have years of unhappiness and probably a history of making poor choices, so that it is only reasonable to predict that change will not happen overnight.

Remember also that many survivors are perfectionists: they expect a great deal of themselves. When they see how much time it is taking for them to heal, such women are prone to "beat themselves up" for not getting it straight and continuing to make mistakes. They would have more patience with a dumb animal than with themselves.

A sweatshirt often seen on little children has a message which says, "Be patient. God isn't finished with me yet." The sentiment is a valuable one for survivors. We are people in process. Our feelings are like the weather — they change. And we change by the day, even by the hour.

One survivor working toward health decided to go for a body massage to help her work on some of her physical symptoms of stress. She was encouraged after the first session because she had found some relief.

During the second session, however, she was "strung out." She curled up in a ball on the massage table and could not complete the session. Afterwards she was devastated and angry with herself for this behavior. Surely she would never be well! What a way to act! What a waste of money!

When she took the time, however, to sit quietly and go over what had happened in the masseuse's office, she began to understand. First of all, the piped-in music set her on edge; it made her feel by turns anxious and insecure. The masseuse would have changed the music or turned it off if the survivor had asked.

And she found in retrospect that lying nude with only a towel around her bothered her. The next time she goes to the masseuse, she can decide to wear shorts or a body stocking if that will help her feel more comfortable.

This is an example of how a survivor learns to be patient with herself. This survivor's reactions were not wrong, and she is not a bad or hopeless person, as she initially believed. She needed only time to think things through, to plumb her feelings, and to deal gently with herself. The second massage could be seen for what it was: a wonderful learning experience.

U. Undergarments.

Sexual abuse robs a woman of joy in her sexual self. She has been demeaned and diminished in that part of herself. These profoundly damaging issues have to be worked through with time in an environment of trust. But while at work establishing her sexual health, there are little things a survivor can do to help heal.

For one thing, she can buy pretty undergarments. These articles of clothing cover her intimately, whether they be underwear during the day or nightgowns and robes for night. If the clothes are well chosen and pretty, in time she may come to feel that she too must be pretty to attend to herself in this way.

The excursion to buy nice underthings can be hard for some survivors, because they are not used to giving themselves this kind of attention. A pair of jeans is one thing, but a lacy bra is quite another.

It might help to take along a friend who regularly treats herself to such luxuries. That friend can lead her to a bin of colored panties or a rack of lacy sleepwear that survivors, with their "abuse blinders" on, would not otherwise see. The friend might encourage her to touch the silky fabrics to feel the beauty. And it might take several trips before she can actually purchase anything.

That's all right. And the garments may stay in a drawer for awhile before they actually get worn. That's all right too. Someday the survivor will be able to wear them. Only she will know what she is wearing under her work clothes, but the thought that she is lovely enough to wear lovely underthings is a positive step.

V. Visit your perpetrator.

While a confrontation with one's perpetrator is certainly not essential, some survivors may be considering the idea. We have given some examples of such confrontations in Chapter 7. Here let us again stress that it is not helpful to go into a confrontation expecting to change anything. In fact, the perpetrator may either ignore the charges, claim you are lying, or hurl a whole new set of accusations at you. If you are not strong enough to handle these possibilities, consider whether you will benefit from the experience. The confrontation is for you and for your own self-satisfaction.

Plan the ground rules in advance. You may want to rehearse the confrontation in the presence of your therapist if you have one. Pick safe or neutral territory on which to meet — perhaps your therapist's office. Protect yourself if there is danger of physical violence; you yourself are the best judge of whether such security arrangements are necessary.

If your perpetrator is dead and physical confrontation is not possible, a visit to the gravesite can be an equally satisfying option. There some women have left a vase or buried a jar in which they can desposit letters or notes. Some speak to the perpetrator, pound on the grave, or shout obscenities. Others feel an urge to deface the tombstone. We do not condone lawbreaking, but this response is understandable and would have to be carried out with the knowledge that it is indeed vandalism. Or, you may . . .

W. Write him a letter.

Often, writing a letter explaining her feelings, but *not* mailing it, can be helpful to the adult survivor. This is a particularly useful exercise for a survivor in therapy or in a group with good support. One survivor reports that the day she read her letter aloud to her support group, she not only gained a great deal of sustenance from her peers but felt a flood of feelings spontaneously expressed and let go — a tremendous sense of relief.

We've seen a lot of letters to perpetrators, ranging from hate letters filled with four-letter words to carefully crafted poems. All are appropriate and helpful.

Many survivors write to their mothers as well. It is helpful to ventilate those feelings toward a mother, perhaps first writing the letter in longhand; scribbling and scratching out can feel good. Most survivors' letters we have seen were then typed before they were sent. We conclude that the survivors wanted to be as clear and legible as possible so that their meaning could not be mistaken.

Finally, many survivors write letters to themselves as children. This can be prompted by studying a snapshot of yourself as a child. Write a letter to that little girl in all her innocence, addressing her confusion and hurt about what is happening to her. The object of the exercise is to see the little girl you were as wholesome, good, and vulnerable, and never, never as guilty for the incest.

X. EXamine your body and see that you are good.

"The body remembers." We hear it again and again. Even after years of therapy, some survivors suffer body pain and discomfort as a result of the incest.

Accepting their bodies as beautiful and good is a struggle for most survivors. Their bodies were used, abused, sometimes mutilated, but the scars were not just physical. The worst mutilation was psychological, the one that, like a hot brand on the flesh, burned its way into their psyches. Like Hester Prynne in *The Scarlet Letter,* they often feel they are wearing a sign of their sin, except that theirs is a sin of worthlessness and ugliness.

How can one persuade oneself that she is lovely, attractive, and physically intact? How can she persuade her body that it is beautiful and good, especially when the body insists on remembering?

Survivors speak of many things that help, and they all say that the process is a long one. One of the more helpful techniques is massage. In the hands of a skilled and understanding masseuse, many survivors find that they are rid of the muscular tension and physical pain associated with memories of incest, pain that can range from annoying to incapacitating. Deep massage seems to relax at a deep level of physical hurt.

A word of caution: Occasionally, deep massage can stimulate painful flashbacks or early abuse memories. For some survivors this type of massage should be used only in conjunction with psychotherapy.

The survivors among us need to learn to be familiar with our bodies, touching them, appreciating them, a task that can be difficult. We need to take long baths, use bubble bath and scented soap, to learn to be languorous and comfortable with the *feel* of our bodies. Then, finally, we hope to look into a mirror to examine ourselves and, little by little, learn to see what is lovely about each part.

Y. YOU — *take care of yourself!*

Many survivors do a good job of taking care of other people but ignore their own needs. Survivors need to learn to nurture themselves.

We are not advocating narrow selfishness or self-centeredness. Rather, the attention to one's own needs, taking care of what one's body and spirit long for, are more in the nature of self-respect and self-love. Women who continually deny themselves for others eventually become angry and resentful. It is hard to love your neighbor as yourself if you do not first love yourself.

There are many methods survivors use to achieve this integrity, this dignity and self-respect that were torn from them ruthlessly when they were children. It sometimes seems easier to see the one flaw in your character than its many good points.

— Celebrate yourself! You survived incest; chances are good that you will not have to live through anything that difficult again.

— Pat yourself on the back when you've done something you

are proud of! You deserve it. You may have been criticized as a child, so your need to accept yourself now is even greater.

— Ask your friends for a list of your attributes, your good qualities. Tape them on the mirror where you can see them when you start the day.

— Listen to compliments and accept the strokes people give you.

— Take care of your physical health needs by keeping regular doctor and dental appointments.

— Give yourself that haircut or permanent wave you need. Make sure you feel good about your appearance.

— Buy yourself a bouquet of flowers, take a nap, waste some time, buy a blouse without feeling guilty. Indulge!

Z. Zero in on building a strong support system.

Survivors often feel singled out and alone in their pain; many feel at some point that they are the only people to whom incest has ever happened. Because they had to endure the incest alone and were compelled to keep the secret, they became accustomed to handling things alone. They were afraid to ask for help, perceiving — quite accurately, perhaps — that they would not have gotten it.

But as adults trying to reclaim their lives, survivors are not alone, and they need to build a support system of friends and acquaintances who will be there when they want them. Uncovering the past in therapy, experiencing flashbacks, and reliving the pain can be almost intolerable for the survivor by herself.

Getting this support system can be a tall order for women who have led solitary lives and have no family or friends. Many survivors choose to join a support group for survivors, a women's group not especially limited to survivors, church organizations, or one of the appropriate twelve-step programs.

This is the time to begin trusting a small circle of friends. Listen to your inner voice. People who seem judgmental, critical, or mean probably will not be part of your support system; in fact, you may already know who would and would not be good candidates. If a person seems friendly, you need to give a little information about yourself, then see how it is received. Take notes. If the response is warm and accepting, give a little more. Friendship takes time and a lot of give and take. It does not mean the absence of *all* criticism, but constructive criticism offered in a spirit of love.

Selecting a Therapist

Therapy may well be the single most important factor in stimulating the healing process. Yet selecting a therapist has been described as a nightmare by many survivors. Here are some points to watch for when selecting a therapist to help you on this journey. And always remember that *you* are the employer seeking assistance in a job you need to do — the job of healing yourself and reclaiming your life.

Unfortunately, most people begin looking for a therapist at a time in their lives when they are least prepared to make good decisions: at a time of emotional turmoil and extreme stress. So if possible, begin the search *before* the crisis becomes full-blown. Otherwise, you may wind up settling for the first therapist you locate.

But first let's clarify the term "therapist." While at one time virtually all therapists in America were psychiatrists (M.D.s), today the holders of a variety of professional degrees share the title. Professionals included in the term "therapist" are clinical psychologists (Ph.D. or Psy.D.), social workers (M.S.W. or D.S.W.), and psychotherapists (usually M.A. or M.S.), trained in a variety of schools and in a variety of disciplines. Legally, at this time of writing, *anyone* can call him or herself a "therapist."

Since there is no certain way to determine which of these professionals might be best suited to your needs, it is important to observe the following guidelines:

1. Begin by asking friends who have been in therapy. But remember that if a therapist was helpful to a friend with a marital problem or with decisions about career changes, that same therapist may not be the best one for you, with your very different set of issues. And just as you might not have selected the same man your friend did for a husband, you might not be pleased with her therapist.

2. Shop around. If you live in a city or town where there are many possible candidates, interview several therapists before choosing. Beware of those who look at you with disfavor when you say you are interviewing several people. A good therapist will understand the necessity of your exercising caution and will know that you need to establish a comfortable relationship.

3. Don't confine yourself to conducting individual interviews. Other potential sources may help you winnow the field more quickly. These sources include outpatient psychiatric departments of local hospitals, particularly teaching hospitals, or reputable postgraduate training centers for psychotherapy. Local township or community mental health centers may offer sliding scales. Consult with the director of the agency, who should be familiar with the staff and the expertise of its individual members. Employee assistance representatives may be able to recommend specific therapists especially skilled in treating issues such as yours.

4. Seek out experts. Therapists are beginning to specialize. If you hear of one who primarily treats survivors of incest, certainly consider her a good possibility. If that sort of specialty is unavailable, ask any potential therapist if she has treated other survivors, if so how many, and what her feelings are about treating them. There is no right or wrong answer to these questions, but the therapist's response will show whether you feel you can trust this person.

5. Join a survivor's group. It is instructive to see how other women resolve their issues, and you may also find a ready-made support system because of your common values. Such groups can be either of the self-help variety or conducted by a therapist. Again, there is no guide better than your own perceptions to determine whether you can benefit from a group or which group is best for you.

6. Don't be afraid to ask questions designed to explore the attitudes and treatment methods of a potential therapist. Your questions may include the following:

Q. Have you had previous experience in treating survivors? A "no" answer to this question is acceptable if the therapist is interested in educating himself or herself. This can be through reading and workshops geared to treatment of the survivor, consulting specialists, and, most important, listening to *you* — the *real* expert on the subject.

Q. How do you feel about working with survivors? A safe answer will express hope and enthusiasm for recovery from incest. It may also indicate the potential therapist's respect for and understanding of the resiliency of adult survivors.

Q. Do you find that clients can learn from a variety of therapeutic experiences or do you prefer to be the sole provider of services? A safe answer will encourage clients to grow and heal in as many ways as possible, searching for and receiving support from a variety of healthy resources.

Q. Do you feel that it is ever appropriate for therapists to have sexual contacts with clients? The only safe answer is "No!" Often sexual attraction occurs between client and therapist, but for a therapist to act on these feelings is never appropriate. It is a terrible violation of the client's boundaries and damages her in much the same way the incest did. It is distressing for Karen Lison to report, as a therapist, that a large number of adult survivors she has treated have been revictimized by their previous therapists.

7. In general, select a therapist or a group with whom you feel comfortable and an atmosphere that seems empathetic, warm, and respectful. Try to avoid therapists who appear cool and critical, or uncomfortable in group situations. Listen to your inner voice and trust your perceptions. Seek a relationship in which you feel safe, understood, affirmed, and appreciated.

A final word about courage. We don't talk as much about virtues and vices as people did in times past, which is perhaps too bad. Classically, courage is one of the seven cardinal virtues, an ingredient of one's character that for centuries has been deemed necessary for a person to grow into a moral being.

Courage comes from the inner impulse that moves us into action, even risk, because we know we want to change. Its opposite is the fear that immobilizes. Fear freezes people. They become stultified and cease to grow. Courage does just the opposite.

It was courage that was so manifest in the incest survivors to whom we talked. Choosing a therapist requires courage, as does confronting the fact of incest. It takes courage to reach outside and trust someone, and to reach inside and trust oneself. It takes courage to admit the ways incest has destroyed pieces of us and courage to find ways to rebuild them. It takes courage just to remember.

Most of all, it takes courage to stand up and say, "This is who I am. Yes, this terrible thing is part of me, but I am not therefore a terrible person. And please do not tell me how I am doomed and crippled because of what someone else did to me. I, too, am a person, and I deserve respect."

Notes

Notes are keyed to the page and line of the text, the first number referring to the page, the second to the line.

Introduction

5/19 Mark 4:21–22. A similar passage appears in Matthew 5:15 and Luke 11:33.

Chapter I

17/5 Figures about sexual abuse range widely and seem to be revised rapidly. The best recent source of figures is John Crewdson's *By Silence Betrayed* (Boston: Little, Brown and Company, 1988), in his chapter entitled "Numbers." He surveys the latest findings in both the United States and Canada and examines the range of figures that different studies have proposed. The estimates stand as high as one in two women and one in three men as having experienced some kind of child sexual abuse. The largest random sample of sexual behavior was the Kinsey report of 1953 (A. C. Kinsey, W. B. Pomeroy, C. E. Martin, and P. H. Gebhard, *Sexual Behavior in the Human Female*, Philadelphia: W. B. Saunders, 1953). Kinsey and his colleagues found that 3 percent of their female subjects had been abused by a male relative before the age of fourteen, a number they considered statistically insignificant. The Kinsey researchers have been criticized both for their sampling techniques and for their view that the 139 women they interviewed who had experienced incest were not harmed by the experience.

More recently, Diana Russell's random sample of 930 women in the San Francisco area in 1977 showed a figure of one in six women who had been a victim of interfamilial sexual abuse (*The Secret Trauma*, New York: Basic Books, 1986). Russell now believes that her numbers are, if anything, "an underestimation" since 36 percent of the households refused to be interviewed, and those persons may have been the most victimized of all (Diana Russell, lecture, May 17, 1988, Waukesha, Wisconsin). Other recent figures include those of the U.S. Department of Justice, which called child molestation "one of the country's most frequent, least understood crimes" and stated that "it might be affecting as many as one of four children" ("Symposium Studies Child Molestation," *New York Times*, 4 October 1984, sec. III, p. 3). The FBI cites information estimating that one in four women will experience sexual abuse before age eighteen, that 10 percent of American families are affected by incest, and that "between 60,000 and 100,000 female children are sexually abused annually, and yet only 20 percent of these crimes are reported" (Robert J. Barry, "Incest: The Last Taboo," reprinted from *FBI Law Enforcement Bulletin*, January–February 1984, p. 1).

17/9 Susan Forward and Craig Buck, *Betrayal of Innocence: Incest and Its Devastation* (New York: Penguin Books, 1979), and Sandra Butler, *Conspiracy of Silence: The Trauma of Incest* (San Francisco: Volcano Press, 1978).

18/11 Figures from a documentary shown in the fall of 1983 by Chicago's ABC affiliate stated that all the inhabitants of the women's penal farm in Dwight, Illinois, had experienced sexual abuse as children.

20/8 For a fuller discussion of dissociation, see pages 46ff.

21/35 Lynn Daugherty, *Why Me?* (Racine, Wisconsin: Mother Courage Press, 1984), p. 11. Another useful definition is that provided by V.O.I.C.E.S. in Action (Victims of Incest Can Emerge Survivors), a national organization of incest survivors. It provides perhaps the most broadly based definition: "Incest is a betrayal of trust involving overt or covert sexual actions — direct or indirect, verbal or physical (which may include — but is not limited to — intercourse) between a child and a trusted adult and/or authority figure."

22/18 Jon Conte and John R. Schuerman, "The Effects of Sexual Abuse on Children: A Multidimensional View," *Journal of Interpersonal Violence*, 2 (1987), 380–390.

23/4 Only now are we discovering the high rate of abuse for boys. Sadly, little research exists to date. See Judith Lewis Herman, *Father-*

Daughter Incest (Cambridge, Mass.: Harvard University Press, 1982), p. 14. For additional information on perpetrators, see Diana Russell, *Sexual Exploitation: Rape, Child Sexual Abuse, Workplace Harassment* (Newbury Park, California: Sage Publications Inc., 1984).

25/6 Alice Miller, *For Your Own Good* (New York: Farrar, Straus, and Giroux, 1983), p. 254.

Chapter 2

36/13 Ruth S. and C. Henry Kempe, *Child Abuse* (Cambridge, Mass.: Harvard University Press, 1978), p. 51; David Finkelhor, *Child Sexual Abuse* (New York: The Free Press, a division of Macmillan, Inc., 1984), p. 93.

38/2 Richard Kluft, author of *Childhood Antecedents of Multiple Personality* (Washington, D.C.: American Psychiatric Press, 1985), and Bennett G. Braun, editor of *Treatment of the Multiple Personality Disorder* (Washington, D.C.: American Psychiatric Press, Inc., 1986) are well-known leaders in the study of multiple personalities. Many survivors, however, have benefited by working with therapists of the client-oriented variety who usually do not use hypnosis and who tend to follow their client's material as the therapy process evolves, permitting personalities to make themselves known at their own pace and allowing integration to occur as a natural, unorchestrated event.

43/23 Natalie Shainess, *Sweet Suffering* (New York: Bobbs-Merrill Co., Inc., 1984), p. 8.

44/9 Samuel Clemens (Mark Twain), *Huckleberry Finn* (reprint, New York: Heritage Press, 1940), p. 39.

46/3 American Psychiatric Association, *Diagnostic and Statistical Manual of Mental Disorders,* third edition, revised, Washington, D.C.: American Psychiatric Association, 1980. Hereafter referred to as *DSM-III.*

46/9 These definitions of amnesia are also from *DSM-III,* p. 253.

47/15 Definitions from *DSM-III,* pp. 236–237.

51/16 Child-abuse expert Hank Giaretto says, "At the heart of the runaway problem is abuse. Most of those kids had been abused. Otherwise they wouldn't have run away from home" (John Crewdson and Lynn Emmerman, "Sex Abuse Extends Beyond Its Victims," *Chicago Tribune,* 25 September 1984, sec. I, pp. 1ff).

61/15 From a paper by Joy Ann Kenworthy, Ph.D., at a conference called "Freud, Incest, Women, and Psychotherapy: Avoidance of the

Truth?" held 14 September 1984 at Governors State University, University Park, Illinois.

Chapter 3

67/32 Vladimir Nabokov, *Lolita* (New York: G. P. Putnam's Sons, 1955), p. 18.

68/24 Even when cases do come to court, convictions of child sex offenders are difficult. For more information, see John Crewdson, *By Silence Betrayed* (Boston: Little, Brown, 1988), Chapter 10.

82/11 See Dan Kiley, *The Peter Pan Syndrome* (New York: Dodd, Mead, 1983). The book deals with what the author sees as the refusal by many American men ever to grow up. Like Peter Pan in James Barrie's story, these men require a "Wendy" for mothering but steadfastly refuse to enter the adult world of shared responsibility.

Chapter 4

88/5 Information from a public lecture delivered October 1984 in Evanston, Illinois.

89/22 Erik Erikson, *Childhood and Society* (New York: W. W. Norton, 1963; revised edition. Hogarth Books, 1965, reprinted by Penguin Books, 1965), p. 241.

89/31 Erik Erikson, *Identity and the Life Cycle* (New York: W. W. Norton, 1980), p. 57.

90/10 M. Scott Peck, *The Road Less Traveled* (New York: Simon and Schuster, 1978), p. 24.

92/1 Ruth S. and C. Henry Kempe, *Child Abuse* (Cambridge, Mass.: Harvard University Press, 1978), pp. 48–49.

92/32 Jean Renvoize, *Incest: A Family Pattern* (London: Routledge and Kegan Paul, 1982), p. 101.

93/10 Roland C. Summit, "The Child Sexual Abuse Accommodation Syndrome," *Child Abuse and Neglect,* 7 (1983), 182–183, 185.

94/6 Karin Meiselman, *Incest: A Psychological Study of Causes and Effects with Treatment Recommendations* (San Francisco: Jossey-Bass, 1978), pp. 112–113.

94/32 Linda Tschirhart Sanford, *The Silent Children* (New York: Anchor Press/Doubleday, 1980), pp. 157–158.

97/34 Renvoize, p. 26.

101/4 See Ezekiel 36:26: "A new heart will I give you, and a new spirit will I put within you; and I will take out of your flesh the heart of stone and give you a heart of flesh."

Chapter 6

156/7 C. S. Lewis, *Mere Christianity* (New York: Macmillan, Inc., 1952; paperback edition, 1960; reprinted 1978), p. 91.

181/24 We are indebted for the explanation of this concept to Professor Linda Williams, University of Illinois at Chicago. We discovered that our terminology in this chapter had been first used by film critic Laura Mulvey, who, in an essay entitled "Visual Pleasure and Narrative Cinema" (*Screen*, 16:3 [1975], 6–18), describes man as "bearer of the look" and woman as its object. It should be pointed out that the world of film and the world inhabited by real men and women are not conceptually interchangeable. Film, by its nature, utilizes voyeurism; that is the way we are cued into the dramatic action. The way men and women act in the nonfilm world was what we were attempting to assay, although the film analogy helps to explain this concept.

Chapter 7

202/31 See Eugene T. Gendlin, *Focusing* (New York: Bantam Books, rev. ed., 1981). Gendlin's "focusing technique" has been a widely applied method of helping people center themselves to recall and get in touch with sources of stress. It is especially valuable for incest survivors because it teaches women how to listen to their bodies and remember old pain.

207/24 Eighteen-year-old Cheryl Pierson was found guilty and sentenced to six months in jail in Suffolk County, New York, for planning the murder of her father, James, who she claimed had sexually abused her. She had persuaded a classmate to do the killing for $1,000. Scores of incest victims wrote to Judge Harvey W. Sherman on her behalf. Judge Sherman said that although he believed the woman had been sexually abused, he could not condone murder (*New York Times*, 6 October 1987, sec. II, 1ff.).

215/16 Beverley Flanigan at the University of Wisconsin-Madison has authored some of the most useful research available on forgiveness in a forthcoming book called *Forgiving the Unforgivable*. Professor Flanigan studied individual cases in five widely varying communities: one in

Utah, one in Virginia, one in Wisconsin, one in Florida, and one in New Zealand. She found incest ranked high among her respondents as an "unforgivable sin" and yet, surprisingly, most women had been able to work through to forgiveness, often without benefit either of clergy or of therapist. Flanigan concludes that forgiveness does not reconcile people or relationships. Rather, what it does is to provide the victim with a way to rebuild herself and her world after the destruction of trust.

Chapter 8

235/15 *The New American Cuisine* by the editors of *Metropolitan Home* (Des Moines: Meredith Corporation, published by Crown Publishers), p. 291.

245/2 V.O.I.C.E.S. in Action (Victims of Incest Can Emerge Survivors), cited in Chapter 6 as a national self-help network for incest survivors, provides a special-interest subgroup for women whose abuse involved animals. For more information on V.O.I.C.E.S., see "Helpful Organizations" in the "Readings and Resources" section which follows.

Readings and Resources

Literature addressing sexual abuse is a rapidly expanding field, we are happy to report, and the survivor can choose from a wide range of sources to meet her needs. We have listed some of our favorites below, with a description of what we consider the strong points of each. If no comment follows a title, that fact indicates that the book is so recent that it appeared while our book was in press. We include the reference, however, to be as up to date as possible for our readers.

A. Recommended Readings

Allen, Charlotte Vale. *Daddy's Girl.* New York: Berkley, 1980. Excellent first-person account.

Bass, Ellen. *I Never Told Anyone: A Collection of Writings by Women Survivors of Child Sexual Abuse.* New York: Harper and Row, 1983. An honest and comprehensive collection of moving stories by survivors.

Bass, Ellen, and Laura Davis. *The Courage to Heal.* New York: Harper and Row, 1988. An invaluable guide, this book is an encyclopedia of information for the survivor and those who live with her and love her.

Beattie, Melody. *Co-Dependent No More.* Center City, Minn.: Hazelden, 1987. Discusses several options for controlling behavior, including self-help programs.

Black, Claudia. *It Will Never Happen to Me: Children of Alcoholics.* Denver: MAC Publishing, 1981. A sensitive and compassionate book that describes survival techniques learned by children in alcoholic families and explains how such techniques cause problems in adulthood.

Brady, Katherine. *Father's Days.* New York: Dell, 1981. Excellent first-person account of a long-term incestuous relationship between father and daughter.

Briggs, Dorothy Corkille. *Your Child's Self-Esteem: Step-by-Step Guidelines to Raising Responsible, Productive, Happy Children.* Garden City, N.Y.: Doubleday, 1970. Offers a guide for parents to encourage healthy child-rearing practices.

Brownmiller, Susan. *Against Our Will.* New York: Bantam, 1976. Explores the social setting that makes sexual assault possible.

Butler, Sandra. *Conspiracy of Silence: The Trauma of Incest.* San Francisco: Volcano Press, 1978; 1985 (updated). Explores the impact of, and society's response to, incest. Includes a framework for community groups interested in looking for solutions to the problem of incest.

Caplan, Paula J. *The Myth of Women's Masochism.* New York: E. P. Dutton, 1985. A comprehensive exploration of the social attitudes that reinforce the erroneous belief that women seek or enjoy pain. Also includes an excellent chapter on how women have been victimized in the therapeutic setting and offers suggestions for implementing change.

Cermak, Timmen. *A Primer on Adult Children of Alcoholics.* Pompano Beach, Fla.: Health Communications, Inc., 1985. A booklet describing issues faced by adults who have grown up in dysfunctional families, especially the issue of control. Because it is a booklet, not a book, it is available only at selected bookstores and from the publisher (1721 Blount Road, Suite #1, Pompano Beach, Florida; toll-free number 1-800-851-9100).

Colgrove, Melba, Harold Bloomfield, and Peter McWilliams. *How to Survive the Loss of a Love.* New York: Bantam, 1976. Describes how loss of love is a form of grieving. Excellent suggestions for dealing with that grief.

Conte, Jon, and John R. Schuerman. "The Effects of Sexual Abuse on Children: A Multidimensional View." *Journal of Interpersonal Violence,* 2 (1987), 380–390. Scholarly study of special interest to professionals looking for the most recent research on the subject.

Courtois, Christine A. *Healing the Incest Wound: Adult Survivors in Therapy.* New York: W.W. Norton & Co., 1988.

Crewdson, John. *By Silence Betrayed: Sexual Abuse of Children in America.* Boston: Little, Brown and Company, 1988. A detailed examination of the widespread occurrence of child sex abuse, along with an analysis of the legal system that frustrates the prosecution of perpetrators.

Crosson-Tower, Cynthia. *Secret Scars: A Guide for Survivors of Child Sexual Abuse.* New York: Viking, 1988.

Daugherty, Lynn. *Why Me?* Racine, Wis.: Mother Courage Press, 1984. A book that many survivors have found helpful in understanding and accepting their incestuous pasts.

Finkelhor, David. *Child Sexual Abuse.* New York: The Free Press, 1984. A scholarly, thoroughgoing, and up-to-date examination of the incidence of child abuse by one of the foremost researchers in the field.

Finkelhor, David. "The Trauma of Child Sexual Abuse: Two Models." *Journal of Interpersonal Violence,* 2 (1987), 348–366. A thorough outline of a new model for understanding the trauma of incest. Especially helpful for professionals.

Fortune, Marie M. *Sexual Violence: The Unmentionable Sin: An Ethical and Pastoral Perspective.* New York: The Pilgrim Press, 1983. The author is a Christian minister who specializes in the problems of abused women. All her writings reflect faith, wisdom, and strength.

Forward, Susan, and Craig Buck. *Betrayal of Innocence: Incest and Its Devastation.* New York: Penguin Books, 1979. Extensive case studies of a variety of incestuous relationships.

Fraser, Sylvia. *My Father's House: A Memoir of Incest and of Healing.* New York: Ticknor and Fields, 1988. A moving, beautifully written account by a woman who discovered late in life how she had divided herself into two personalities as a child to survive abuse, and how at last she healed herself.

Gendlin, Eugene. *Focusing.* New York: Bantam Books, 1981. A classic primer for learning how to isolate the way past events influence present functioning.

Gil, Eliana. *Outgrowing the Pain.* San Francisco: Launch Press, 1984. A book for and about adults abused as children, termed helpful by survivors who have consulted it.

Goodwin, Jean M. *Sexual Abuse: Incest Victims and Their Families.* Littleton, Mass.: Wright-PSG, 1982. Scholarly overview of the entire scope of incest.

Hancock, Maxine, and Karen Burton Mains. *Child Sexual Abuse: A Hope for Healing.* Wheaton, Ill.: Harold Shaw Publishers, 1987. Written from a Christian perspective, this brief book examines the psychological damage to the survivor, then leads her through a program of prayer toward healing.

Hazelden Meditation Series. *Each Day a New Beginning.* Center City, Minn.: Hazelden, 1982. Excellent daily meditation book written especially for women.

Herman, Judith Lewis. *Father-Daughter Incest.* Cambridge, Mass.: Harvard University Press, 1982. The most literate and compassionate explanation of why incest occurs, with a useful compendium of state statutes at the end.

Kaufman, Gershen. *Shame: The Power of Caring.* Cambridge, Mass.: Schenkman Books, 1980. Helpful to anyone trying to understand how shame damages us in childhood.

Kempe, Ruth S., and C. Henry Kempe. *Child Abuse.* Cambridge, Mass.: Harvard University Press, 1978. A pioneering work by the late pediatrician and his wife, the two people most widely seen as responsible for bringing the attention of the medical community to battered, abused children.

Lerner, Harriet Goldhor. *The Dance of Anger: A Woman's Guide to Changing the Patterns of Intimate Relationships.* New York: Harper and Row, 1986. Helpful in understanding the sources of anger and what to do about its crippling effects.

Masson, Jeffrey Moussaieff. *The Assault on Truth: Freud's Suppression of the Seduction Theory.* New York: Farrar, Straus, and Giroux, 1984. A landmark book that throws into question the basis of Freud's Oedipal theory and asserts that Freud decided to suppress real case histories of incest because he and his colleagues were not ready for the truth.

Meiselman, Karin. *Incest: A Psychological Study of Causes and Effects with Treatment Recommendations.* San Francisco: Jossey-Bass, 1978. Ample documentation and case studies, although designed more for the professional than for the general reader.

Miller, Alice. *For Your Own Good.* New York: Farrar, Straus, and Giroux, 1983. Interesting case histories, but most useful for its list of children's rights at the end.

Morris, Michele. *If I Should Die Before I Wake.* New York: Dell, 1982. A vivid first-person account that shows real courage.

Norwood, Robin. *Women Who Love Too Much.* Los Angeles: Jeremy Tarcher, 1985. Especially helpful to women involved in self-defeating relationships with men.

Peck, M. Scott. *The Road Less Traveled.* New York: Simon and Schuster, 1978. A guide to becoming a responsible adult and healing spiritually.

Renvoize, Jean. *Incest: A Family Pattern.* London: Routledge and Kegan Paul, 1982. A British writer visiting America and interviewing experts about incest. Much information ranging across the whole spectrum of family relationships. The very range, however, makes the book difficult to read.

Roth, Geneen. *Feeding the Hungry Heart: The Experience of Compulsive Eating.* New York: Bobbs-Merrill, 1982. A sensitive and helpful book that explains the origins of eating disorders and the purposes they serve.

Russell, Diana. *The Secret Trauma: Incest in the Lives of Girls and Women.* New York: Basic Books, 1986. The first large-scale and scientific sample to test the incidence of incest. Powerful evidence from an academic researcher.

Russell, Diana. *Sexual Exploitation: Rape, Child Sexual Abuse, Workplace Harassment.* Newbury Park, California: Sage Publications Inc., 1984. Especially good for developing an understanding of perpetrators.

Rush, Florence. *The Best-Kept Secret: Sexual Abuse of Children.* Englewood Cliffs, N.J.: Prentice-Hall, 1980. A pioneering work that examines the laws (written and unwritten) from the Old Testament to the present modern world which have, in effect, sanctioned child sexual abuse.

Sanford, Linda Tschirhart. *The Silent Children: A Parent's Guide to the Prevention of Child Sexual Abuse.* New York: McGraw-Hill, 1982. A comprehensive parents' guide and general resource book that attempts to trace the complex cultural reasons for the victimization of children.

Sanford, Linda Tschirhart, and Mary Ellen Donovan. *Women and Self-Esteem: Understanding and Improving the Way We Think and Feel about Ourselves.* New York: Penguin Books, 1986. Discusses how the messages we received as children influence how we feel about ourselves today. Explores methods of building self-esteem.

Schaef, Anne Wilson. *Co-Dependence: Misunderstood — Mistreated.* New York: Harper and Row, 1986. Author proposes to look at co-dependency as a form of addiction and gives hope for recovery.

Shainess, Natalie. *Sweet Suffering.* New York: Bobbs-Merrill, 1984. Her view of "female masochism" is somewhat controversial, but Shainess does try to explain the dynamics of revictimization.

V., Rachel, ed. *A Woman Like You: Life Stories of Women Recovering from Alcoholism and Addiction.* New York: Harper and Row, 1985. Series of autobiographical stories from women recovering from alcoholism and other addictions.

Viorst, Judith. *Necessary Losses: The Loves, Illusions, Dependencies, and Impossible Expectations That All of Us Have to Give Up in Order*

to Grow. New York: Simon and Schuster, 1986. Describes our journeys to maturity and self-knowledge.

Wegscheider-Cruse, Sharon. *Choice-Making: For Co-Dependents, Adult
Children, and Spirituality Seekers*. Pompano Beach, Fla.: Health Communications, 1985. For co-dependents and adult children from dysfunctional families.

Wegscheider-Cruse, Sharon. *Learning to Love Yourself: Finding Your
Self-Worth*. Pompano Beach, Fla.: Health Communications, Inc.,
1987. Helpful step-by-step manual teaching ways to get rid of self-
defeating messages and to make positive changes.

Whitfield, Charles. *Healing the Child Within*. Pompano Beach, Fla.:
Health Communications, Inc., 1987. An excellent guide to discovery
and recovery for adult children of dysfunctional families.

Woititz, J. G. *Struggle for Intimacy*. Pompano Beach, Fla.: Health Communications, Inc., 1985. Very useful book for learning intimacy and
why it is so difficult for adult children of dysfunctional families.

B. Helpful Organizations

Alcoholics Anonymous: General Service Office
468 Park Avenue South
New York, New York 10016
(212) 686-1100
　　Callers can obtain information regarding AA meetings in their areas.

American Anorexia/Bulimia Association, Inc.
133 Cedar Lane
Teaneck, New Jersey 07666
(201) 836-1800
　　Offers callers referrals to clinicians and treatment centers specializing
in eating disorders; free reading lists; newsletter.

Children of Alcoholics Foundation
200 Park Avenue — 31st floor
New York, New York 10166
(212) 351-2680
　　General information packet is offered free of charge; referrals to
groups and treatment programs throughout the country.

Women's Center
46 Pleasant Street
Cambridge, Massachusetts 02139
(617) 354-8807
 Referral service and educational literature provided.

Incest Survivors Anonymous
P.O. Box 5613
Long Beach, California 90805-0613
(213) 428-5599
 A self-help peer program for survivors. National office will provide callers with the phone number of the nearest group.

Narcotics Anonymous
P.O. Box 9999
Van Nuys, California 91409
(818) 780-3951
 Refers callers to the NA office or group in their area; low-cost literature on addiction and how NA works.

National Child Abuse Hotline:
Childhelp USA
P.O. Box 630
Hollywood, California 90028
(800) 4-A-CHILD ([800] 422-4453)
 A twenty-four-hour hotline offers crisis counseling by professionals, referrals to services in local areas; literature available.

National Committee for Prevention of Child Abuse
332 South Michigan Avenue, #950
Chicago, Illinois 60604
(312) 663-3520
 Offers general information packet at no charge, including a catalog and directory for other organizations and resources.

National Council on Alcoholism (NCA)
12 West 21st Street
New York, New York 10010
(212) 206-6770; (800) NCA-CALL (622-2255)
 Refers callers to nearest affiliate. Free catalog of publications.

Overeaters Anonymous — National Office
4025 Spencer Street, Suite #203

Torrance, California 90503
(213) 542-8363

A self-help, peer-group twelve-step program with no dues, fees, or weigh-ins. The national office refers callers to the nearest OA meeting and offers a free pamphlet.

Parents Anonymous
6733 South Sepulveda Boulevard, #270
Los Angeles, California 90048
(800) 421-0353

Referral to organizations in callers' areas; serves abusive parents. Crisis counseling link with Childhelp (see previous entry).

V.O.I.C.E.S. in Action
P.O. Box 148309
Chicago, Illinois 60614
(312) 327-1500

Offers a national network of support and communication for survivors of incest.

In Canada

The best source in Canada for information and help is

Addiction Research Foundation
33 Russell Street
Toronto, Ontario M65 2S1
(416) 595-6056 for general information
(416) 595-6111 for direct help

The Foundation has an 800-person staff, and its services include treatment and research facilities, educational resources, and community assistance. The Foundation also serves as a clearing-house for services within each province.

Information regarding eating disorders is available from

BANA (Bulimia and Anorexia Nervosa Association)
Faculty of Human Kinetics
University of Windsor
Windsor, Ontario N9B 3P4
(519) 253-4232, ext. 3063

Offers fulltime staff and treatment programs. Free information available.

In Toronto two highly regarded facilities that treat eating disorders are

Clarke Institute of Psychiatry: (416) 979-2221
Wellesley Hospital: (416) 926-7014

In cases of suspected child abuse, it is wise to contact the provincial government to be put in touch with the appropriate agency. Information and aid can also be obtained from

Institute for the Prevention of Child Abuse
25 Spadina Road
Toronto, Ontario M5R 2S9
(416) 921-3151

Index